Searching for Mercy Street

Searching for Mercy Street

My Journey Back to My Mother, Anne Sexton

LINDA GRAY SEXTON

LITTLE, BROWN AND COMPANY

BOSTON   NEW YORK   TORONTO   LONDON

First Edition

Permissions to quote from copyrighted material appear on page 308.

Library of Congress Cataloging-in-Publication Data

Sexton, Linda Gray.
    Searching for Mercy Street : My journey back to my mother, Anne
Sexton / Linda Gray Sexton. — 1st ed.
            p.   cm.
    Includes index.
    ISBN 0-316-78207-6
    1. Sexton, Anne — Family.   2. Sexton, Linda Gray, 1953–   —
Family.   3. Women poets, American — 20th century — Biography.
4. Mothers and daughters — United States — Biography. I. Title.
PS3537.E915Z86   1994
811'.54 — dc20
[B]
94-8889

10   9   8   7   6   5   4   3   2   1

MV-NY

*Published simultaneously in Canada
by Little, Brown & Company (Canada) Limited*

Printed in the United States of America

For Nicholas Gray,
who kept watch as I typed,
with love for your love

If I can write everything out plainly, perhaps I will myself understand better what has happened.

— Sherwood Anderson
Collected Short Stories

Now nearly all those I loved and did not understand when I was young are dead, but I still reach out to them. . . . Eventually, all things merge into one, and a river runs through it. The river was cut by the world's great flood and runs over rocks from the basement of time. On some of the rocks are timeless raindrops. Under the rocks are the words, and some of the words are theirs.

— Norman Maclean,
A River Runs Through It

Contents

Acknowledgments

I would like to thank

Anne Sibbald and Mort Janklow
for their friendship, loyalty, and perspicacity.

Fredrica Friedman,
for challenging me to tackle the last wall of resistance.

My sister, Joy, for her patience and support.

My husband, John, for those many
late evenings after work when he read the manuscript drafts.
These pages bear the mark of his dedication and courage.

Searching for
Mercy Street

The Letter

꩜

I will go now
without old age or disease,
wildly but accurately,
knowing my best route.

— Anne Sexton
"Suicide Note"

THE LETTER, written on a single sheet of legal-length yellow paper, was folded several times as if it had been in an envelope. It lay in my dresser drawer, on top of the stash of letters housed in a rectangular metal box that had belonged to me since I was twelve, a storehouse for all my most important and private documents: an envelope with a hank of my hair cut by my mother on Mother's Day in 1963; a record of all the money I had earned baby-sitting to defray the cost of my riding camp during adolescent summers; my report cards through high school; letters from a boy I had loved. This was a box I would never be without; a box I perused from time to time as I relived small moments of my own history.

I put my hand out and touched the letter with one fingertip. Had I found it? Had I at last discovered the missing suicide note my mother must have written just before shutting herself into her car and starting up the engine? Only a fool would accept the idea that the woman who had made a documentary out of her life would leave this world without a word. What more perfect, safe place could she have selected for the last letter she would write?

It was 1974, a few months after my mother, the poet Anne Sexton, had killed herself. I was twenty-one, alone in the house that had sheltered my sister and me through our adolescence, the house that had witnessed the dissolution of my parents' twenty-five-year-old marriage, heard the increasing clamor of my mother's mental illness, and — a month previously — overseen her suicide in the garage.

I picked it up, my hands shaking. Neither the heading nor the closing of the letter was visible, but the black scrawl was immediately recognizable. My mother had begun this letter with a dull pencil and then continued on in her traditional thick black felt-tip pen. Around me, the house was silent, wrapped in the still November night. I opened it and began to read.

Wed. 2:45 P.M.

Dear Linda,

I am in the middle of a flight to St. Louis to give a reading. I was reading a *New Yorker* story that made me think of my mother and all alone in the seat I whispered to her, "I know, Mother, I know." (Found a pen!) And I thought of you — someday flying somewhere all alone and me dead perhaps and you wishing to speak to me.

And I want to speak back. Linda, maybe it won't be flying, maybe it will be at your *own* kitchen table drinking tea some afternoon when you are 40. — *Anytime* — I want to say back.

1st I love you.

2. you *never* let me down.

3. I know. I was there once. I, *too*, was 40 and with a dead mother whom I needed *still*.

Just this Sunday Daddy and I had a fight and I called the police and the whole thing was so awful. — *That's* when I'm writing this. The Wednesday after. And you rode out to the fish place with Daddy last night & told him you were sorry — about your role. You know — all that.

Well, Linda — it was my fault too. I was jealous and I *provoked* him — but you know I didn't mean to. I want to say to you how sorry I am for any pain the fight caused you. Daddy *knows* you adore him! And I know you love me. We *both* think you are great. You told the police what you *felt* happened. That's all right — *even* with Daddy.

I want to thank you for not letting me down — for sticking by
me even when you loved Daddy so much.

I want to thank you for loving me, *too!*

But that is over!

This is my message to the 40-year-old Linda. No matter what
happens you were always my bobolink, my special Linda Gray. Life
is not easy. It is awfully lonely. *I* know that. Now you too know it
— wherever you are, Linda, talking to me. But I've had a good life
— I *wrote* unhappy — but I lived to the hilt. You too, Linda —
Live to the HILT! To the top. I love you, 40-year-old Linda, and I
love what you do, what you feel, what you are! Be your own woman.
Belong to those u love. Talk to my poems, or talk to your heart —
I'm in both if u need me. — I lied, Linda. I did love my mother
and she loved me.* So there!

xoxoxo Mom

* She never held me but I miss her so that I have to deny I ever
loved her — or she me! Silly Anne!

It took time for the truth to infiltrate my muddy, excited brain.
This was no suicide note but rather a letter I had indeed seen before, back in 1969, even though I read it now as if for the first time.
A letter from my mother was always precious — her natural abundance well suited to the expressive nature of letter writing — and I
had saved nearly every one I had ever received. During my years at
summer camp she had written me several times a week; I waited eagerly by the mailbox for her words from home, overflowing with
her personality and her vigor, rich with anecdote and advice. Some
of those letters were safeguarded in this very metal box. How odd,
then, that this yellow sheet of paper had not set off any tremor of
recognition. When I had received it at sixteen, I must not have
wanted to see or hear its words. Why not? What revelations had it
contained that frightened me into blocking its existence from my
mind for nearly five years?

Mother had been on her way to give a poetry reading in St.
Louis: high in the sky, on an airplane, she had written to me not
as the girl I was at that time, but as the woman she knew I would

become. It was a letter from my past, directed to the Linda of some indistinct future, a strange collision of worlds and times and places and people. In it she correctly assumed that by the time I was forty years old, she would be dead.

The letter began by apologizing for the violent fight my parents had had the night before the letter was written, a fight during which my sister and I had felt compelled to separate them physically and then speak with the police, whom Mother had summoned. When Mother returned home from her trip shortly afterward she must have given me the letter, and I, probably still angry over the incident with the police, had shoved it into my box, deliberately forgetting about it.

But was that anger sufficient explanation for why I had not wanted to remember her words? I kept reading, and the letter moved on beyond mere apology: "That is over!" she said. "This is my message to the 40-year-old Linda." Wasn't the phrase "40-year-old Linda" the crux of it, the core of my resistance to reading and understanding this letter with my heart? She was writing to a woman whom, at age sixteen, I had no desire to imagine, much less become, and she was speaking from the perspective of a mother who is gone — a mother speaking from the grave to her daughter who sits at her kitchen table, alone. A mother saying good-bye.

Over time, I have come to understand that this letter is, most certainly, the suicide note I sought that night in 1974. A metaphorical one perhaps, directed solely to me, but a trumpet call heralding her intentions nevertheless. No wonder I had fought acknowledging it in 1969.

She had written of her love for me, but — more important — she had spoken frankly of her death, of the loneliness of the life she had led. Most telling, she let slip an admission I had never heard from her before: that despite her difficult relationship with her own mother, there had actually been some love between them, love that it was now painful for her to acknowledge because its loss was even more painful. She knew that I, too, would face such a day.

She touched on several generations of womanhood in this letter that summed up so much of her life: her daughterhood and her motherhood; and my daughterhood and my motherhood. All these emotions tangled in front of me, snagged on the words of her letter. Would I, too, admit one day to a love for a mother I had rejected? Would I regret harsh words, or all that I had not been able to say?

That night I was physically alone in the house where my mother had killed herself only a month earlier, yet still she sat by my side. I was unmarried. I was childless and motherless. I was young and without voice. I still had not come close to the point in my life of which she spoke: my fortieth year. I sank down on the twin bed of my childhood room, atop the flowered pink spread with which her body had been covered until the ambulance arrived. I was not a child. I was not a woman, quite.

I read her words again, felt her surrounding, consuming presence, and filled with longing. Overwhelmed, I cried with bitterness for all the arguing we had done just before her death, for the separations I had thrown between us in my desperation to grow up and out and away from her presence, for all the confusion I felt at hearing her difficult words, however uplifting I might ultimately find them.

I missed her. I hated her for having left me. I hated her for remaining with me as strongly as she did, for following me around with words such as these, words I had no choice but to listen to. We had shared and endured so much together. She had been my mentor, my guide, my girlfriend, my teacher, my confidante. My creator — for she had shaped me as surely as God shaped Adam. My Romeo — for she had adored me, for a time, without reservation.

While marking the beginning of the end of her own journey in this world, her letter to the "40-year-old Linda" was the map that marked the start of my own long journey — though at the time I was not able to recognize it as such, and had I done so, I would have turned away in despair and rebellion. But as it developed, the journey became an unconscious one, an inevitable requirement of living and maturing, a journey made by all daughters who have lost their mothers and who come to that time in their lives when they must examine the loss and love inherent in this, the most important of all our relationships, the one upon which all others are based — our first. I had no choice about whether to accept the proffered map.

The sojourn, in her mind, was to take twenty-four years, but now I doubt if such a hegira can ever be completed. Resolution of my emotions about my mother may be unattainable, however much I crave it, perhaps reached only when death forces it upon me. My mother's journey back to her mother lasted only sixteen years, cut short by the suicide this letter foretold. My mother would never know what it was like to be fifty or sixty years old and pondering her relationship to her mother, Mary Gray. Perhaps this exploration meanders throughout our lifetime — regardless of the death of the other person involved. Attempting to define and understand ourselves within the context of this relationship constitutes the very fabric of life and, as such, precludes resolution.

My mother spent all of her life seeking the metaphorical home she called "Mercy Street." In the last years of her life, her sense of desperation intensified as she began to sense she would never find this place of which she often dreamed. She had by then prepared her last book of poetry for publication, entitled *45 Mercy Street,* which contained poems written between 1971 and 1974. In the poem from which the book takes its title, she describes the obsessive quality that had begun to characterize her search:

> *In my dream,*
> *drilling into the marrow*
> *of my entire bone,*
> *my real dream,*
> *I'm walking up and down Beacon Hill*
> *searching for a street sign —*
> *namely MERCY STREET.*
> *Not there.*
>
> *I try the Back Bay.*
> *Not there.*
> *Not there.*

And yet I know the number.
45 Mercy Street.
I know the stained-glass window
of the foyer,
the three flights of the house
with its parquet floors.
I know the furniture and
mother, grandmother, great-grandmother,
the servants.
I know the cupboard of Spode,
the boat of ice, solid silver,
where the butter sits in neat squares
like strange giant's teeth
on the big mahogany table.
I know it well.
Not there.

In Mother's mind, "Mercy Street" was the place where past and present reconciled, where confrontation joined hands with forgiveness. Perhaps she believed unconsciously that because she had not found Mercy Street by her forty-fifth year she would never find it, and perhaps this contributed to her despair as she approached her forty-sixth birthday in 1974. Or perhaps she sensed that even if she should find Mercy Street it would not be what she expected or needed. And so, in the poem, she wakes herself from dreaming of this mythical destination to look squarely at what is left to her in daylight — her art:

Next I pull the dream off
and slam into the cement wall
of the clumsy calendar
I live in,
my life,
and its hauled up
notebooks.

Nearly two decades have passed since my mother's suicide in 1974, years in which I have edited three of her books of poetry and a book of her letters, and written four novels of my own. Mother's reputation as one of America's finest contemporary poets is secured, an authoritative biography of her life has been published, and my work as her literary executor has at last diminished to a manageable level. Nevertheless, this year may be only a resting spot along the path of my travail on this road of mourning and celebrating my mother. Once again I attempt to seize hold of our relationship — if just for a moment, if only here on this page, to capture it with words. This year, in which I turn forty, provides me with a vista that overlooks the continuum of my motion as I have run to and from my mother, to and from myself. As I sit here today at my word processor, I can see both what was and what is yet before me. I become my own character: my life, this book.

I address the sky and the uncharted airplane that carries a tall dark-haired woman with a felt-tip pen. *Mother, are you listening? This is what I have seen and heard and learned. I am the forty-year-old Linda and I am ready to speak back.*

In Exile

§

My heart pounds and it's all I can hear — my
feeling for my children does not surpass my
desire to be free of their demands upon my
emotions. . . . What have I got? Who would want to
live feeling that way?

— February 6, 1957
Anne Sexton to her psychiatrist,
Dr. Martin Orne

*M*Y STORY as a daughter and my mother's story as a mother begins in a Boston suburb, back in the 1950s, when I was exiled from my childhood home to make room for someone else: Mother's mental illness, which lived among us like a fifth person. At ages one and two and three, I could not understand that Anne Sexton's experiences with mental institutions, insanity, and the underside of her own unconscious would one day be put to good use in the crafting of a poetry recognized worldwide. I knew only that I was small and alone, sent off to live in the home of relatives until her "condition" improved; I had been taken away from my mother at the period of childhood in which separation anxiety is acute for even the most secure, beloved child. This rupture in the fabric of our family was the event that defined my childhood, just as her responsibility for casting me out was the event that defined her motherhood.

How I came to be exiled evolved into a legend with many variations, recounted by a number of narrators. My mother and my paternal grandmother, Nana, had each told me the story as I was growing up; while the details often differed, the basic theme, sung over and over, consisted of this: as a three-year-old I had overwhelmed my mother, my needs too intense for this fragile, dependent twenty-eight-year-old woman. Increasingly burdened, she was unable to care for me or my baby sister, Joy, and had had a psychotic break during which the voices in her head spoke so loudly she could hear nothing else.

> Ugly angels spoke to me. The blame,
> I heard them say, was mine. They tattled
> like green witches in my head, letting doom
> leak like a broken faucet;
> as if doom had flooded my belly and filled your bassinet,
> an old debt I must assume.

> — "The Double Image"

She had begun seeing a psychiatrist shortly following Joy's birth in August of 1955, when she began to feel disoriented, "unreal," and agitated. By March of 1956, this feeling had deepened, and she became terrified of being alone with Joy and me. At this point, whenever my father traveled for business, Mother found it impossible to eat, paced the house twirling her hair, or lay in her room masturbating and crying. Her loss of control accelerated, and this manifested itself in alternating bouts of depression and rage — a rage wherein she often slapped me or tried to choke me. She saw faces on the wall and heard voices directing her to kill either herself or my sister and me. The delusion was strong enough that she wanted to tear the wallpaper off the wall from which the voices spoke, but she found herself frozen with fear.

In mid-July, to end her desperation, she decided to kill herself. She took down to the back porch the bottle of pills the doctor had prescribed to help her sleep. There she sat for a while, long enough for my father to discover her and call her psychiatrist, who hospitalized her for a three-week stay at Westwood Lodge, the same private mental clinic that had once treated her father for his alcoholism.

"I was too sick to be your mother," she elaborated as I grew old enough to listen to this story, her eyes mournful as she drew deeply upon the cigarette, a Salem menthol, that she held clasped in her long elegant fingers. With her black hair and eyes of aquamarine, she was as beautiful and dramatic a woman as a daughter could hope for. How I would pray to look just like her — tall, slender, statuesque, and dark.

Small and blond, with a shy smile and blue eyes that held a tentative expression, I had been, Mother said later, an impossible three-year-old. "You cried all the time," she explained. "You whined. You were a difficult, annoying child." She told the story of my childhood quite richly, as if it were a fairy tale about different people, people we didn't know and would never meet, people who had gone through a difficult time but who were living happily ever after now.

I averted my eyes with shame when she told me how hard I was to care for: perhaps my ugly nature was to blame for my mother's difficulties with being a mother. What I remembered from those early years was my own fear, the anxiety that lived inside me like a boa constrictor and made it hard to breathe. My mother had been hospitalized in a terrible place, my mother had left me, my mother — the center of my small universe — was as fragile and precarious as the translucent Limoges my Nana kept on high shelves at her house. Who knew when or how she would next break? The years would bring suicide attempts, trances, fugue states, fits of rage — and depression so intense that she sat for hours staring into space, or paced restlessly like an animal in a cage, or spoke to the voices inside her head. Fear was the four-letter word with which I lived, locked inside me like a dirty secret.

Before Mother's first hospitalization in the summer of 1956, when I turned three, Nana had always taken me to her home during the times Mother couldn't cope with me, and I had found it a place of warmth and love. After Joy's birth, however, Nana became physically debilitated herself, and caring for two small children was out of the question.

She came to pick up Joy, and Mother begged her not to, following her up the stairs to the bedroom. "Just give me another chance, Billie," she said. "I'm feeling better, I'll be all right now."

"You can't be serious, Anne," Nana answered. I was trailing behind the two women, and all of us now reached the landing.

"I *am* serious. I don't want you to take her!"

"Your doctor says Joy's to come with me. They're not safe with
you." And with that, Nana, her jawline thrust forward, went in to
pack up Joy's booties and blankets. Joy, the interloper in the bassinet, oblivious, the baby who brought no joy to me.

"But I'll be good — I won't hurt them even if Linda whines for
an *hour*! I promise!"

My grandmother did not relent and when she had finished
packing up, she set Joy in the crook of her arm and started down
the stairs. "You can't take her!" Mother screamed, enraged.

Nana kept right on going, her shoulders square with determination.

Mother turned on me, eyes electric with hate. "It's all *your*
fault," she shouted, putting her face down close to mine. "*Your*
fault!" I sucked my thumb, cringing against the green-and-gold
wallpaper. Mother turned and ran to her room, where she slammed
the door. I could hear the sound of her cries through the wall.

Every child is engaged by a story in which she plays one of the
main characters — even if cast as the villain rather than the heroine, even if the story recalls pain rather than happiness. Remembering such a story is also another way of validating the experience,
a literal picking at the scab so a clean scar can form. For many years
I retold the story in a detached manner, a classic way of denying
how much that moment at the head of the stairs hurt me. It took
time before I could acknowledge it with either anger or tears.
A long time before I could acknowledge the fury and sadness
that day created in me, or the hostility that choked me like a poi-
sonous noose and made me resent Joy, whose birth had seemed
the cause — however innocent — of my abandonment.

Though Nana had volunteered to take both of us again, my
mother's mother, Mary Gray, decided this would be too taxing for
Nana. And so I was sent to the same lonely home in which Mother

herself had been miserable as a child, cared for mostly by nurse-maids and housekeepers; the same place the voices inside her mind had first made themselves heard; the same garden where the seeds of her mental instability had taken root. She remembered her own childhood as a time scarred with incidents of emotional pain. In their "big house with four garages," Mary and Ralph Harvey par-tied a lot, drank heavily, and expected their daughters to stay on the *qui vive*, an expression that meant they must be appropriately dressed and groomed and ready to receive visitors at any moment. Appearances took precedence, even at the dinner table, and any one of the three could be dismissed because her complexion rendered her unpresentable. Ralph used the strap to discipline his girls. These memories overflowed Mother's psychiatric sessions and later would fill her poetry.

My departure from my parents' house happened rapidly, a tumble down a long, rocky hill. Events moved too quickly for un-derstanding; they packed me up and took me to Annisquam, a wealthy retirement and vacation community on the northern Mas-sachusetts shore.

The Harveys were prosperous, Ralph having made a fine living running the woolen mill that bore his name, where my father also worked after he and my mother eloped in 1948. Daddy was a trav-eling salesman, assigned to the South and the Midwest, away from home a great deal. Once I arrived in Annisquam, my grandparents hired a young woman named Esther to care for me. My grandfa-ther was a large, intimidating man with a deep voice and broad face. I have few memories of him, none of being touched, and I never knew his lap or his laugh. Each night, however, my grand-mother Ga-ga did allow me to sit briefly on her lap in her rocking chair on the long porch that overlooked the ocean.

Mary Gray Harvey was a pretty, blond woman, small of frame and a bit stout in her later years. Her clothes were impeccable, her jewelry elaborate. Her lap provided me comfort during this time of turmoil. The evening air felt cool against my flushed face as I, wrapped in a thick white towel, could come to her only fresh from

my bath. Just past the strip of lawn, the rocky ledge plummeted to
the lip of the sea, which glistened like a giant gray mirror streaked
with fire, reflecting the sun as she lowered herself over the rim of
the world, slowly, like a woman into her bath.

After dark each night, however, the voice of the wind and the
surge of the ocean against the rocks frightened me. Wolves, I
feared, skulked beneath my bed. I never got in or out of bed without leaping as far from the edge of the mattress as possible, feet up
fast. Later Mother would take this memory of mine and use it in
her poem "The Fortress."

> *No,*
> *the wind's not off the ocean.*
> *Yes, it cried in your room like a wolf*
> *and your pony tail hurt you. That was a long time ago.*

Within a month or two, fifty-five-year-old Ga-ga and Grampa
also became frustrated and overwhelmed with housing a young
child who suffered from nightmares and anxiety. And then, too, the
amiable Esther, who had filled my lonely days with game after
game, was scheduled to return to school as fall approached.
Mother, however, was no better. I could not return home.

On the day before her twenty-eighth birthday, while my father
was traveling in the Midwest, Mother attempted suicide with an
overdose of Nembutal. Nana drove her to the Emergency Room to
have her stomach pumped and then told my father over the telephone. Mother's psychiatrist, Dr. Martin Orne, hospitalized her at
Glenside Hospital, a grim public institution totally unlike any
other mental hospital to which she would ever be committed again.
"Her family was not very sympathetic about her problems," commented Dr. Orne in 1990. "Seeing her at Glenside, they recognized
that things were serious. Moreover, Glenside cost less than Westwood Lodge, and that mattered." Glenside was the hospital
Mother wrote about in her poem "You, Doctor Martin," the hospital where, she later described to me, she was strapped to a bed

with her arms tied to prevent her from making any other attempts
on her life.

> *I speed through the antiseptic tunnel*
> *where the moving dead still talk*
> *of pushing their bones against the thrust*
> *of cure. And I am queen of this summer hotel*
> *or the laughing bee on a stalk*
>
> *of death. We stand in broken*
> *lines and wait while they unlock*
> *the door and count us at the frozen gates*
> *of dinner. The shibboleth is spoken*
> *and we move to gravy in our smock*
> *of smiles. We chew in rows, our plates*
> *scratch and whine like chalk*
>
> *in school. There are no knives*
> *for cutting your throat. I make*
> *moccasins all morning.*

While the Harveys neither understood nor empathized with
their daughter once she was an adult — any more than they had
when she was a child — they nevertheless did make an effort to
help her through the mental crisis she was undergoing by doing
what they could to ease her distress in a practical sense: they had
taken me into their home, they were paying some of Mother's psychiatric bills, and twice a week they sent down their cleaning
woman, Mary ("Me-me") LaCrosse, so that Anne would not be
burdened by housework. Perhaps seeing their daughter hospitalized
at Glenside had sobered them just the way Orne hoped it would.

Ga-ga sent me off to stay with my mother's sister Blanche, in
Scituate, Massachusetts, and once again I was condensed into a
suitcase. As they were growing up, Anne, Jane, and Blanche had
rarely gotten along, consumed as they were by jealousy, minute
games of power, and one-upmanship. Or, at least, so it seemed in

Mother's eyes. Intense sibling rivalry flourished there like weeds in a neglected garden. Mary and Ralph had been self-involved, distant parents, adults consumed with their own problems; the three Harvey girls never stopped squabbling about whose turn it was, what belonged to whom, and who got the most. Though we saw Jane and Blanche only at Christmastime, and Ga-ga and Grampa equally rarely, my parents seemed to have no compunction about leaving me with any of them.

"[My sisters] certainly didn't care about me — my awful sisters!" Mother confided to her psychiatrist, Dr. Orne, in 1961. "I still hate them." The fact that Blanche was willing to take me into her home did not appear on the scorecard of love my mother kept in her own mind.

How strange it seems that despite Blanche's ambivalent relationship with my mother, she did offer me the best foster care she could manage. As the middle sister, she had always played mediator within the family, the one who took care of the others; thus, she stepped forward at a time when Jane's situation was far more conducive to taking on a stray child. Jane lived close by, in Wellesley, in a large house. Her husband made a fine living and could have more easily provided for an extra child.

The Taylors, on the other hand, were poor. My uncle Ed, an alcoholic, had trouble keeping a job, and he hung around the house in an undershirt. Blanche already had two daughters, just in elementary school, as well as two sons, one my age and one Joy's age. She had no help with either her house or her children, and there were neither the emotional nor monetary means to care for — much less love — a fifth child who belonged to a sister about whom she felt, at best, ambivalent. In this place of exile, secrets fermented.

It was a long car ride to Aunt Blanche's, one made longer by fear. I was to sleep in my cousins Lisa and Mary's room and try to be brave. Soon my mother would be well and I would go back to Newton, they said. I tried not to wonder or to ask questions; I tried not to cry but failed.

I remember this: how desperately I wanted my doll, a floppy baby with a stuffed cloth body, her white-blond hair a match for my own. I needed a familiar object to confirm who I was, or, more important, a familiar body with which to cuddle. I would rock her in my arms like a good mother. Aunt Blanche telephoned to ask for her, and my parents promised to send her down. I checked the mailbox every day, but it rang empty as a drum. It hurt to be so alone. It hurt to be forgotten.

I snuck into my cousin Harvey's room and stole his plastic ruler for a game I called "shoe man"; it got caught in a crack between the floorboards and snapped in half. My mistake with the ruler brought out Uncle Ed's strap. This strap was a snake that lived by eating the mistakes children made. The more you made, the bigger and stronger he got. I see my uncle now, how he moved toward me, slowly, a big sweaty man with a leather belt in his hand. We were in the master bedroom, and he wore only his undershirt and shorts. Sitting on the edge of the bed, he bent me across his lap, peeled my panties down, crushed my face against the white chenille bedspread. This was how he beat me. This was shame: stripped naked, butt under his rough palm, the fire of his snake on my skin.

No one rescued me, or any of my cousins: especially not at night, when we hid behind doors, under beds, in closets. The noise started downstairs, then spiraled upward, like the smell of something burning. Aunt Blanche's cries did not cover the sound of Uncle Ed's fist as he hit her. *Thud-thud, thud-thud*, a hammer striking a rubber mat. I counted the number of blows: if there were too few it would be worse for us. After a while there was silence. Then a click, the refrigerator door opening, the hum of its motor coming on. The sound of a bottle set down hard on the metal table. None of us children moved. We knew intermission when we heard it.

No one said *stop* as he lurched up the stairs. His voice wheedled our names, thick and sweet, as if he were tricking a dog to come over so he could whack it black and blue. No one stopped him. Did anyone care?

Even drunk, Uncle Ed was good at finding our hiding places.

My thumb, however, was an old friend. It had been with me as long as I could remember, and its comfort never left my side. It had a special taste: a little sweet, a little sweat. Thirty-seven years later I can still remember that taste and the way my thumb fit between the softness of my tongue and the hard roof of my palate. I might have gone to high school being a closet sucker if it hadn't been for Uncle Ed.

I remember this: me, three years old, hunkering down in front of a low bookcase that resides in that shadowy house of my memory. It stood beneath a window that let in a wash of late afternoon sunlight, and I squatted in front of it, running my fingers over the fat books with their spines of bright colors. I wondered when I would be able to read them. Already being read to was my favorite activity — a way to escape. These were thick stories that would last long enough to provide a respite of many hours. My mouth watered as if they were food. Thumb in my mouth, I caressed the titles one at a time.

"Get that out of your mouth!"

Uncle Ed strode across the room and jerked me to my feet by one skinny arm. His face was close, right up against my cheek, the unshaven stubble prickly. His eyes held the same fury Mother's often had. I shrunk from the electricity there.

He rubbed the soggy, wrinkled skin of my thumb between his fingers, hard, and then squeezed until the nail turned white. It hurt, as if I had closed it in the car door. I held very still. Didn't speak. Didn't breathe. Already I knew the power of words: what they could make happen, what they could bring down on your head. I was learning fast.

"Next time," he whispered, "I'll cut that thumb off and scramble it in my eggs for breakfast."

With his angry eyes and ugly voice, he left no room for doubt, and so I lived with that threat, repeated often, whenever I forgot to get the thumb out of my mouth in time. Terrified, I tried to keep my hand mostly in my pocket. I did not understand why sucking my thumb was bad or why it made him so mad. Seeing me purse my lips around that tender little digit sent him sky-high — and that was all I needed to know.

These months away from my parents encompassed the most complete terror I have ever known. I wondered if perhaps my mother had died and I was never really going home. Perhaps I had killed her — me and my tears, my demands, my need to be loved. What had I done that I should be punished this way?

At night, I lay awake in the dark to plead my case with God. *If I am very good tomorrow could you please make my Mommy better? If I eat all the broccoli on my plate will you help me not to make a mistake? If I don't suck my thumb anymore maybe could I please go home?*

Nights, from my bed, I watched the moon shift its shape through the sky. After a while, I stopped praying, stopped talking to God after dark. At three I had learned the litany of despair and knew its truth with all my being: depend on no one. Not the wide, empty sky, nor the distant yellow moon. Not a teacher, not a minister. Not God. Not grown-ups. No one will give you what you crave: a doll, a cuddle, permission to suck your lovely soggy thumb. No one will rescue you.

༄

In later years it never occurred to me to ask how long I stayed away from home because I already knew: a two-year sentence. It never occurred to me to ask why I was dispatched because I already knew: Linda was a child who could not be satisfied, a monster of demand who drove her mother into an institution in search of relief. Reiteration of the point lay in the fact that my mother's parents had also banished me. Even then I understood implicitly that motherhood was a dangerous state of being, one that could overwhelm even strong and wise grandparents, one that could drive a sensitive woman to a mental hospital.

Though I am no longer a child, to write of these things feels forbidden, to give voice to memories such as these, taboo. Family matters: dark and secret. I remember the snake who comes in the dark, the taste of fear sour in my mouth, the blackness of a bedroom not my own, and worst of all the voice whispering: *If you tell they will not love you anymore. If you tell they will send you away again.*

The specter of the isolation I endured while away from my mother remained with me, affecting my choices and my behavior as a teenager and as a young adult. I have only just discovered how much I need to regain the power taken from me so many years ago, when I was a frightened and guilty child, shuttled from place to place. Power accompanies words: the ability to speak your mind, to tell your own story, to say what you want, to communicate — this is a right for which we fight from the moment we discover the ability to speak during our second year of life. It is a right humankind has pursued throughout its history.

For part of my life I refused to remember my own difficult memories, much less speak or write of them, even to myself; words and memory can be a gift — but they can be a threat as well. Memory may carry insight and even illuminate my life, but the scenes that it reveals can be dangerous. How much am I willing to endure *in order* to remember? Do I truly *want* to be empowered by memory or language?

My sons, Nicholas and Alexander, are now eight and ten. As they were growing, I often looked at them and wondered about my own childhood, reexperiencing it through their developmental struggles and crises; I began to ask myself if my mother had worried about me, far from my familiar places in Newton, living with an aunt we sometimes saw only at Christmas. I cannot imagine sending my own children so far from me at such an early age, even in my most depressed moments, even at my most despairing. Who could understand Alexander and Nicholas as I do, who could anticipate their needs, protect their vulnerabilities? If I conjure up my own children in a similar exile, I am able to cry for the three-year-old I once was.

How had Mother *felt* about sending me, alone, to live in a strange place? She clearly understood how *I* must have felt at three, for years later in "The Fortress," a poem written for me, she captured my mood of isolation and despair perfectly:

> The wind rolled the tide like a dying
> woman. She wouldn't sleep,
> she rolled there all night, grunting and sighing.

She knew the sounds with which I went to sleep. Was not this "dying woman" of the tide both a metaphor for and the reality of my childhood and my adolescence? The mother in Anne had not seen it as clearly then as the poet would later, for if she had, surely she would have rescued me and brought me home again. Or so my fantasy went. No mother would willingly consign her daughter to such emotional pain. The separation she allowed between us established the boundaries of our relationship for the next twenty years, and it was one of the aspects of my childhood hardest for me to forgive.

But how much control had she really had? Was there any realistic possibility that a woman who sat frozen in fear all day long could have prevented my abandonment? Once I had not asked questions like these; I had been only angry. Years after her death, I finally brought up the subject with my father, choosing the safety of dinner table conversation in a quiet French restaurant. It was 1985, the first time the two of us had ever discussed this period in our lives. It may have been the first time we ever really talked — however indirectly — about Mother's illness.

"How did I get sent to Blanche's?" I asked, cutting into my lamb.

"I didn't have much to say about it," he answered.

"I don't understand." I was puzzled: if my father hadn't had control, who had?

"I was traveling," he said, beginning to tell his part of the story as he sipped his wine. "And I'd flown back in. Nana picked me up at Logan and told me what she and Mary Gray had decided to do."

"You didn't know before then?"

He paused. "Well, your mother had been getting sick when I traveled for a while by then, and Nana often took care of her, and you. Usually I knew what was going on, but I couldn't do anything because I was too far away. Then Joy came and having a baby just made things worse for Anne. That first time she tried to kill herself Nana called me and told me over the phone."

"So you came back and Nana met you at the airport . . ."

He nodded. "She and Mary Gray were taking care of things. This was how it was going to be — a fait accompli!" He drank deeply now and his blue eyes dimmed, shifting away from mine. "I was upset. I thought we should all stay together. I didn't want you girls being taken away like that. Joy was so little."

"Why didn't you tell Nana what *you* wanted to do?"

He snorted. "For God's sake, Linda, you know perfectly well you couldn't tell my mother anything once her mind was made up. There was nothing I could do. Anyway, Anne was too unreliable then. We couldn't trust her with you."

I watched him as he told the story, shielded by the rim of my wine glass. I could see how upsetting it was for him to talk about all this — but even so, I wasn't convinced that he couldn't have done something to make everything different. It wasn't just Mother who had abandoned me after all. Daddy, too, had had a part. "It was terrible for me," I said quietly. "I hated it there."

"I didn't think you should go," he repeated. "It was Mary Gray and Nana who made all the plans."

My parents had been in their late twenties — children no more. Yet within reach of their own parents they always seemed to act like children. I could just see him with my grandmother, driving out of town through the Sumner Tunnel in her big blue Oldsmobile, as she told him what she and Mary Gray had decided was best for our family. Daddy, sitting there, fifteen pounds skinnier than he was now, nodding while he clamped his teeth down hard into the filter of his cigarette — but nodding just the same. I knew he couldn't hear what I was telling him now — that I had been hurt then, that I wanted him to say he was sorry for that time in my life.

Suddenly I understood why my memories of him from this early time were so few: he had been on the road selling wool and garnets at least half of every month, sent there by a father-in-law who had promised to make him heir to the business. And I knew in my heart — despite my judgmental anger — that probably he had had very few choices except to accept the help offered by these powerful parents: he could hardly have quit his job to stay home with us himself. He, too, had been trapped.

That night I let my father's answers stand unchallenged and did not say what I really thought or share the anger and hurt I felt. I wasn't willing to take the risk of alienating him and being "banished" from his affections again. I, too, was in the midst of repeating old patterns well learned.

I had always believed that Mother was in the mental hospital for the entire, interminable time I lived with Aunt Blanche and Uncle Ed. I had imagined her weaving straw place mats, making moccasins, unable to manage — that's why she hadn't visited or sent my doll and books. But after her death, when, as her literary executor, I began to read through the files of correspondence, diaries, and manuscripts to research the book that would eventually be published in 1979 as *Anne Sexton: A Self-Portrait in Letters,* I saw that she had actually come home after a brief hospitalization of a few weeks. She spent the remainder of the time I was in Scituate at home: keeping her appointments with her analyst, lunching with friends, having her hair done. She slept in her own bed and wandered through her own house.

Stunned, all the excuses and rationalizations I had used to cushion myself from the truth collapsed inward. If she had been at home, why hadn't she sent my doll? Were such small things *so* overwhelming? The more I read, the more furious I became, especially at the parade of her psychiatrists, pompous as kings, who in later years made me ashamed of my anger, counseling me not to feel exasperated with her sickness, not to admit that I wanted only one thing: to have a mother who was normal.

When, during adolescence, I saw a psychiatrist for the first time, I began the story of my life by speaking of the two-year exile to Blanche's. Mother, who often asked for an accounting of my psychiatric sessions, had corrected my recollection: though it had seemed like two years, she'd admonished me, I had really been there only two *months.* This revision of my story became the fact until years later when I read an early draft of Mother's biography that pinpoints the length of my stay at six months. To me, our time apart felt longer than it had actually been — forever; to Mother, it had seemed shorter than it actually was — not long enough.

I have other memories of my early childhood as well, and some of these bring me joy instead of pain. Sometimes they jibe and sometimes they conflict with the tales my mother told, but they are seeded in my mind like pockets of light in a dark field, providing intense clarity. These memories summon forth moments when my mother was most certainly mothering me, allowing me to depend upon her. As such, they bring me a pleasure as sweet and slow as that of a butterscotch sucker. I revel in the warmth of each, for as long as possible, as if they were all small campfires scattered across an enormous expanse of darkness.

To dry my tears, Mother had rituals. A lap that seemed wide enough to hold me and arms that seemed strong enough to keep me. Her deep raspy voice, singing, "Don't you be my melancholy baby, cuddle up and don't be blue." I put my head against her breast and held her tight with my own small arms. At night she came in to read *Goodnight Moon* and to cuddle. "Goodnight house, Goodnight mouse." The shades were drawn, the room fell dark just as the story had foretold, objects fading, shadows growing; the sheets were cool and smooth, ironed by our housekeeper, Me-me, the scent of fresh linen. Mother created a song just for me and sang it every night she was home with us: *"Night-night time has come for Linda Gray, Night-night time, the same time every day, It's night-night time, It's night-night time, night-night time has come."* To my ears this simple lyric was the most beautiful poem she ever wrote. I treasured it; I adapted it for my own children when I became a mother. These were the magic times. Safe times. Knowing, for that moment, that I could count on her: she *would* take care of me; she *was* my mother; she was *here*.

As I grew older her love of poetry fueled another ritual: how she labored, when I was six, to teach me John Masefield. From every corner of the house we practiced in tandem: "I must go down to the sea again, to the lonely sea and the sky." She explained what spume meant, how to project my voice, and — without any words at all — gave me lessons in love: here was the attention, laughter, and tenderness I craved. High on the upward swing of a mood, she sometimes danced from room to room, leaping like a gazelle, pretending to be a ballerina. How I adored her in those moments and how earnestly I wished that kind of giddy, impulsive joy could last forever.

‍ڡ

If my mother was the strongest influence upon me during child-hood, her importance to me was defined by her repeated absences. In contrast, the second-strongest influence during my childhood was that of an equally powerful woman — whose importance to me was defined by her nearly continual presence, except for those six months when I lived away from home. In my mind my father's mother, Wilhelmine Muller Sexton, whom we called Nana, became more of a mother to me than Mother herself. She was not a large woman, but I always think of her that way — solid and strong enough to take on all our burdens. Known as Billie to her friends, she was attractive, with chestnut hair and blue eyes, her figure trim. She dressed beautifully in a conservative Bostonian fashion and her makeup (which she called "her face") was always in place. She stood in stark contrast to my mother, who alternated between wearing flamboyant clothing, makeup, and jewelry — a stunner — and sitting slumped at the kitchen table in her coffee-stained bathrobe, her hair tangled from her fingers as they twirled endless knots, her eyes empty. When I was a teenager, other parents be-lieved Nana *was* my mother: she was the one who drove both Joy and me to our after-school activities and to the doctor or dentist, and she certainly looked young enough. As I think over the story of my childhood, I recall how Nana always entered calmly, bringing with her safety, security, and the sense that an adult had arrived to take charge. How I loved her for this.

In 1958 our family returned to some semblance of normality, all living under one roof again when Joy came back from Nana's at three years old. I was five. Nana baby-sat for Joy and me at our house and took us for long weekends to her house in Weston, only a few miles away. She stopped by at any and all hours, clip-clopping up the driveway on her high heels to bring us small treats, like a loaf of my father's favorite bread or a box of cupcakes from Hazel's Bakery, or an armload of the mending and alterations she did for my mother and for us, "the girls." She moved through the house like a silent soldier, rearranging drawers, surreptitiously straightening the mess in which we lived, and beginning to prepare dinner when the stove stood bare at five o'clock.

In the dining room, my mother sat hunched over her desk, her back rounded under her cotton shirt, twirling her hair around her index finger from time to time. If we plucked at her elbow, she sent us back to Nana in the kitchen. Her concentration was fierce, trancelike, as she sat there typing with two or three fingers, as she created elaborate rhyme schemes on manila paper with a scratchy lead pencil. How often I wished she would stop and read me a story. Just one.

Nana did instead. Whenever she was the one putting us to bed, she lulled us to sleep with ritual: stories and back rubs. As she stroked our backs with hands roughened by washing dishes and mopping the floor (despite her wealthy Bostonian upbringing, the stock market crash in 1929 had brought an end to luxuries such as maids, and so she did all her own housework), she regaled us with tales of my father and his sister, our aunt Joanie.

Joanie still lived in her mother's home, having returned after the dissolution of a short marriage. Petite, vivacious, and attractive, she had worked as a stewardess, travel agent, antiques dealer, and teacher of the mentally retarded — but what she most craved was the security of marriage and raising her own children. Over the years, Joanie became our favorite, which irritated Mother no end: Joy and I argued over who got to go on the next picnic with Joanie, to the beach, or on an overnight with her. As we grew into teenagers, Joanie also became a confidante — someone we could tell our troubles to without being required to hear her troubles in exchange.

Nana told wonderful bedtime stories, especially those embellished accounts of her children as they were growing. Joy and I always clamored for more, pouting when she ran out of anecdotes.

The love in her voice testified to the worth of her own two children, now grown but still by her side: a good childhood, it appeared, never had to end — especially in light of Joanie's living
situation. Nana spun love in a fine mesh net and hung it under the
tightrope upon which my mother and our family teetered in our
desperate act of balance.

Despite my early feelings of anger and hate for my sister, living
side by side again tied us together in a tight emotional bond. As we
grew, we became fierce rivals for the love and tenderness that were
in such scarce supply, while simultaneously banding together to
help each other through the daily crises. Although we each played
distinct roles as time went on — me acting as bossy adviser to my
younger sister, who was adoring, needy, and constant — we were
anchors for each other in a stormy Sexton sea. We depended on
one another. Even as each of us wished that she could have all the
available love and attention, neither of us wished to trek solo down
the lonely road of childhood. When Mother started twirling her
hair or staring into space, Joy and I exchanged looks of worry no
one else could understand. We held hands on the lip of the pit that
was Mother's instability, united in a double helix of love and hate.
So when Joy, at six, cut the hair off my favorite doll, I, at eight,
made certain my parents heard of and saw the disfigurement. Later
that evening, however, I crept into my sister's room — where she
had been sent without supper — smuggling beneath my dress a
push-up popsicle.

The stress in our home did not come merely from my mother's
mental instability. My grandmother herself, wonderful as she was,
created her own set of difficulties. She had always hewed to a rigid
set of rules regarding the proper conduct for a wife and mother.
She left Cornell after her junior year when she became engaged
to George Sexton, because she believed it inappropriate for a
wife to have more education than her prospective husband. Her
daughter-in-law, Anne, however, broke every rule, and this offended her deeply. By eloping with my father at nineteen, my
mother had created the circumstances that pushed him to give up

his education — instead of the reverse, as my grandmother had done. The fact that Anne had mistakenly believed herself to be pregnant lowered her further in my grandmother's eyes.

My parents had been crazy in love when they met at the Longwood Cricket Club for a date and eloped a month later. Romance filled their first year together, as they returned to Colgate, where my father was entering his sophomore year as a premedical student and my mother tried her hand at being a housewife, baking pineapple upside-down cakes and asking her parents to send her a Mixmaster. Mother's wild energy brought out some daring on the part of my otherwise quiet father, while Daddy's supportive nurturing was exactly the kind of succor Mother craved.

After that first year, however, my father could no longer stand the humiliation of being, as he put it, "on the dole." He and Mother returned to the Boston area after Ralph Harvey got him a job as a "sample boy" in a friend's woolen mill; no one would ever accuse my mother's father of nepotism. Though my father worked hard, hauling himself up through the ranks over the years, all my grandmother's hopes for her blond, blue-eyed son, whom she had sent to a good private school and seen complete a successful first year at Colgate, now seemed to lie in ruins because of his marriage to this flamboyant, pretty child who wore too much lipstick and slept all morning while the housework lay undone. Right from the start, Nana assigned my mother the role of villain and my father the role of victim.

My mother's worst transgression, however, lay in the fact that by becoming mentally ill — and both branches of the family viewed this illness dubiously — she had rendered herself incapable of caring for her children, whose protection and guidance were — to my grandmother — a decent woman's main responsibility in life. It seemed to my grandmother that Anne had never grown up. Right after my parents had married, she had asked my mother to run down to the store and pick up a bottle of milk. She was stunned to see her daughter-in-law throw herself full-length on the floor, drumming her heels and fists and shrieking that she would not go. My mother never managed to erase this picture from Nana's mind, as her behavior continued to seem egocentric at its best and frightening at its worst.

For Nana, family was sacred. She herself remained resigned to her marriage with a man who was a philandering alcoholic, who had taken her inheritance of two million dollars and lost it all by buying on margin before the stock market crash, and who in later years drifted from job to job. She struggled to anchor her family and keep it afloat, cruising the bars to look for her husband and then sending in my father, only a young boy, to find his father and haul him out. In those years an unaccompanied woman could not enter a bar — but she could run the family. When George Sexton was killed suddenly in a car accident in 1960, just a year after Mother's parents died, Nana grieved but kept right on coping. Her genteel upbringing had prepared her for none of this, but quickly she had discovered her own inner mettle. As time passed she became more matriarchal, more stubborn and controlling. The situation often demanded such attributes, and when it did not, the pattern had become too ingrained to abandon.

My mother and her illness, I am sure, seemed to Nana one more disaster in a life that had already thrown more obstacles in her path than she could ever have imagined. Nevertheless, she would have managed to deal even with this had it remained a private or straightforward issue for which she could always set the course the family would follow. However, despite her illness, my mother turned out to be remarkably resilient and equally determined to control *certain* aspects of the family's life, an attitude that both frustrated and enraged Nana. If Mother was strong enough to write poems all day long, meet other poets for lunches and readings, or even go to week-long poetry retreats, surely she must be strong enough to make a meatloaf for supper, surely she did not need such extensive, expensive, psychiatric help.

Had Mother simply acted like a docile sick child, all would have been clearer. Nana would have taken over entirely and run the life of the family from the position of the matriarch she considered herself to be, without interference. Instead, by writing the sort of revealing poetry that was to become her trademark, my mother took control of her illness — at least some of the time — and then went public with it, achieving a perverted glory that brought her a great deal of attention. In Nana's eyes, Mother had betrayed her family's privacy and brought shame upon us all. This insult to family commitment and honor shocked my grandmother.

Nana was not alone in her distaste for my mother's tendency to disrobe verbally in public. Initially my mother's family was similarly dismayed to find their weaknesses and foibles captured so forthrightly on the pages of Mother's ever-expanding black binder full of poems. After her parents' deaths, Mother felt she did not need to hold back and so wrote ever more boldly about her childhood and her parents.

Her feelings for her father and mother grew even more complicated as their deaths revealed more betrayals: Ralph's profligate lifestyle, his lavish gifts, expensive clothes and cars, and the perpetual consumption of alcohol, had cost him his company. Secretly, year after year, he had sold off shares to his partner for cash, all the while duping my parents into believing that — with hard work and determination — my father would inherit the family business upon Ralph's death. Following his death from a stroke in 1959 — just months after Mary Gray's death from breast cancer — Mother's grief, devastation, and betrayal found voice in some of her most accomplished poems: "The Division of Parts," "The Double Image," "The Truth the Dead Know," "A Curse Against Elegies," and "All My Pretty Ones."

> I hold a five-year diary that my mother kept
> for three years, telling all she does not say
> of your alcoholic tendency. You overslept,
> she writes. My God, father, each Christmas Day
> with your blood, will I drink down your glass
> of wine? The diary of your hurly-burly years
> goes to my shelf to wait for my age to pass.
> Only in this hoarded span will love persevere.
> Whether you are pretty or not, I outlive you,
> bend down my strange face to yours and forgive you.

When my grandparents died they seemed to me as distant and unknowable as steamships on the horizon of a smooth and lonely sea. I grieved over them only because my mother once again became erratic and despondent, sitting and staring into space, twirling her hair around her finger, over and over, hour after hour. I knew what she was thinking about: suicide. Even at six, I knew the meaning of the word, whispered by the adults around me. When a boy down the street taunted me, "Crazy! Your mother is crazy!" I sucked my thumb, and my mind seized up with fear.

Once again Daddy and Nana packed Mother up and took her away from me. When I think back on it I realize now that while she often went to the hospital, she rarely went in an ambulance; there were few sirens save those that sounded in my heart. While only nine times did she actually go so far as to attempt suicide, there were many more hospitalizations than that and these were preceded by warnings: that vacant look in her eyes; twirling her hair until it snarled; crying and not being able to stop; frozen desperation. All this brought me nauseated anxiety. Like an old woman with arthritic bones who can predict the weather, I learned to anticipate my losses. Within a matter of days, or hours, someone would take her to Westwood, or McLean, private hospitals that specialized in treatment of the mentally ill.

And so when Ga-ga and Grampa died, I did not mourn them, but instead my mother and her absence. When she left, my world teetered and slid, then came to rest precariously on the safety of routine for the next few days: get up, get dressed, go to school. *Please, God, let her be home when I come back this afternoon.* Every time she left I asked myself if she would come back at all this time; and I could not imagine the place they had taken her. "She's sick," my father said. "She's in the hospital." I wanted to care for her at home. I knew my job. If I took care of her maybe she would never be sick again.

〜

Ralph Harvey's will delivered the last blow and sealed forever Mother's attitude toward her father. He had sold out, piece by piece. Mother threw his framed picture to the floor, shattering the glass with her heel and grinding her foot into the image of his face. Ralph's failure became a blow from which neither of my parents would ever recover: my father's career had now been irrevocably altered, for he would never own the family business, never become the wealthy merchant of whom he had dreamed when he had left college and his plans for medical school behind him. My mother had endured her husband's repeated time away from the family for nothing. Kayo would never be in a position to run the company rather than travel for it.

As the years passed, Mother's feelings about her parents and her willingness to write about them with frankness did not improve the already contentious relationship with her older sisters. Jane and Blanche and their childhood family were the characters peopling the famous world Anne Sexton's poetry soon became. They grew angry with my mother, and at her vivid depictions of a miserable childhood punctuated by rejection and physical discipline.

Mother could never forget how her father had banned her from the dining room table because he could not bear to look at the pimples of her adolescence; nor could she banish from her psyche the enemas and genital examinations she remembered bearing at the hands of Mary Gray. All this found voice in her poetry — "Oh the enemas of childhood, reeking of outhouses and shame!" — but never catharsis, as I realized one night when I was a teenager. Mother sat at the kitchen table before supper, crying and near hysteria, arms and legs intertwined as if to lock up her body. That night she lived again in some other world as she cried out over and over, "Mother, don't look!" Joy and I watched her with horror, averting our eyes, praying that she would stop. Eventually we took her upstairs and put her to bed, where she fell into a sleep-drugged trance.

With poetry like this representing the home in which they all had been raised, who could blame Jane and Blanche for being angry? What they fervently believed ought to be private was now being published; even worse, many of the events she wrote of did not conform to their own recollections of the past. They complained that she was just as much of an inventor as she had been when she was a child.

My mother herself felt misunderstood by them all, and, in fact, the entire family did appear puzzled by this odd woman they had spawned. Later, Blanche would explain to me that as the years went by, none of them could understand why Anne wanted to breach the code of old Boston ethics upon which they had been raised by making family matters public. Nor could they understand what all her complaints were about: my mother had a privileged childhood, Blanche insisted earnestly. Who cared about incidents like their father's beatings with straps? None of the rest of them were upset by any of it. And so, ultimately, they suspected my mother's mental illness was nothing other than posturing for attention, her poetry nothing more than Anne once again acting out her most dramatic, disgusting impulses.

～

Unlike the Harveys, Nana kept most of her objections to Mother's work silent. Despite the obvious, if unspoken, disapproval of my mother's flagrant literary exposures, I wonder if perhaps secretly, in a silent guarded part of her soul, my grandmother did not envy all my mother accomplished as well as hate it. She kept a clipping file of every article and review written about Mother; she hemmed and altered all the dresses Mother used for poetry readings; she cared for us whenever my mother had a seminar or a reading that took her out of town; she ran all the errands that made it possible for Mother to work at her art full-time.

My grandmother was a woman of no little intelligence. She had had aspirations but had given them up. In keeping with her times, she had forced her creativity into outlets such as cooking, sewing, and telling bedtime stories. Her son's wife, on the other hand, managed to get out of dealing with all such boring routines: with the help of Me-me and a mother-in-law who ran her household, Anne had the time available to write poems and stories that were, during a meteoric three-year rise, suddenly becoming available in all the best magazines, and even in bookstores. My grandmother

did not understand many of the poems, or the violet pitch of emotion that fueled them, but most of them shocked her anyway:

> *I am in the domain of silence,*
> *the kingdom of the crazy and the sleeper.*
> *There is blood here*
> *and I have eaten it.*
> *O mother of the womb,*
> *did I come for blood alone?*
> *O little mother,*
> *I am in my own mind.*
> *I am locked in the wrong house.*
>
> — "For the Year of the Insane"

Billie Sexton knew what it was like to be locked in the wrong
house. Her own marriage had put her there, but she was too proud
to admit it. And so, as much as she sometimes did not like her
daughter-in-law's frank expression of these emotions any woman
might feel, she did *understand* those emotions — all too well. What
a luxury it must have seemed to her, to put those feelings onto paper and so purge the anger that undoubtedly haunted her days. Perhaps these feelings in common were part of what made Nana so
angry with my mother at the same time she was so helpful to her.

For, whatever Billie Sexton might say, whatever she might imply,
however later histories might judge her relationship with her
daughter-in-law and her poetry, it was she who provided the freedom that enabled the poet to do what she did so well. And ultimately it was a mutually satisfactory arrangement: while my
grandmother complained about her daughter-in-law's lack of ability in the wifely arts, secretly she felt glad that Anne gave her room
to take over and that her son still needed her; while my mother
bitched about having her space invaded, secretly she felt relieved to
have a domineering mother-in-law who commandeered the household and cared for her as if she were another one of the children,
freeing her to become, quite simply, a star.

These stories of my family's early life together make up a fabric of many colors: the thread of the tapestry is rich and the weave so dense it is difficult for me to see clearly how it was made. I strip it down to look at it more clearly and come to this, just simple facts that make me ache as if I were still a little girl: my father drove up and down the eastern seaboard, a sample salesman for his father-in-law's woolen mill, just doing his job. Nana ran the house, perfectly. On the days her sickness allowed her, my mother wrote poems dark and rich as chocolate. As for Joy and me, we came and went. But in us grew a craving worthy of Rapunzel's rampion: never to be abandoned again.

First Metaphors

I give you the images I know.
Lie still with me and watch.

— Anne Sexton
"The Fortress"

THE PAST is a deep drawer in my mind, filled with a clutter of memories, dreams, fantasies, and images. When I open that drawer I learn about myself and about the others I have lived with and loved. It seems to me now, at this midpoint of my life, that all of us must experience the strong wish that accompanies every act of remembering: the desire to believe that whatever we remember is the way an event actually happened — the truth of one particular moment, one particular day. Intellectually we accept that the nature of truth as we experience it must be subjective, yet we insist, quite emotionally, that our version is the only one possible: I remember, therefore it was.

Mother defined her truths, interior and exterior, through her poetry, in which she naturally took a great deal of literary license. My mother imparted to me her enduring belief: what actually happened is not nearly so important as how you *feel* about what happened. Emotions are the bedrock upon which she built, with craft and artistry, her poetry — a poetry dubbed by many as "confessional," for in it she spoke baldly of the intimate and private aspects of her life.

For example, in *Mercy Street* — Mother's autobiographical play, which was eventually produced off-Broadway in 1969 — she explored an image she could never pinpoint definitively as memory, but that she could never quite dismiss as fantasy either: her father, a bottle of Scotch in his hand, sitting on the side of her bed late one night, kissing her lewdly and rubbing his hand between her legs. If it didn't actually happen exactly this way, surely the scene stood as a metaphor for the ways in which she feared her father and yet craved his love.

To write about such an event required only that she could *feel* it; thus she learned about herself, and, as a part of that process, perhaps she could also learn something about humankind. Her memories and fantasies were important to her, above all, in this way. Like Freud, she was her own laboratory.

We transcend many experiences — angry parents, fierce teachers, the taunts of both enemies and friends — particularly if we write of them. Whether captured in language or not, these experiences ultimately toughen the soul; to them we owe our mettle. Mother was not interested in castigating her father for a transgression that she freely admitted might have been only fantasy in her mind. She was captured by the idea that through the process of writing about a memory the poet can make it *more* real, *more* significant, than the actual event would have been in any case. What is told — as opposed to what is known — becomes the central concern. Or, as Mother told Dr. Orne in a therapy session in 1961: "What you write is better than what you are." Words can capture truth or promulgate lies. Words can clarify or disguise. Words can cleanse or make one's soul more filthy. Words have magical powers.

If childhood is the place and the time in which language wakes and allows us to begin capturing our reality in an enduring fashion, then the deep drawer filled with early memories should overflow with all manner of treasure. I open this drawer now to see, in one corner, half-hidden, a snapshot. I pull it out, unsure if it is memory or fantasy, dream or metaphor. Such distinctions no longer matter, however, when what I seek is only the truth of how *I felt*, a truth far more revelatory *about me* than any exact history.

Here is Mother, sitting at the kitchen table in our small kitchen, elbows propped on the rectangular pine table with iron legs. Sunlight slants through the window, signifying midmorning. The air is hazy with smoke. Between her fingers a cigarette angles, making a yellow stain on her skin. The ashtray full, she smudges her butts in the saucer of her coffee cup. The other hand drifts up to her head, as if forgetting what it was meant to be doing, as if determined to put something right. Smoothing and patting her hair one minute and then beginning to twirl curls the next. Ropy twists around the long bony fingers, her rings snagging. Sparkling and twisting. Smoke rises. Dishes from breakfast are still on the table. All morning long she is silent, staring. I sit at the table like a watchdog. I make pictures with my two-tier box of crayons: the colors are solid and bright — azure, forest green, magenta, carmine, and harvest gold. I am afraid to leave her.

"Mommy, can we have lunch?"

"Not now."

"I'm hungry."

When she turns to me I see her locked inside herself, staring out at me from another world. Her eyes are smoking, as if she has stuck her finger in an electric socket and all that jittery juice is burning its way out through her eyes. Her hair snakes up from her head. She looks at me with hate. I look away fast.

Time passes. My thumb's in my mouth, but it doesn't help my tummy. "I'm hungry," I say again, getting up to come around the table.

"Go away."

I stand there and stare at her. I am so scared. Her eyes flare, a jolt, a flash, her hand strikes. My cheek burns with the long print of her fingers. I start to cry.

꒱

As a child I already felt I was my mother's watchdog — a gate-keeper of sorts. When I was twenty-five, I drew a pair of eyes, black and threatening, on a piece of paper while attending a lecture; this felt-tip sketch frightened me so much that I hid it. Those eyes evoked in me the most intense anxiety. They were smoking as surely as Mother's eyes in the scene described above.

What did those eyes mean? I sweated it out for days, arriving finally at a single association: *the eyes are behind bars.* At first this meant nothing either. But gradually I began to think of my own eyes, those eyes whose vision was too dangerous to be borne. As a child

I had witnessed that motherhood, womanhood, and adulthood were hazardous states. Adults were often out of control, burning up, electrified. Sometimes mothers and fathers were violent, sometimes women were insane. Sometimes a mother slapped her little girl. Sometimes a mother wanted to kill her to make her stop crying.

At the front of the drawer is another snapshot that brings with it a flood of intense, precisely detailed memories. I am in my parents' bedroom with its gray-and-yellow flowered wallpaper. The twin beds are joined by a single gray headboard, on the wooden bedside tables stand lamps with mirrored bases. I have been watching television, while my mother lies on the bed behind me, staring off into space. I turn to ask her a question and she doesn't answer. I stand up and go over to her. Naked from the waist down, she is making noises and her fingers curl through her crisp black pubic hair. She pushes her long clitoris back and forth against the thick lips of her vagina. I drop my eyes, ashamed. She does not stop even though I am in the room. Her eyes don't seem to see me or know I am here. I am scared. Maybe she is having some kind of fit? Maybe they will take her away to the hospital again?

I close my eyes on this scene and try hard not to see it, though it happens again other times, once in the bathtub, more times on the bed. I shut my memories up in the prison of my mind; I know without being told that I shouldn't see things like this. This is bad. If I am to take good care of my mother, then I must make sure no one knows. The watchdog must keep quiet.

And so, for a long time, I keep my eyes, and my voice, behind bars. I am determined not to be like my mother, spilling secrets like water from a cup, writing out a family's shame. I will lock our dirt up tight.

To write these words frightens me. What sin do I commit by remembering and speaking at last? Like some long-craved-for food finally in my mouth, words have power. Mother used to own all the words. Now I own some of them too. Once I hated her for using her voice. Now I understand why she did.

࿓

Pull the drawer open again, Linda. The drawer will give you the fuel to continue. I bend slowly to look, and suddenly I see it there square in the middle, next to the yellow balloon of first grade: summer, the beach. An expanse of white, fronted by rolling blue, backed by dunes high as cliffs. Mother loves the sun more than food, and the beach provides heaven for us all: sun for her, a family outing for us; we are relaxed; everything is "all right," a phrase that embodies, at that time of my life, safety and therefore happiness. The ocean tumbles at our feet, and Joy and I, best buddies, build mud castles in a race with the tide. Crane Beach, just north of Boston — packed with other people and their children, normal people doing normal things. The bright orange, red, and yellow of beach blankets. The green canvas umbrella that no one ever sits under. The strong wind that can bring goose bumps even when it is ninety degrees, that fills our heads with a muffled roar indistinguishable from the sound of the sea.

Dad has packed the round red-plaid Scotch cooler with ice and bottles of beer without their labels. "Pass me the brown soda," Mother jokes, mindful of the lifeguards sitting atop their tall white chairs and the signs that forbid alcohol on the beach. We eat potato chips and egg salad sandwiches on white bread. Mother and Dad let us sip the brown soda. Coppertone on the back, sand up the butt, the sound of the waves pounding the rhythm that would never leave my head, that would soothe me for years to come whenever I heard it, carrying with it the contentment of days such as these. Above us the gulls wheel, shrieking their raucous joy at the pickings we leave. Mother smiles. We are content. For a while we, too, are normal people doing normal things.

Summer again: this photo does not fade with time. My parents, hand in hand, walk out the front door and down the walk. From my bedroom above, I watch them, strolling down our street in Newton Lower Falls after Sunday supper. Mother is dressed all in white to accentuate her deep tan, her long legs finished in flat white sandals, her toes painted with bright red polish. Tonight she looks like the nickname my father has given her: "Princess Anne." My father, in chinos and a madras shirt, is as slender as she, just Mother's height, his blue eyes sparkling, his hair lightened near to blond from the hours spent on yard work under the sun. This summer he has landscaped and planted a brand-new lawn from scratch all by himself — mixing the rich loam and the stinky fertilizer, pressing the scatter of seed into the earth with the weight of a rusted water barrel. Stakes bearing small white flags of surrender now surround our yard.

As my parents stroll down the sidewalk, the neighbors watch. Later Mother will tell me that they comment on her and Daddy, on how the handsome Sextons seem nearly an "integrated marriage": "They think I'm as dark as a Negro," she whispers with delight. As dusk creeps up among the rhododendrons, she and Daddy return to our front door. Dark lacing through light, their fingers still form a caress.

꒳

Autumn: a weeknight after dinner. The fluorescent overhead in the kitchen glares down on the abandoned table, the plates with their cold remains. I am eight. Dinner is calves' liver, fried up tough and dry. Liver makes me gag, so I just eat the bacon off the top and my baked potato. Usually I can't get away with this, but tonight Daddy and Mommy are distracted. Joy has already dropped a lot of her liver under the table for the cat, sending me nervous little grins with every piece she lets fall. My mother keeps smoking and watching me. She's twirling her hair and stirring the melting ice in her martini with her finger. She and Daddy had a long cocktail hour tonight and dinner was late. Leaning against the wall next to her are the crutches she got over the weekend after twisting her ankle.

"Linda, you're big enough to do the dishes after supper," Mommy says.

I stare at her in dismay. "Do I have to?"

She lights up another cigarette and rests her elbows on the table. "You and Joy clear them and scrape them and then I'll show you what to do." She motions with her hand for me to start, and the cigarette leaves a trail of smoke in the air.

I pout. I want to run up to my bedroom and the new library book I took out that afternoon. The thought of the story makes my mouth water. I've done all my other schoolwork just so I can go up now and read before bed. Dishes are her job. Daddy already fried the liver.

"She's too young," he says now, irritated. "Leave her alone."

"She's big enough."

"Anne, you just don't want to do it yourself."

My stomach clenches itself into a fist. They are going to "have a discussion" now. That's what we call it. We never say "fight." At school if two boys punch each other on the playground it's called a fight, but at home when my parents punch each other it's called a discussion. Already I am learning something important: at home words can mask reality but they do not change it.

"I hate how you want to baby them!" Her voice sharpens, bearing down on him like a drill. "You talk about how you hate Billie but you're just like she is!"

I blink my eyes fast, once, twice. I get up and start to clear the plates, but they don't even notice. This is no longer about the plates.

His blue eyes snap and shrink back into slits of hate.

Hands shaking, I stack the dishes in the sink in a clattering, slipping pile, hoping my noise will stop the rising hurricane.

The words are a blur now. She's taunting him, and I can see how stupid he feels.

"Stop it, Anne!" He clutches his upper arms, thick as tree trunks.

I wonder where "Princess Anne" has gone.

"*You* stop it!"

They are shouting, harder, louder, words sharp enough to chop through thick ice. My father is huge with anger, face sunburn-red.

He grabs her.

"Come on!" she screams, shoving him back. "You want to hit me? Go right ahead!"

They stumble over each other, Mommy trips over her crutches, Joy and I stand still, tears sliding down our cheeks.

What should we do?
Should we stop them?
Should we call Nana?

"Go ahead and hit me!" Mommy yells. "It'd be a relief to have you kill me!"

Daddy doesn't answer. He is gone somewhere inside his head. He doesn't hear her, he doesn't see us, he doesn't even look up, his fist is a tight knot by his side. He swings it up and into her face. *Thud-thud. Thud-thud.*

Joy and I cry harder. "Don't, Daddy, don't!"

We catch at his arm but he shakes us off, fleas from a dog's back. His arm is like a rock, we leave no imprint. "Don't hurt Mommy!"

He shoves her back into the dining room, into the corner, against the wall. Her head snaps back and forth as he shakes her shoulders, and then he bangs her head against the wall. *Thud-thud, thud-thud.* The noise is terrible. I imagine her skull, thin as the turkey wishbone Joy and I snap after Thanksgiving dinner. She screams again and I see her own hand, clenched into a fist, punch her thigh. Again, he bangs her against the wall. *Thud-thud.* Her head hits the round metal thermostat.

Is there blood? Will he kill her? Will any of us survive?
Oh, Daddy, please let us be a family again.

They stumble into the hall. "Finish the job!" she shrieks. But Joy is behind Daddy, still trying to catch his arm, and he trips over her. She goes down on her knees. Somehow this stops him, he sees our frightened faces. He reaches down and sweeps us into his arms. The anger is gone, like some fierce autumn wind that comes and then just dies down, scattering behind it fallen leaves in new patterns. Nothing will ever look the same.

He carries us into Mommy's writing room and sits beside us. I see tears on his face, too. He hugs us to stop our trembling and suddenly I'm not afraid of him anymore. He tries to explain: sometimes people fight, but they can make up, too. "Sometimes," he says, "people come to a meeting of the minds."

"What is that?" I ask, sniffling my runny nose.

"Like on the golf course," he answers. "Like meeting up with someone and seeing them again, the way I meet my friends for golf. And you talk and you go on."

Suddenly Mother is back, shouting at him through the glass French doors that open her small writing room onto the living room. "It's not fair, Kayo," she screams, "to get them on your side!"

He starts after her but she runs away. What side is she talking about? I wonder as we all run now, to try to catch her, to explain how much we love her. How can there be "sides" in this tornado of fear? Isn't this about living and dying?

When we get to the kitchen she is nowhere; the green Ford's engine screams to life in the garage, the tires squealing as she floors the accelerator. Down the driveway, off into the night — she who was not meant to drive on her hurt ankle. I start to cry again. It is my fault: I should have done the dishes. This punishment is worse than being sent away. Or maybe they *will* send me away. Maybe when she comes back she won't be all right. Maybe she will have to go to the hospital.

Daddy takes us both upstairs, washes our red and puffy faces, and puts us to bed. I do not understand this tenderness from a man who has been so terrifying only a moment before. How can hands that hit be so gentle now? Why was Mommy hitting herself at the same time he was hitting her? Why did she tell him to punch her? I push all these questions out of my mind and burrow deeper into the sheets, squeezing my eyes shut against the images that jab at the air in front of me. I am glad that my father is here, taking care of me.

In my memory, a single image serves as the touchstone for that night. On the kitchen floor, pointing toward the back door in an alignment reminiscent of geese lined up for a sojourn south, lay the wooden crutches. My mother had abandoned me once again. My old fear returned: I was three, four, five, and six. Alone. Afraid.

༶

Here's a photo of my aunt Joanie: backlit by the riot of autumn color, taking me on a farewell-to-summer picnic. Picnics were her specialty, with specially packed lunches, along with afternoon crafts projects and ice cream treats.

That year the trees have already begun to harden toward winter, branches etching their premonition of cold against deep blue Indian Summer sky. She spreads a fringed, plaid wool blanket on the bank of the pond and unpacks our lunch: peanut butter and bacon sandwiches, and a tall thermos full of steaming tomato soup.

Joanie is beautiful in ways different from my mother: her hair piled high to show off her smooth neck, her petite figure lush, her deep blue eyes tinged with a little sadness always, but with laughter as well. We laugh, giggle hysterically, and talk; she tells me stories about her boyfriends, what she wore on her last date: the opera, with a tiara in her hair and the off-the-shoulder black number she wears in the portrait that hangs in Nana's den. This day I ask her about her marriage and subsequent divorce, about how it feels to get pregnant out of wedlock and then miscarry a child. "Oh, Lord," she says, turning away. "How did we get into that?" She stares out over the pond. I look down at the ground and draw a design with a stick. I am embarrassed, upset that I have brought up a subject that can hurt her. Yet, despite my curiosity, I find relief in her reticence, in her carefully drawn boundaries, so different from what I am used to with Mother, who talks about anything and anyone — Mother, who told me when I was ten that Joanie had miscarried her baby in order to please Nana's need for a sick daughter who required attention.

The mallards float by, the bullfrogs poke their heads up through the sludge and algae at pond's edge, just to remind us, every once in a while, that there is indeed a world beyond ourselves. Joanie passes over the package of chocolate cookies. "I love you, Linny Pie," she says.

On the raft of memories such as these rides the love that got me through the tumult during my years of living with my mother. At the hands of Nana and Joanie I learned there were adults you could depend on.

~

It's Sunday night dinner at Nana's house. Mother hates going there, and yet we go, nearly every week. In the car we ride in silence, Mother chain-smoking. At five o'clock there is cocktail hour. Chit-chat. Hors d'oeuvres. Mother crosses her long legs, smokes some more, and is bored. She stares out the big picture window at nothing. Dinner occurs precisely at six.

Daddy carves the roast, sits in his father's seat at the end of the table opposite his mother. Joy and I sit on one side and Mother is on the other. Sometimes it feels to me as if she is in opposition to everyone in the room. I make sure I don't let my love for Nana, or for Joanie, show.

"I can't eat this meat," Mother announces. "I'm sorry, Billie, but I can't." She lights up a cigarette, even though she knows Nana hates smoking during the meal.

Nana's face is startled, hurt. "But this is a prime rib. I had the butcher give me the best!"

"Look at this." She spears it and holds it up for us all to see. "It's too . . . *red*." She lets it fall back onto her white china plate as if it were a bleeding rodent.

"For Chrissakes, Anne." My father cuts a piece and defiantly shoves it into his mouth. "Mother, it's delicious."

"Do you want more vegetables then?" Nana offers.

"No." My mother shakes her head and gestures to the tiny mound of mashed potatoes and the green beans that lie scattered like straws across her plate. "I feel too sick to eat."

I look around at everyone else's plate, heaped high with food. My throat closes up. I push my potatoes around so it looks like I am eating something. Under the table Joy begins to kick the rung of her chair.

"Joy!" My father reaches over and raps his knuckles on the side of her head. "No kicking. Eat your dinner."

Joy obediently fills her fork with string beans. She eats all the beans, and then starts cutting tiny pieces of roast beef. Daddy frowns. "Why do you do it like that?" he complains. "You're supposed to take bites of each thing, around and around. What's the matter with you?"

Joy's eyes shine with tears. She doesn't understand that he's not really angry with her, that he wants to control the way she eats because he can't control the way her mother doesn't. I want to hold her hand under the table but I'm afraid to.

Mother puts her drink down with a click. "What I want," she announces, "is some gravy bread."

Nana sits, silent, buttering a piece of her roll. Every Sunday now there is a new argument about the gravy bread; gravy bread is a euphemism for white bread soaked in the beef juices that flood the carving board. Joy and I like to drink the juice in a little cup and Nana delights in saving it for us. Recently Mother has been insisting that she be given the juice because she can't eat meat. As if to prove her point, she will put a piece of meat in her mouth and try to gag it down. Sometimes she succeeds in swallowing it, other times it comes back up all over her plate. Watching her vomit a piece of roast beef is an extremely convincing argument for why she should get the prized beef juice, although I can't quite understand why she wants it: if, as she insists, she's grossed out by the bloody meat, why does she want the blood itself?

"Anne, you know I save the juice for the children," Nana says quietly.

"It's all right," I interrupt anxiously. "We don't mind."

"Well, I mind. You children are the ones who need the nutrition here. You're the ones who are growing."

"I need it too," Mother insists. "They're already healthy, Billie. I can't eat any meat, and it should be mine."

My grandmother shoves her chair back angrily, her jaw thrust out and her mouth grim. My father looks at his plate stonily and keeps eating, shoveling the food into his mouth. Joy and I stare at our laps and swallow hard so we won't cry. We don't care about gravy bread: we just care about not setting Mother off. Why is mealtime always so difficult? I wonder. Why does it loom like a black pit at the end of every day? Sundays at Nana's are the worst.

Sometimes in the car on the way home, Mother will start making mean remarks about Nana, and when she and Daddy get inside our house they start to fight. *Please, God, don't let that happen tonight.*

Nana slaps the gravy bread down in front of Mother. She hasn't put it on the good china, but on an old chipped tea saucer instead. It seems to me this slice of cold red bread with the fat congealed along the edges is a sacrifice we all make to appease a tempestuous God. Mother forks it up greedily. I remember Grimms' fairy tale, Snow White, where the queen eats the heart of the boar and licks her fingers with pleasure, believing that the raw red muscle belongs to her step-daughter.

۶

The last week of October: just before Halloween Daddy drives us to the pumpkin patch and lets us squabble over which pumpkin is best. Joy and I wander through a field of orange globes, hundreds still at this late date. Dad rolls them onto their sides, looking for one with a minimally flat back, a strong and sturdy stem. The man at the stand weighs our choice. We pay by the pound. Riding back home in the car, we sing.

At home everyone has a role in the Halloween drama: Joanie has helped us design our costumes, and Nana has been sewing for weeks — one year a Chinaman, the next a bunny rabbit, once a Kyoto lady with a fan and chopsticks in my uptwist hair. Joy and I drink cider and plot our strategy: if we go up Clearwater Road and then down Pierrepont before cutting through the Jenks' backyard, will we cover more houses?

Three days before the important night, we make the pumpkin into a jack-o'-lantern. The entire family gathers in the kitchen for this project after supper. Mother decides what the face will look like while Joy and I cover the kitchen floor with layers of newspaper. We strip to our undershirts and scoop deep into the cool stringy innards with our hands, getting slimy all the way up to our armpits. We set the seeds aside for frying in the black iron skillet with a handful of salt. Daddy does the final hard-press paring on the inside so that no stray strings will catch in the candle, and then he begins to carve the lines Mother has drawn. He notches the top with precision so we can line it up properly when we put it back on. I am awed by the way he thinks through this small detail.

Halloween night itself: Mother's spaghetti sauce, simmered all day long from whole tomatoes so that I walk into a wall of fragrance when I come home from school, ready to start getting dressed even though there are hours more until dark. This, one of the few meals she is happy to make, is a family favorite. Later, spaghetti and garlic bread warming our stomachs, Joy and I fly out into the dark, picking up friends along the way. Trick or treat! On our own, with no parents to caution or reprimand, we are free in the night, walking house to house. The cold autumn air presses against our heated cheeks, and cools throats already slick with chocolate. Mother and her sickness are banished to the back of my mind. As my paper sack gets heavier and heavier, and my arms begin to ache, I become another, carefree, Linda. Mounds, Milky Ways, Rollos, Tootsie Pops, Mary Janes, Bazooka. I give Joy each piece I don't like — licorice, Good 'N Plenty, Snickers, Mars Bars — and still every year my candy lasts until Easter. I eat one piece a day. Who says you can't control your life?

꒰꒱

I don't remember what I did to deserve it. I wasn't good all the time, so I'm sure there was something, some regular childlike thing, that got me into trouble. Maybe it was the time I came back from skating late. Whatever. In our home, if I didn't get spanked then I got slapped. I was never sure which was worse: a slap was more personal, in your face, as if to say, "I hate you. Go away." But spanking hurt more. This time it is spanking, so she pulls me onto her lap and shoves my underpants down around my ankles. I cooperate and don't wiggle or try to get up. I remember Uncle Ed, and the chenille bedspread at Blanche's that made my nose itch when I bit it to keep from crying when he made my fanny hot with his belt. Mommy doesn't use a belt. She reaches down and slips off her sneaker. Size nine. Big enough to cover a lot of skin. I try not to squeeze my fanny cheeks tight because that makes it hurt worse, but after the third spank it doesn't matter what I do. It hurts so bad, it's hot, it's like fire poured over all my soreness, my private places. She keeps spanking and I can't help crying now, my nose-running face slippery. She never counts. She just does it till she isn't angry anymore. When she's finished I lie on my bed, face-down. I hate her. I hate me.

ॐ

Another season: winter. A dark night, probably a weekend. The air is clean and cold, scented by the smell of wood fires from neigh-borhood chimneys. We pile into the car, a little cramped because we have a house guest, Tony Hecht. I know he is a poet, just like Mother, but I do not think she has ever read any of his poetry to me. I love him because he is fun.

When Tony comes to stay Mother turns on like a Christmas tree, brightly colored and gay. She doesn't hang around in her bathrobe. She puts on her lipstick before breakfast. She gets up for breakfast! She laughs a lot, her wonderful throaty laugh, and hap-piness fills me with joy. She flutters around the house, cooks meals, and, best of all, she and Daddy do not fight. We have house guests only occasionally, and when we do Joy has to come and sleep in my room, but I don't mind when it is Tony who has displaced her.

That winter night we drive to the toboggan slide. Though it is not far from home, we have never before been there; as a family we rarely take vacations together, or day excursions, because Mother is too unpredictable. On the one camping trip we took as a family, Mother got upset at using the public bathroom on the camp-ground. "I can't go here," she whispered to me after the second day, starting to twirl her hair around her finger nervously. "I'll stay with you," I offered, and I did, but my presence didn't help. We trudged back down the hill to our campsite. Daddy sighed. "For Chrissakes, Anne. I'll go to the store and get you a laxative." She shook her head. "I want to go home." She reminded me of a child at the play-ground. "The kids will be so disappointed!" he protested, not say-ing how disappointed he would be. She shook her head again and went to sit facing the woods, her back to us. Joy and I helped

Daddy pack up the tent, the frying pan, the sleeping bags. Anger hardened inside me like a thick column of ice.

But this night Tony is here, and Daddy pulls our toboggan down off the roof of the car, and in the dark we climb up the tall ladder to the top of the slide. I don't see how the sled gets to the top. A chute of ice lies before us, the ground miles away, snow-covered and silent. We all pile onto the long sled, and I am thrilled to be right behind Tony. I wrap my arms around his middle, hold tight, excitement and fear in my throat; I revel in being so near to him. I press my face against the wool of Tony's jacket, make a small moist patch there with my breath. And then we are off, down, down, my stomach leaping as we hurtle over the ice and through the dark, faster than I have ever gone on my bike, snow and stars blurring to tears in my eyes. Bumping out to slow on the ruts at the bottom, I surprise myself by clamoring "again, again."

Handsome and funny, Tony Hecht is my favorite. Later he will become one of America's most famous poets. At nine I love him absolutely — my first crush on an older man. When he leaves, I stand at the window and cry. It never occurs to me that Mother may have a crush on him as well.

As an adolescent, I wondered if Mother and Tony were lovers. After Mother's death I read their correspondence and realized that they were not. Tony, it seemed, was one of the few who held Anne the Seductress at arm's length — perhaps one more reason I liked him. In 1961, after one of his visits with us, he sent my parents a pair of wine glasses as a gift and asked that she and my father drink a toast to one another. Love, he taught my mother, *could* be platonic.

ᢙ

Winter brings skating as well. Mother, hardly an athlete, likes going outdoors for one activity only — sunbathing. Nevertheless, once in a while she breaks her own rules about abstaining from exercise and accompanies us skating. She straps on her old pair of white figure skates, and Daddy dons his college hockey blades, and we all troop out to the frozen pond that has formed in a depression on the public golf course behind the house. Round and round we go on the patch of ice nature has provided as our own private — if bumpy — skating rink. When we come indoors, Mother makes hot cocoa, chocolate wafting through the kitchen to tease our noses, our faces flushing hot in the steamy, animal warmth that rises from the radiator covered with wet wool: caps, socks, scarves, and mittens.

꒳

A spacious fifty-gallon fish tank, filled with salt water tropicals, pure white sand, and coral of various hues. Aquariums are one of Daddy's few hobbies, and I am thrilled to be allowed to share this with him. By now we live in Weston; I am fourteen. Carefully we choose each fish from the darkened aisles of aquariums at the store: the bright blue Queen Angel, the white-spotted Tomato Clown, the magenta-and-yellow Royal Gramma I name Tamar after studying the Bible in English class that month. The long-nose Hawaiian Butterfly with its camouflage eye set in the middle of its yellow tail seems the smartest to me, designed to last. It is a world of underwater mystery, running in precise control, feedings clocked to the hour, the salinity kept balanced, the temperature always maintained in the eighties. Daddy and I work in tandem, in a silence that comforts. I would like to live in this serene tank, be ministered to so fastidiously, lead this kind of uncomplicated life. I would like to feel my father's attention beam down on me day by day. But if not — then there is this, just the two of us, elbow deep in warm water.

Until one Sunday morning, when Daddy comes into the kitchen with pain and fury in his eyes. "They're all dead," he informs me bluntly. He smacks his fist against the beige kitchen counter. Fear revs inside me.

I run to the living room to find them floating belly up, all their beautiful colors bleached, all their intricate motion stilled. Yesterday: life. Today: death. Just as unpredictable as always. I start to cry while Daddy begins to scoop them out of the tank with the mesh net, his expression grim and angry. "What happened to them?" I ask, wiping my nose on my sleeve.

He bends to the floor and holds up the electrical plug to the tank's heater. "This was unplugged. Overnight. They couldn't take the temperature drop."

"But we never unplug that."

"*We* didn't!"

"Then who?"

"Those creeps of your mother's, that's who."

Saturday afternoon Mother's poetry-rock band, Anne Sexton and Her Kind, had come to practice. I remember now that the electric keyboard had been in this corner; Bill must have unplugged the heater for the tank so he could plug in his instrument. I had sat on the step down into the living room, tapping my feet, swaying to the rhythm, fancying myself a grown-up part of things. Now I am ashamed. My father hates this band — another part of life that takes Mother away from him — and maybe he is right. The band killed our fish, destroyed our tank, the metaphor for peace that existed right in the midst of our unpredictable, chaotic household.

Mother comes to the entrance of the living room and leans against the door frame. "I *told* you I was sorry, Kayo. Nobody meant to kill the fish. It was an accident."

His face is set, and he doesn't answer her.

"You can buy more," she says with a shrug, dragging on the cigarette in her hand. "They're only fish."

Her words sting us. I see Daddy tense, and then turn away. She stands there for a minute more in her cotton shirt and her double-knit slacks and then walks back to her writing room. The clatter of her typewriter resumes. From the kitchen the radio plays. Inside of me hate boils, looking for a way out. Daddy and I finish collecting the dead and then go to the bathroom to flush our treasures down the toilet.

⌇

A late afternoon as daylight peters out. The sky is gray and the world looks dirty. Daddy and Joy and I drive into Boston to Massachusetts General Hospital. I look up at the enormous stone face of the building. It makes me feel very small even though I am about to be eleven. On some high floor my mother is locked up. I have

read her poem about the mental hospital, "Music Swims Back
to Me."

> *Wait Mister. Which way is home?*
> *They turned the light out*
> *and the dark is moving in the corner.*
> *There are no sign posts in this room,*
> *four ladies, over eighty,*
> *in diapers every one of them.*
> *La la la, Oh music swims back to me*
> *and I can feel the tune they played*
> *the night they left me*
> *in this private institution on a hill. . . .*
> *It was the strangled cold of November;*
> *even the stars were strapped in the sky*
> *and that moon too bright*
> *forking through the bars to stick me*
> *with a singing in the head.*

I cannot remember if I have ever visited her before. Most of the
time when she goes to McLean or Westwood Lodge it's only for a
few days, and Joy and I have never gone, I think, to see her in those
places. I rememeber the poem and wonder if this mental ward is the
kind where they strap her to a chair, where there are bars on the
windows. Will there be old ladies in diapers? Or is what I imagine
worse than what is?

A big metal elevator takes us up. At a barred door we stand
silently and ring to be admitted, and at last a male nurse comes
and unlocks the door with a hoop of keys attached to his belt
like a prison guard. *My mother lives in this place,* I think. *This is her
home for now.* I bite my lip so I won't cry. Joy and I hold hands.
Nana has insisted we dress in our Sunday church best. I feel as if I
am suffocating.

Mother looks up at us shyly. She hugs me, and it feels strange. "I
love you, Pie," she says, her voice thick and sticky with the tranquilizers. "I love you too, Muggy," I answer, my voice thick with all
the tears I squeeze back. Her hair lies close and slick against her

skull. Is this woman really my mother? Will she be my mother to-morrow and the day after? Will she ever come home?

She has her own room here, small with beige walls and a twin bed in the corner. Stacks of books are piled high on the floor, just like beside her bed at home. She sits on the bed, her radio playing, happy to see Daddy with the cartons of cigarettes. She takes us for a walk down the corridor, as if we are touring a museum. There are no toothless ladies in diapers, there are no women bound with straightjackets. In the living room a few people sit and rock and stare while the television spills its images into empty space. In the kitchen, there is an enormous refrigerator with four different kinds of juice. We all take a cup, pretending drinking juice in a hospital kitchen is an everyday activity. The taste of the V-8 lies thick and furry on my teeth. A nurse plays table tennis with Joy, and I watch. Mommy and Daddy have a minute alone. This place isn't what I expected, but the vacant eyes of the patients frighten me anyway. I get a queasy, off-balance feel as I watch them sitting silently, still in their bathrobes, in the late gray afternoon. Anxiously, I eye the big metal door.

"When are you coming home?" I ask Mother when she and Daddy kiss each other good-bye.

"Soon," she says. "There's a new medication they're trying. It makes me feel a little funny, kind of — " she cocked her head to the side, searching for the right word — "like my brain is stuffed with wool. Woolly. It's called Thorazine."

"Maybe it will help," I say hopefully.

They lock the big metal door behind us. Two weeks later she will come back home — until the next time. I try to learn to live with this.

෴

Smells come from the drawer of the past as well, smells that stir the roots of memory: a woody musk that recalls sunlight baking the wooden steps and the dirt of the small tulip bed beside the breeze-way of our house at 40 Clearwater Road, essence of summer com-fort; dark wine and onions, beef stew on winter nights; a perfume of gardenias that says *Nana*; or this one here — the smell of ginger

snaps baking, warm and spicy on a dark winter afternoon. Mother
sends me to borrow ginger from our neighbor. In the icy street I see
a dead cat, run over by a car; clambering over the snowbanks I turn
my head away and do not let myself recognize that it is one of our
cat's newly grown kittens.

Mother and I mix the stiff, sticky cookie dough in the V-shaped
beige bowl, ridged along the outside, that holds potato salad during summer. We roll it out, arms aching, in the dim yellow kitchen,
grease the cookie sheet that twenty years later will come to rest in
my kitchen drawer. She laughs. She wears her black hair cropped
short, and wraps an apron around her waist. Rings sparkle on her
fingers as she wields measuring cups and spoons. Ginger snaps —
her favorite cookies. Ginger snaps — not the comfort of oatmeal,
not the richness of chocolate chip. Ginger snaps: an exotic mix of
sugar and bite, just like Mother.

From the oven, the sweet caramel of sugar baking. For me, this
smell will always signal safety: if you can bake cookies, you can't be
too crazy.

Snapshots, seasons, smells, and memories, too. Though I would
like to forget it, one memory leaps up insistent as a dog. Mother
calls for me to climb into her bed late on a Sunday morning to
cuddle. She never gets up before nine if she can help it, and Daddy
has nicknamed her a "pad rat." I have already been to Sunday
school and back, driven by our neighbors while Mother attends St.
Mattress. This morning is like many others: Mother wants to "play
nine." Playing nine means that I — the real nine-year-old — slide
up in the bed and she slides down, puts her head on my chest while
I pat her head. "Now you be the Mommy," she says. "And I'm your
little girl."

I comply, though unwilling. I hope this time she won't get stuck
in the game and be reluctant to trade places. Often when we play
this game she scares me by refusing to be my mother again.

Time passes. An hour maybe. I try to be a good mommy and
take care of my little girl, but her head is so heavy, like a giant's.

How can I take care of a little girl when I am only nine? I try to imagine my mother is my doll. That doesn't help, and I scrinch my eyes shut to help myself not see. Her head gets heavier and heavier, weighing on my chest and making it hard to breathe. I am beginning to feel as if I'm trapped underneath a truck as big as the one that comes on Mondays for our trash, as if I am being crushed by the arm that compacts the newspapers and wire hangers. I can feel Mother's chest rising and falling against my side as I stroke her head with my hand. She's talking and talking but I don't understand her words.

"Nana," she says. "I love you, Nana."

I'm getting smaller and smaller with each minute. I can't breathe.

"Anne loves cuddling with Nana."

Tears thicken in my throat. I keep patting her head.

"I love being nine," she says drowsily. "It feels so good."

"I like you to be thirty-four," I choke out at last. "Could you be thirty-four now?"

"Pretty soon," she promises.

I am suffocating, and the big tears squeeze out the corners of my tightly shut eyelids. I try to hang on, to take good care of her — just like I promised God I would when he sent her home from the hospital. If I take good care of her she will never have to go back to the hospital again.

"Mommy?" I plead. "Please?"

"No," she pouts. "I'm nine!"

"Please," I say and start to sob, my chest heaving its burden up and down.

"I'm nine!"

"Please be thirty-four!"

"I can't be thirty-four — I'm just a little girl. I'm *your* little girl. Don't you want me anymore?" She twirls her hair around her finger. "Should I go live someplace else?"

Fear scalds me. "Please," I whisper. "I want *you* back."

Years later I discovered she had told the story of "playing nine"

to her psychiatrist this way: "We spent about an hour pretending . . . I really liked it . . . I probably relate to Linda as a child
would to a mother, crawl up next to her as a child would to a
mother . . . I can save myself through my children because there's a
bond."

The memory of playing nine hurts because I keep seeing my
own small face, so desperate and so afraid, overwhelmed with the
responsibility I feel toward keeping Mother sane. And anger comes
too: her cavalier description to her doctor shows how little com-
prehension she had of the terrible fear she ignited in me each time
she indulged herself with this game. "It's something like a trance,"
she continued to Dr. Orne. "I really liked it, was acting out for
about an hour and a half. She went along with this and then became frightened."

Why couldn't I just have gone out after church, like my friends
did, to play hopscotch in the street? While the game brought comfort to my mother in its return to her early cuddles with her own
Nana, to me the game aroused over and over all my fears of losing
my mother. At nine I was required to *be* the mother because my
own mother had descended once again into childlike behavior —
just as she did when she became so sick she could not take care of
herself. The game was a metaphor for all that was to come, the increasingly blurred nature of our relationship, mother versus daughter. Who was who?

At the very back of the drawer lies another memory of cuddling,
but this one fills me, as I lift it out, with peace. In this memory lies
the luxury of rest, of love in proper proportion. This time I am
nine, and Mother is indeed thirty-four. It is a dark afternoon, late
Thanksgiving day. Mother and I nestle beneath a thick wool
afghan on top of the bed in Nana's bedroom. We are meant to be
taking a nap, but, as usual, we are talking, sharing what we see and
feel. Without knowing it, in this exchange of ideas and emotions
Mother passes on to me her powers of observation; she shows me
how to watch, how to see, how to record what transpires in the
world around me. This is how I inherit her greatest gift.

The world outside is wet, suffused with the gray light of a late rainy day. Through the large glass window past the ivory dressing table, the two of us watch the underwater action: a pheasant struts, staccato, his tail combing the yellowing grass. The tree I have named the broccoli tree stands like a sentinel, silent and upright. It is not large, but it is sturdy and distinct. Mother's body curls around me in warm shelter. I am utterly cocooned. I am happy. Her fingers, long and lovely, trace a dance of tenderness across my face. Feelings become memories; this memory becomes emblematic, the truth of that particular day.

I remember the safety and warmth of that afternoon. I remember the love, sturdy as the tree, immutable as the poem she would later write to make our moment endure. She titled it "The Fortress" because on that day love did indeed build a strong wall around us:

> Darling, life is not in my hands;
> life with its terrible changes
> will take you, bombs or glands,
> your own child at
> your breast, your own house on your own land . . .
> I cannot promise very much.
> I give you the images I know.
> Lie still with me and watch . . .
> We laugh and we touch.
> I promise you love. Time will not take away that.

Mother, you were right: time did not take away that.

A Maker of Myths

~

The speaker in this case
is a middle-aged witch, me —
tangled on my two great arms,
my face in a book
and my mouth wide,
ready to tell you a story or two.

— Anne Sexton
"The Gold Key"

A THICK, symmetrical tree, tall enough to brush the rafters of
the cathedral ceiling in the living room. My father's choice.

A tree with a crooked spine, still on the lot the week before
Christmas, looking for a home. My mother's choice.

Any kind of tree — preferably with needles and an evergreenish
sort of smell — one that allows me to continue to celebrate this
most Christian of holidays, even though I am now Jewish and living
on the West Coast. My choice.

Why did Christmas matter so much to my family then, and why
does it matter so much to me now? As I look through this window
into my childhood, I see December twenty-fifth as the one day we
could count on: it arrived every year predictably and reliably and
came complete with its own set of rules and expectations. The sur-
prises of Christmas were all to be found under the tree: safe, tamed,
wrapped in gay paper. With fervor the entire family joined together
to create the myth and write the story that was Christmas, precisely
because it symbolized the "normal" family we so longed for.

Christmas at our house was full of magic and superstition, but
none of it was religious: Jesus got lost in the shuffle. It was the rituals that were important, the rituals that kept us safe and beat back

the chaos of living with parents who were so unpredictable. When Christmas came, we told ourselves that we were safe from the nights where Daddy could bang Mommy's head into the wall, or the days where Mommy could sit like a statue, twirling her hair into snakes and mumbling to herself. Christmas was like a new start: "Oh," Joy and I would say to each other, "those other things will never happen to us again."

But the mainstream of time that flowed between the stepping-stones of each Christmas continued, with fear still twining itself around our ankles. Joy and I held very still and lived in our dream world: 1957, '58, '59, and '60. And when the hammer fell, *thud-thud,* we closed our eyes and prayed the next time would be different. All year we waited for Christmas to come around again, praying that this year there would be consummate peace in our home long past the holiday season. December twenty-fifth may have been a myth we needed quite desperately, filled with mystery and make-believe, but it was a myth all the same; ultimately it could neither heal nor hold back the rising tide of our fear and Mother's instability.

No one in the Sexton house ever missed Christmas — for illness or any other reason — not even Mother. Or, perhaps, especially not Mother, because Christmas was clearly just as magical to her as it was to us, a time when she could once again revisit a positive part of her childhood. She, too, fervently believed in the holiday's restorative powers.

The season began when my mother made her yearly trek up the attic stairs. The attic, with its sloping rafters and dusty floor, was crammed with the multitude of objects Yankee frugality dictated she and Dad save rather than pitch: mattresses; scores of woolen blankets becoming progressively more moth-eaten; two bassinets; a baby bathing table; lamps with broken necks; dozens of empty boxes; Mother's maternity clothes; oil paintings; family silver; crates of disintegrating paperback books; a copper tea service complete with oil burner; stacks of magazines. There, barely visible in the dim yellow light emanating from the bare swinging bulb, Mother would rummage with determination until she found the "bubble tree" and the large silver punch bowl she used to hold the incoming Christmas cards, a weighty trophy won by her parents, who had owned show-quality bulldogs.

Her parents had had their own traditions, important ones that were engraved deeply on everyone's memory. When Mary and Ralph were alive, we celebrated the holidays with them; after they died, we carried on many of the traditions for them as a way of transferring their myth-making abilities onto ourselves: an appearance by Santa, who was played by Ralph (and later my father) in a red velvet suit from Abercrombie and Fitch, carrying a pillowcase full of oranges; lobster tails and shrimp with cocktails, prime rib *and* turkey for dinner, floating island pudding for dessert. The Harveys observed details like these with rigor. Setting up the bubble tree was only one such ritual, but it was an original, handed down directly from Ralph and Mary Gray.

The bubble tree, which Mother always set prominently in the window of the living room, facing the street, was a small electrical evergreen whose short branches were studded with sockets into which colored lights the shape of candles were screwed. The lights compensated for the fact that the tree was artificial because they lit up in a variety of pleasing colors and bubbled their tinted oils as they began to heat.

Every night I lay on the living room rug, or on the couch, and contemplated the tree after Mother had plugged it in. Lit only when full dark fell, it stood elevated in front of the window on a small folding TV table also inherited from Ga-ga and Grampa. It took a while before the bubbles began to percolate and as they did they warmed me, one tree and then its reflection in the black glass panes of the window. The colors were mellow, yellow-gold, deep blue, dusky red; the tree stood in solid defense against the dark December night and the cold that leaked in around the cracks of the window sill. It pleased Mother that both Joy and I loved the bubble tree as much as she did.

Newton Lower Falls was a small middle-class suburb of Boston, and Clearwater Road was lined, at regular intervals, with square three-bedroom wooden houses set back by equally square morsels of lawn. All had been made to look marginally different by creative combinations of paint and siding. My parents had brought me to this house from the hospital after I was born in July of 1953. However, raised in the prestigious, wealthy, and elite suburbs of Chestnut Hill, Weston, and Wellesley, they always felt the neighborhood was beneath them. Mother carefully taught us finger-bowl etiquette and the use of the correct fork, and how to scoop soup from the back of the bowl to the front. She prided herself on being a Boston lady even as she slouched in her chair at the dinner table in direct defiance of her own mother's perfect posture. Though my parents did make close and enduring friendships while they lived in Newton Lower Falls, from as far back as I can remember I knew and worried that one day we would move to a "better" suburb where the lots were bigger and the neighbors of more like background. The idea of moving anywhere terrified me, bringing forth memories of other displacements.

While the neighborhood began to celebrate the Christmas season immediately after Thanksgiving, stringing lights on the outdoor bushes and decorating their trees with "tacky" blinking lights and too much tinsel, my parents were purists. *Twelve* days of Christmas, my father declared. And so we kept it, sacred as the Bible. The emergence of the bubble tree signaled that our Christmas season had begun in earnest.

Over the years the bubble tree began to age and then deteriorate; each year Daddy added more tape to hold the bulbs on the branches, more picture wire to hold the branches on the tree. When I was eleven, we made the inevitable move to Weston and reluctantly consigned the tree to the trash. Grieving, we conducted an annual search for another like it, but failed.

Buying the Christmas tree and setting it up always introduced a chill tension into the glow of the season. My parents' feelings about which tree to buy reflected their self-esteem more than anything else. My father loved large, full trees, mirroring his longing for success and perfection. But my mother, whose voice was more than loud, craved a tree that no one else wanted. She liked the drama of the statement: she liked having something unique, even if it was unique in a negative direction. One weeknight in mid-December after my father had come home from work (weekends drew crowds and my parents hated crowds) we made the family pilgrimage out to the country to the Christmas tree lot. There, in the dark, our breath pluming visibly in the frigid air, the debate would begin as my father started to examine trees in detail. Joy and I tagged along, trying to agree with everything everyone said and so keep the peace.

Mummified with heavy twine, the trees stood with their arms pinioned skyward. Despite the lot owner's insistence that customers not unwrap the trees, my father carried a steak knife with him for just such a purpose. His small gloved hands reached into the prickly interiors to push and prod, looking for bare spaces where branches had broken off, or not grown to begin with. Mother, dressed in slacks and a camel hair coat, spent her time lobbying Joy and me: she painted the lonely soul of some small straggly tree in colors of merciless pathos. Choosing a Christmas tree was my first experience with the democratic process, however: the majority ruled, and Joy and I always voted with Daddy.

Once we moved to Weston in 1964, with a cathedral ceiling in the living room that was sixteen feet high, Daddy's desire for arboreal splendor could be indulged totally. And so it was that my father strapped the fullest, most glamorous tree of the lot onto the roof of the car, swearing the entire time — though his pride would not allow him to accept the assistance offered by the exasperated owner of the lot. Daddy spent the ride home carrying on about how they had picked his pocket: Christmas tree–lot owners were a bunch of thieves. In the backseat, Joy and I basked in the dark drowsy heat, glad the hurdle of choice had been overcome and sure that they wouldn't argue about the price. Mother didn't care how much things cost. She just leaned her head against the seat and drew deeply on her cigarette, saying nothing, steeped in a silence totally out of keeping with her nature.

As Daddy hoisted the tree off the roof of the car, however, I prepared myself. Once it was brought into the house, he would try to insert it into an antiquated green stand with three colored bulbs in its base that hadn't worked since I could remember. Then, swung erect and balanced, it would be left to stand for a day or two to allow the branches to relax into the proper position for decorating. Mother always made fun of Daddy's meticulous preparations, but we went along with them nonetheless.

Setting the tree up, however, was the most dangerous event of the evening, possibly of the entire season. Daddy loosed the behemoth from the top of the car and hefted it, his face getting as red as his red-plaid wool hunting jacket. He cursed his way into the living room, leaving a trail of pine needles in his wake. Joy and I stood by helplessly, knowing that to try and help would make him angrier.

As the years went by and his yen for the ever-taller tree grew, the stand appeared to shrink. Struggling to get the base over the thick trunk, he resorted to the saw, the hammer and tongs. His cursing was now awesome. Joy and I both looked away, trying not to let our anxiety spill into the room. I fiddled with the boxes of ornaments so as not to have to look at him. Eventually he jammed it on. "By God," he said, "that friggin' tree better be flat on the bottom."

My desire to leave the room was now as strong as a morning urge to get to the toilet quickly. This lust of his for a gigantic tree always made him forget how difficult the masculine feat of getting such a tree upright and balanced could be. The three of us heaved and shoved and pushed it to stand, running to the other side as it threatened to keep right on going. Sometimes we rigged it to the ceiling with wire, a trick that inevitably resulted in Daddy hammering his thumb and screaming at someone. My mother just sat on the sofa and smoked, a smile on her face, as she savored a small-tree revenge sweet as eggnog. She never said a word, but everyone knew what she was thinking. For once, she was the one acting like a grown-up. I'm certain that Daddy was not the only father on the block who lost his temper when it came time to swing the tree erect, but because his loss of control recalled how closely we lived to no control, the fear I felt was intense.

One year every ball in our arsenal had gone onto the tree and neither parent had lost his or her temper over anything. It was late, and we all climbed to bed wearily. From my bedroom a while later, just as I was drifting off to sleep, I heard an enormous crash. The air seemed to vibrate with the force of it. Daddy hurried downstairs just in time to catch the cat trying to extricate itself from the top branches of the sixteen-foot monster.

Daddy had never really liked our two cats. Their attempt to scale the Christmas tree as if it were a rooted evergreen did not improve matters. The shattered glass, the broken branches, and the hysterical barking from our two Dalmatians made the scene even more Kafkaesque. Daddy picked up the cat and threw her across the room, where she hit the wall with an ugly thump and then ran off to hide. Joy and I tried to help him get the tree upright, but he screamed at us to go to bed, so we slunk off like the cat, and left him with the mess. While Mother slept on upstairs, bedded down deeply under the influence of her sleeping pills, Joy and I lay awake in the dark, listening to the vacuum cleaner, which seemed to roar on for hours. And the next morning it was as if nothing unusual had happened. The tree was lit, my father happy once again.

Most years, of course, the cat didn't try to climb the tree and our anxiety stayed at a manageable level. Most years my father simply cursed, and we all pushed and pulled and got the tree upright without disaster. Once the tree was up, my father underwent a transformation. He relaxed. Decorating was the best part, nearly worth what we had to suffer through to get there. Daddy's smile lit the room. He was a handsome, charming man, his mood as infectious when he was happy as it was when he was angry.

At this point Mother would rouse herself from the sofa to turn on the Christmas music. "Ave Maria" was her favorite, and we all covered our ears and giggled when she began to sing. Daddy rolled his eyes. She had never been able to carry a tune, but she loved to pretend she could and so floated through the room, yowling off

key, making us laugh as Daddy began to string the electric lights —
which definitely did not blink (too "low class," they said) — and
as Joy and I began to argue over who would hang which ornament.
The only ornament Mother ever hung in the later years was a gift
from Nana: a tiny gold typewriter with minuscule rhinestone keys;
the piece of paper rolled into its platen read *dear Santa*.

Joy and I hung hundreds of glass ornaments, some of them collected by my parents but most inherited from my maternal grandparents, together with some handmade by Joanie, who had an
artistic streak. There were silver balls hand-painted with sleigh
scenes, there were rose-colored glass balls with the words *Merry
Christmas* in scrolled glitter. There were long hand-blown ovals,
carefully preserved in boxes over the years. Definitely not your ordinary five-and-dime glass balls.

Decorating the tree took a considerable amount of time, witnessed by the fact that we had to replay the Christmas carol record
ad nauseam, and Mother belted out "Ave Maria" until we begged
for mercy. After the balls came the glittery ropes of "garland,"
which we inevitably forgot to put on before we hung the balls, and
so we were forced to resort to icicles or tinsel, which my parents
scorned as being tacky and which were impossible to separate from
each other fresh from the pack. Still, we fretted, determined to give
a last bit of shine to the tree. Another hour went by replete with
groans of frustration.

The tree was finished. It had taken a lot of work. It had taken a
lot of emotion — expressed and repressed. We were all ready for
bed. Joy brought a pail of water to fill the base. Dad turned out the
lights and we sat there quietly, just admiring the glow and the mystery that emanated from this creation that drank and breathed and
filled the house with the heady scent of balsam: every year a tree
took root in our memories as it stood there on our living room car-
pet. The tips of Mother and Dad's cigarettes glowed in the dark.
The record played one last time and for once Mother did not sing
along with "Ave Maria."

ᐧᔭ

As the big day approached, my mother slid into her role as the Christmas Wizard. As soon as she had had her own children for an audience, she had drawn my father into re-creating the series of traditions that had enriched her childhood. These were the dramatic staples with which the extensive cast of Staples-Dingley relatives had entertained for many years as she was growing up: enormous Christmas trees with piles of presents, lavish food, an appearance by Santa in the living room, and a special Christmas song and dance written and performed by their clan every year.

Our day began with Mother and Joy and me kneeling on the wooden toy chest in front of the window in my room, searching the barely lightening sky for a glimpse of Santa's sleigh. Every year, against the bare bone branches of the winter trees, Mother would point and exclaim, "Look, girls! There he is!" Excited, we jumped up and down as we, too, sighted the brief flash of red silhouetted in early morning light. Then there were moments of suspense as we waited to hear the familiar "Ho, Ho, Ho" from downstairs.

Mother and Dad's morning began even earlier than ours, when they woke in darkness to begin the rituals. Working carefully, Mother helped my father don the treasured Santa Claus suit that had been used for countless years during her childhood. As her own mother had once suited up her father, she now suited up mine, gluing on a real theatrical white beard, long and full, and eyebrows that were realistically bushy. These were the rituals of her own childhood; what the poet might have scorned as bourgeois the child still alive in Anne remembered and reveled in. This childlike quality in my mother was one of the reasons the holiday itself was so much fun: she was determined to re-create as much of the Harvey Christmas myth as possible.

Over his shoulder went a pillowcase filled with the oranges that later Mother would squeeze for the mandatory fresh juice at the breakfast table; with typical lack of self-control, she would down several glasses and give herself terrible heartburn. With the sack on his back, Daddy would creep downstairs to wait for some signal — still mysterious to me — that would indicate the time had come to begin ho-ho-ho-ing.

Though the ritual was elaborate, it was actually a scaled-down version from her own childhood, when the Dingley great-aunts would stomp through the attic in rubber galoshes, jingling sleigh bells, to mimic the sounds of reindeer on the roof. We had no available great-aunts and we, suggestible children, presumed the reindeer landed in the backyard, where we had set out a pan of water to assuage their thirst.

At the sound of Santa's hearty voice — my father became a marvelous actor on this day, anyway — we ran pell-mell down the stairs to stand in shy confusion before the great man. He took us on his knee and gave us each an orange from his sack. He stayed only a few moments and then disappeared as soon as our attention became focused on the stockings hung on the fireplace screen, stuffed to overflowing in piles on the floor.

It was not until I was nearly nine that I turned back from my stocking to see him peeking at us around the living room arch and, with a quick stab of recognition, saw that his merry blue eyes were my father's. Even so, I quickly blocked the thought from my mind. Later that year, one hot summer afternoon on our way to my grandmother's for Sunday dinner, my mother referred to the fact that we well knew by now that Santa "wasn't real," and I burst into such a storm of tears that my father had to stop the car until I could get my grief under control. I did not want to relinquish the myth that made us seem for one day at least, a "normal" family.

Even with the "let's-pretend" apparatus running full bore, Christmas could provoke depression as well as happiness in my mother. She tried hard, at least on the day itself, to lose herself in the rituals; still, depression could and did flood her during the season, especially after her parents died, and some years she would sit twirling her hair, trancelike, at the kitchen table, dragging herself through the season. Then the rituals became painful symbols of all she had once possessed and all she had lost at their passing. Never close to her sisters, she had even worse fights with them after the death of their parents. In later years, other members of the family would remember that when Ralph's body had to be transported to the crematorium, Jane jealously guarded the task, saying, "You can't come. I'm going to do this myself. He was *my* father!"

Back in Annisquam the daughters divided up the contents of their parents' home, a painful, bitter experience Mother would recall in "The Division of Parts":

> *A week ago, while the hard March gales*
> *beat on your house,*
> *we sorted your things: obstacles*
> *of letters, family silver,*
> *eyeglasses and shoes.*
> *Like some unseasoned Christmas, its scales*
> *rigged and reset,*
> *I bundled out with gifts I did not choose.*

This too brought squabbling among them, and Mother later claimed that Jane had gone in first with a moving truck and taken all the valuable items. Blanche, she said, had been left no money. Mother managed to grab some of her grandfather Arthur Gray Staples's books, her mother's writing desk — and the family Santa Claus suit.

Gradually my mother and her sisters became estranged, and so we rarely saw them. She broke off all communications with Jane when Jane borrowed the Santa Claus suit and then did not return it, claiming that it had "disappeared."

Many years later, after my mother's death, Blanche mentioned that Jane had found the suit and had lent it to Blanche. When my sister phoned to ask Blanche if she could borrow it so that her husband could play Santa Claus for my children, the suit had once again been mislaid. In our hearts we consigned the Santa Claus suit to the same category as the bubble tree: precious and gone — and just one more example of family politics.

In my home today, some of the traditions my mother made a part of our lives do continue, however. Plenty of presents. A Christmas tree, on which I hang Mother's typewriter ornament as the final flourish. Christmas breakfast on a gay red, white, and green tablecloth inherited from my mother's mother, Mary Gray, now carries its own, Sexton-inspired rituals: pecan waffles (made in the old metal waffle iron my parents received as a wedding gift) with maple syrup, sausage links brown and crisp, fresh-squeezed orange juice. A lunch of lobsters, beer, and potato chips. For dinner I choose to serve a boneless prime rib because my husband takes no masculine pride in carving a difficult roast. Mashed potatoes are mandatory. As a child, I peeled them for my father, who made them simply with butter and milk. Today Nicholas peels mine and then I whip them with sour cream, garlic, and crushed celery seed: ritual makes way for creativity.

My husband, John, never had any yen to play Santa Claus. Returning one evening from our class in Judaism, which was preparing me for conversion prior to our marriage, I realized with sorrow that I could never re-create this part of the ritual for my own children in the future. I would have to give it up. And I did, but not without regret. When my brother-in-law, Steve, arrived on the family scene, willing and able, we rented a cheap Santa suit and watched the kids mill about him with excitement.

Two years ago, when I stood before the congregation of our temple to chant my Torah portion in Hebrew at my Bat Mitzvah, I found myself newly confronted by the question of Christmas. When I converted thirteen years ago, I had shrugged off suggestions that as a Jew by choice I should not celebrate this Christian holiday. I did not entertain that possibility even once, and it didn't bother me. This time, however, with Alexander enrolled in Hebrew school, Nicholas in religious school, and me fresh from the bima, my younger son stirred up a family controversy when he came into the kitchen one day in August and announced that we shouldn't be celebrating Christmas because we were Jews.

I was flabbergasted and threatened. I didn't want to give up my holiday. Friends from our temple agreed that it would be hard to give up but, ultimately, for the best. In my heart, I thought about the myth: that, as a child, this day meant something special to me because on this day I could believe in our "normality." Now, as an adult, I didn't need the myth anymore. I had a family of my own, one in which each day held many good moments. I thought to myself I was ready to give up the myth of the Sexton Christmas the way I had once given up the myth of Santa Claus.

In November we held a family conference over the dinner table. Each member had an opportunity to talk about how he or she felt, and then we took a vote — we employed the Democratic process, but not about the mere size of a tree. John voted against Christmas; in a last-minute reversal the boys and I voted for it. I was ashamed of myself, of my weakness in needing and wanting it, but Christmas, it seemed, was already a part of our family. We could have done without it, but we didn't want to. We agreed, however, to compromise: John and I would give the boys only Chanukah gifts, leaving the Christmas presents to my family; and next year we would try to let Christmas go altogether.

Christmas Eve, hanging the ornaments on the tree, my children asked for the history of each and every ball, sleigh, and angel. Their eager interest warmed me, brought back the love of my childhood holidays in a wash of nostalgic pleasure. I turned to my husband and thanked him for being tolerant. My eyes filled with tears. "I don't want to give it up," I said then, thinking of my mother and the happy memories of this day which I hoard like treasure.

John put his arm around my shoulders. "I don't want you to either."

And so we decided to keep Christmas, to celebrate its richness of tradition with our own modifications. The tree will never have a star on top because that makes John uncomfortable. Chanukah will be the holiday for which *we* give the children presents. Stockings will still be hung, but are to be stuffed by the kindness of the Boston Santa, who lives at my sister's home.

When Christmas and Chanukah overlap, our December twenty-fifth dinner table bears a centerpiece fashioned by the confluence: my grandmother Mary Gray's Christmas tablecloth; the candlesticks John and I received as a wedding gift flanked by the three silver menorahs we have acquired since the children's births; a brass angel from Nana's collection; the silver flatware belonging to Joanie and before that to my great-grandmother, Christina; gold foil Chanukah gelt scattered about; round beeswax candles in glass holders given by my father's new wife, Peggy. Mother herself drifts through the room like Elijah at the Passover Seder, pleased, I am sure, by the eclectic mix that constitutes our centerpiece, delighting as she did in just such oddball combinations. The lights on our holiday table push back the darkness of being far from family, just as the lights on the bubble tree once beat back the darkness of my mother's madness and my parents' instability — if only for one day.

I see that I, too, have become a maker of myths. When we go to buy our Christmas tree on a sunny sixty-degree day in December, I tell Alexander and Nicholas the story of the dark snowy lots of my childhood, of Grandma Anne's scraggly tree, and they laugh. I promise them more stories, more love. Time cannot take away either.

More Than Myself

Not that it was beautiful,
but that, in the end, there was
a certain sense of order there;
something worth learning
in that narrow diary of my mind,
in the commonplaces of the asylum
where the cracked mirror
or my own selfish death
outstared me . . .
I tapped my own head;
it was glass, an inverted bowl.
It's a small thing
to rage inside your own bowl.
At first it was private.
Then it was more than myself.

— Anne Sexton
"For John, Who Begs Me Not to
Enquire Further"

*T*URNING THE DOORKNOB as silently as I could manage,
I tiptoed into Mother's study with the iced martini I had made, the
olive bobbing up and down at my hesitant step. She sat hunched
over, back to the door, her desk awash in manila paper covered with
elaborate rhyme schemes and revisions scrawled in pencil. Her
rhyming dictionary, a Bible in those early years, lay open and
shoved to one side. Her long fingers clacked away unevenly on her
beige Royal manual; she had never learned to touch-type. A poem
was in progress. Magic time. No interruptions allowed.

I set the drink down on the edge of the desk with absolute still-
ness. Out of the corner of her eye, she caught the movement of my

hand. Startled, she leapt from her chair and screamed. I jumped back. We started to laugh. The martini, miraculously, still stood, rim-full and waiting. I was eight and she thirty-three.

The art of writing had always been a part of Mother's family identity, carried on the shoulders of her grandfather, Arthur Gray Staples, known as A.G.S., a published essayist from Maine, and the editor and publisher of the *Lewiston Evening Journal*. A collector of rare books, he was proud of his daughter, Mary Gray, a graduate of Wellesley College, for her ability to spin a catchy phrase, usually in the medium of letter writing, but also occasionally in verse written for birthdays and family events.

Considering the depth of the intellectual stimulus A.G.S. offered Mary Gray, as well as her Wellesley degree, it seems surprising that she did not actively encourage her own daughters in any sphere beyond that of the proper Bostonian wife and mother. Of her daughters, only Blanche completed college, and both Jane and Anne married as teenagers, with their parents' blessing. Once, when drunk, Ralph Harvey knelt to beg Mother's boyfriend to marry her, though Mother was only seventeen at the time. Two years later, when Mother thought she might be pregnant, Mary Gray encouraged her to elope with my father. My mother's only role model was her namesake, Anna Ladd Dingley, an independent woman and sister to A.G.S., who eventually became a reporter for and part owner of the *Journal*. Mother herself emphasized to me a standard entirely different from the one Mary Gray had offered her: she stressed repeatedly that early marriage generally proves a terrible mistake, and that a woman needs a "center" outside of the home.

Nevertheless, over time, Mary Gray had earned the title of family poet, and it was her desk at which my mother sat as she began to write her first poems after her initial bout with mental illness, when Joy was young. "[My mother's] father was a writer and she should have been a writer — I'm my mother, only I did it and she didn't," she remarked to Dr. Orne in 1961. A few weeks later, she revealed one of her happy memories about time spent with her mother: "I think she was actually pretty nice . . . How did I learn to love books unless she taught me?" This legacy of a love for books was one aspect of mothering she learned from Mary Gray and that she would indeed pass on to me.

Between the years 1957 and 1965, my mother became more than my mother, for in these years Anne Sexton the poet emerged from her chrysalis. When Dr. Orne recommended that she try to express some of her powerful emotions rather than becoming overwhelmed by them, she began trying to write poetry — one month after her first suicide attempt, in November of 1956. She would be in treatment with Orne for nearly eight years for her frequent suicidal thoughts, as well as for her more overt attempts to take her life by swallowing overdoses of her sleeping pills and tranquilizers.

At that time her mental illness was labeled "hysteria." Between 1955 and 1964 she was taken to the Emergency Room at the Newton-Wellesley Hospital at least five times to have her stomach pumped and was then hospitalized there on a short-term basis. There were other proactive hospitalizations during this time as well — generally those in response to suicidal ideation or to psychotic episodes, such as hearing the voices that directed her to kill herself or her daughters.

These years were tossed with the swells of my mother's illness, which took different forms, but which often included strange and alarming behavior. During four years of her treatment with Dr. Orne, she would often fall into a trancelike state in which she had no control over — nor subsequent memory of — her behavior. These trances often occurred during their appointments, a state from which she could not be awakened, a kind of inadvertent self-hypnosis that cleverly kept her from remembering the content of any of their sessions. Orne had devised an equally clever tactic to defeat her unconscious desire to obliterate the material she was revealing: he audio-taped the sessions, then required her to replay the tape and make detailed notes while listening. She would return for the next session armed with the knowledge her unconscious had previously prevented her from "hearing." As a child, I remember watching her as she sat hunched over the long green pages of a spiral notebook in which she scribbled down — sometimes in pencil — a transcription of what had unspooled from the tape recorder in front of her. She worked as hard at understanding these sessions and her illness as she did at her poetry.

As late as 1963, in an appointment with Orne, she entered one of these dissociated states; before the appointment even began, the doctor had discovered her on the floor of the office bathroom, already in a trance. Once in the office with the door closed, she hugged the air conditioner, lay again on the floor, and called for her Nana to return to her. When she returned home, this behavior continued. At her appointment the following day, Orne scolded her for acting out in front of the family, telling her how she had frightened all of us. "[Kayo] was all set to commit me," Mother retorted. "He had to leave [for a business trip], and I didn't want anyone in the house with me. He said, 'What about the kids?' and I said, 'I won't talk to them, just leave me alone.' He called from every place the plane stopped. The kids went off to camp, which they can do by themselves."

In 1963, Joy was eight years old and I was ten. We went off to day camp with Mother refusing to speak, holed up in her bedroom, talking to the voices of dead people. My father, tortured with worry, called her from every airport in which his puddle-jumper landed. The undertow of an episode like this reminded us, once again, of all the hospitalizations that had come before and all those that threatened to pull us under again. On her bedside table stood the rows of bottles of medication that would provide her the means to end her life, and we lived daily with the threat of their presence. That day I wondered whether or not she would be waiting for me when I walked back in the door from camp, or whether Nana would have carted her off to the hospital. Would she be lying in her bed, comatose with pills? In a trance? Looking straight at me and talking to Ga-ga or her own long-dead Nana?

Orne's prescription, for her to try to examine her feelings through poetry, came partly because he sensed an underlying creativity in her imaginative associations and partly as an attempt to help her establish some self-esteem — a finger in the dike of her suicidal impulses. She spoke frequently of her belief that she was fit for nothing except prostitution, and once after an evening session with Orne, even invited a stranger into her parked car, where she performed fellatio on him.

One night following Orne's suggestion, and having just watched a PBS special hosted by the poet I. A. Richards on the writing of sonnets, she went downstairs to the kitchen table and scribbled out the rhyme scheme for a sonnet. "I thought, well, I could do that," she later recalled. "Interestingly, I called up my mother to read it to her — she suggested a better image, for one thing. I wrote one another day, and I took them to my doctor. . . . He said they were wonderful. I kept writing and writing and giving them all to him — just from transference; I kept writing because he was approving."

To be a writer was a family tradition, silently conferred upon the bearer of the magical middle name "Gray," which was Mother's maiden middle name. When Mother began writing poetry in earnest, however, her own mother became threatened. Mother appealed to Mary Gray for financial help so that she could go to college: she wanted to learn more about writing poems and begin educating herself about language and literature. Her urge to improve was enormous, and she felt driven to explore the possibilities that perhaps, just perhaps, she might have something to offer the world other than her failures. However, as Mother recounted the story to Dr. Orne, Mary Gray replied in the most scornful of tones when Anne asked her for assistance. "No. Why should I? It seems to me I deserve some fun in my old age. . . . You could never do the work. You have no idea of how hard it would be." A few months later Mary Gray began to write poetry again, as if goaded by her daughter's ambitions. Their styles at this stage were eerily similar:

> I sit upon the floor and play a game —
> O lunatic ancestor . . . give me another name.

I sit on this floor and crazily break
the pieces apart . . . for my children's sake.

— Mary Gray Staples Harvey, unpublished

A firm rivalry was established, if only in my mother's mind, and in later years this kind of rivalry would serve as a role model in my mind as well. What happens when a daughter chooses to make her mark in the same field as her mother?

However, in 1957, my mother resolutely pushed aside her need for Mary Gray's approval or financial support and went on to find for herself the formal instruction she so craved. Feeling terribly shy and nervous, she begged our next-door-neighbor, Sandy Robart, to call and get information on the time and location of a poetry class she had heard about and then talked her into accompanying her on the first night. So it was that Anne Sexton was able to join a poetry seminar led by the eminent poet John Holmes, which convened one evening a week at the Boston Center for Adult Education on Commonwealth Avenue. In this sort of class — better known in our home as a "workshop" — students brought poems still under construction with them so that teacher and students alike could critique the work aloud in a roundtable fashion — generally quite vigorously. In the warm but competitive atmosphere of this workshop, Mother wrote her first sixty-five poems and formed relationships with three other young poets — George Starbuck, Maxine Kumin, and Sylvia Plath — who would go on to sharply influence the poetry world in the sixties.

And so poetry moved into our home at 40 Clearwater Road with a vengeance, taking over a corner of the dining room until a writing room was added on to the back of the house in 1961. Mother spent her days creating and revising and sometimes stayed up late at night as well, refusing to take her sleeping pills and typing long into the early hours of the morning. I could hear the sound of her typewriter clacking away as I tried to fall asleep, and the staccato action of the keys filled me with anxiety, for I knew she

was in the grip of a vision that in its intensity could seem frighten-
ingly close to the grip of insanity.

Mother and Maxine quickly became inseparable friends, spending hours on the phone each day "workshopping" each other's latest efforts. Poetry had become the fierce center of my mother's life,
and she pursued it relentlessly, producing draft after draft even if
this meant a poem could take as long as a month to write. Between
January and December of 1957 she wrote over sixty poems.

And so, in 1958, that which had begun as a therapeutic exercise
blossomed into a vocation: Mother began to send her poetry out to
a variety of literary journals and magazines and by 1958 had discovered success that accelerated weekly. Her parents' reaction was
mixed: Mary Gray kept on writing poems and so gave credence to
Anne's accomplishments by competing with them, while Ralph
bought up copies of the *Christian Science Monitor* that included two of
his daughter's poems and distributed them to all his friends. He
enjoyed playing the role of the proud and exuberant papa.

Houghton Mifflin published Mother's first book of poetry, *To
Bedlam and Partway Back,* in 1959, and in 1961, both Mother and Maxine won fellowships to the Radcliffe Institute, a newly created part
of the women's college Radcliffe in Cambridge, Massachusetts.
The two women thus elevated themselves beyond the status of
housewives with hobbies. Before she died in 1974, Mother would
publish nine more volumes of poetry, write a play that was produced off-Broadway, and write four children's books together with
Maxine. She would receive numerous honorary doctorates from a
variety of prestigious universities, including Harvard, and have fun
forming her own poetry-rock band, Anne Sexton and Her Kind. In
1967, at perhaps the height of her career, she won the Pulitzer Prize
for her book *Live or Die.*

How she must have regretted that her parents — and Mary
Gray in particular — were not alive to see that day, for the messy
little girl of whom they had despaired, the young woman who
barely managed to graduate from high school, had gone on to become a woman of letters and degrees, a woman whose name was

recognized and celebrated, a highly respected writer. She had indeed fulfilled the implied promise of her middle name — and much more successfully than had any other family member before her.

Though a sketch of my mother's fifteen years as a poet implies that success came to her easily and quickly, in fact only the latter was true. The speed with which Anne Sexton found acceptance within the cadre of the literary elite was indeed remarkable, but it belied the work required. Every poem she wrote in those early years had been revised to an extraordinary degree. As a poet, she was tenacious, believing that only once in a great while did God or the Muse hand down the gift of an inspired poem in some close-to-final form. More often, a poem went through twenty or thirty drafts with amazing numbers of alterations. Scores of her early poems were never published at all, were never seen by anyone other than her fellow students at the workshop. My mother applied herself to her art more diligently, more stubbornly, more raptly than to anything else she had ever before undertaken, except for her analysis — and it paid off.

I remember remarkably few feelings about her obsession with her work from those very early years, when I was four and Joy still lived with Nana, but some remain with me still.

Every day Mother sent me off to the nursery school conveniently located in the basement of our next-door-neighbor's home. All I had to do was walk through the hedge.

"I started you at Mrs. Grant's nursery school when you were two," she explained to me when I was older. "She didn't want to take you, she didn't take anyone until they were three or older, but I begged her, and she gave in because I was so desperate."

"Did I like it?"

She shrugged and hurt flared in me. Didn't she care how I felt about it? "That part of the story is kind of funny," she answered. "I got you ready that first day and sent you out the back door. You didn't want to go, you were kind of teary and sucking your thumb a mile a minute, but I told you you'd be fine." She smiled and lit a cigarette. "You were so shy! 'You'll have a wonderful time,' I said, and I closed the door so that you would know you had to go over. So then I went back to my typewriter, you know, using every minute you were gone to write in. About three days went by and Peg Grant called me to ask if you were sick — she wondered why you hadn't been to school!"

"I don't understand," I said slowly, feeling confused.

"You weren't going across the hedge at all — you were hiding in the garage until it was time to come home!"

I looked at her, dumbfounded, flooded with my memories of that garage, dusty, dark, with snow tires piled in one corner and broken lawn furniture in the other. Tools encrusted with dirt gave it a musty smell, and in every corner were elaborate spiderwebs. As a child I was almost as afraid of spiders as I was of wolves under my bed and hornets with their long stingers; how could I possibly have stayed in that garage for three hours every morning, two years old and all alone, with nothing to do? No juice. No bathroom. How terrified I must have been.

And then, when I did come out of my hidey hole for lunch, no matter how long I had stayed away, she slapped lunch down on the table, but didn't eat herself, just went back and hunched over her typewriter. I saw how she left it only reluctantly when I pestered her for a cookie or a story; how she resented my questions and my need to be near her. I wanted to cuddle in her lap, but she wanted to concentrate. In desperation she would put on a record or set me down in front of the television and go back to her desk. In a picture from that time, I sit strapped into a stroller, while she looks up from the drafts of the poem in her lap with a scowl on her face.

As she explained to Dr. Orne, "Any demand is too much when I'm like this. I want her to go away, and she knows it . . . I've loved Joy, never loved Linda . . . Something comes between me and Linda. I hate her, and slap her in the face — never for anything naughty; I just seem to be constantly harming her."

I want to cry with rage for the little girl I was. I see myself, small and blond, only a few years old, thumb plugged into my mouth for comfort. Did I huddle on top of a pile of old lawn chairs in the gloomy garage as I waited? Was I scared by the spiders? Did I cry?

I compare this to my son's first day at nursery school. How I trembled with anxiety — for him and for myself. When he shrunk back in shyness and fear, I carried him up the walk into the building. I stayed with him those first days until he was ready for me to leave. I made his first separation from me as different from my own separation from my mother as possible. Why? Out of love for him, but also out of my own fear reexperienced, and the drumbeat in my head: *Be different than she was, be a better mother.*

Perhaps I am not truly surprised that I have so few memories of this time when my mother began to pour herself into her poetry. Maybe the numbness, the blankness, kept me safe. Or is the reason even simpler than that, even less dramatic? Perhaps that time of my life did not feel so bad to me *then* as it appears to me *now*. Perhaps, in fact, it was a somewhat happy time. After all, I had been returned to my mother, for whom I longed, even then, acutely. Perhaps I felt so grateful simply to be home, to have escaped my prison term at Blanche's, that to be ignored — or sometimes hit — was worth it. What was a slap or a spanking compared to exile, what was a few mornings in the garage compared to six months in Scituate with Uncle Ed?

My father's feelings about this time were much clearer. He resented Mother's writing almost as much as he resented her psychotherapy: he didn't understand either, and they both took her away from him. He cocooned himself in the belief that with time the beautiful, laughing girl he had married would return to him, and the angry crazy woman who typed alone into the dark hours of the night would leave. His wife's sessions with her psychiatrist constantly highlighted his every word and deed in their marriage; he got the endless scrutiny while Dr. Orne sat on high, handing down judgments. Perhaps worse, he fast grew jealous of her involvement with the Boston literary community: it took her away from home during her "best" hours, those times when she was energetic and lucid, focused on more than her own difficulties. She had new friends to whom he couldn't talk easily and whose world he could not share. As she left him further and further behind, he became more and more lonely.

When the poetry workshops were held at our home in the evenings, and Mother's new friends filled our living room, my father could do little more than pretend to be a congenial host and act as their bartender. To play this sort of subsidiary role humiliated him and underscored one of his deepest insecurities: how could he keep pace with people who had college educations when he had left college after marrying my mother in order to support his family? In defense, he found fault with what he called "those poetry types" and became critical when they did not meet his conservative standards. As the years passed and my mother waded out further and further into the Boston literary scene, this rift between my parents worsened.

By the late fifties, they had begun to fight about these issues with a deadly earnestness. It struck him as unfair that she still couldn't (or wouldn't) take responsibility for attending to her children, but seemed totally capable of waltzing off on Saturdays for poetry readings and workshops with her new friend, Maxine Kumin. The rest of the family complained as well — especially Nana, who took up much of the slack in "mothering" us.

One Saturday afternoon, Mother and Maxine had scheduled a lunch date with another very influential poet and editor. Mother was up at a reasonable hour for once, preparing to leave. Daddy had been walking around tight-jawed for a while already, clearly angry that she was going.

"It's a Saturday, Anne," he complained finally. "I don't see why you have to go and leave the family on a weekend. It's selfish."

"It's important," she said, putting her coffee cup, rimmed with bright red lipstick, into the sink.

"It's an indulgence — just like all these hours with a psychiatrist are an indulgence! You can't expect my mother to take care of the kids all week long because you're too sick and then make a miraculous recovery on the weekend when there's something you feel like doing!" His face was getting red, his eyes like blue flint. "I'm sick and tired of explaining your behavior to Mother! Of defending you to your parents!"

"I don't need you defending me — if Billie's going to be a bitch, let her!" Mother's voice was shrill and defiant. "Don't try and defend me when you don't even understand what I do!"

"What do you mean?" He turned toward her slowly.

"My work is beyond you — but you won't admit it!"

"You just shut up, Anne," he said, his voice dropping, and his hands grasping his upper arms in a clutch that looked like a desperate plea for self-control. "Just shut up!"

"It's all a mystery to you, isn't it?" she sneered. "You can balance a checkbook, but you can't make a smart stock deal. You're a dope!" She started to laugh, wild and crazy and loud. "A little old maid!"

"Shut up!" he howled, and started toward her across the kitchen. She leapt to her feet and ran to her desk in the dining room. She picked up her typewriter and heaved it across the room. "Is this what you want?" she screamed as the heavy machine crashed into the wall. "I'll get rid of it *for* you — you certainly couldn't do it yourself!" She picked up sheaves of worksheets and her therapy notes and began to tear them top to bottom.

"Shut up!" He came at her and once again she ran, into the living room this time. They wrestled, and he hit her, fist to jaw.

She started to cry. "Come on!" she screamed. "Do it right!"

He hit her again, and then she began to hit herself as well. They were down on the floor, totally out of control. "Kill me," she sobbed, "please just kill me."

He stopped, panting.

"You win!" she said, putting her hands up in front of her face. "You win, I won't go to Dr. Orne! I won't go to lunch! I won't write anymore!"

"Stop it, Anne. You know you have to go," he said, brokenly, defeated. "Come on." He pulled her to her feet and into the kitchen, where he made her an icepack for the bruise on her jaw. Later,

Mother developed a remarkable insight about this kind of incident: "Maybe why I want Kayo to beat me up is to prove he's a man and I'm a woman," she mused to Dr. Orne. "I want him to be aggressive."

My father had expressed his frustration, and his fear, that she was leaving him, emotionally and intellectually; he hit her to keep her, to hold her under him symbolically. Mother expressed her rage that he would not recognize the most important achievements of her life by ripping them up with her own hands, by taking control over them: I made them, she seemed to be saying, I can destroy them. The message, even then, seems clear as the gin of her nightly martini.

Already I could see that if I wanted to share my mother's life it was the poetry I must share her with. If I wanted to be close, indispensable, a companion, then words and language would be the bricks with which I would build the bridge. Perhaps I knew even then that I wanted to be a writer.

Companionship

*I love you. You are closest to my heart, closer than
any other human being. You are my extension. You
are my prayer. You are my belief in God. For better or
worse you inherit me.*

— Letter from Anne Sexton to Linda,
July 23, 1969

$\mathcal{B}$Y THE TIME we moved to Weston in 1964, our home
overflowed unabashedly with the evidence of Mother's total im-
mersion in her writing: books stacked high on all available surfaces,
drifts of paper and worksheets, breakfast dishes in the sink, beds
unmade, ashtrays overflowing with sour old cigarette butts, the
acrid smell of spaghetti sauce scorching on the bottom of the big
aluminum pot. She refused to make the bed she and Daddy shared,
she refused to do the dishes that stacked up in the sink. I would
come in the door from school and set right to work, not wanting
my father, or my grandmother, to see the mess.

Perhaps none of this would have mattered in a home where
emotional stability lay as a base. But for us there was always the
sense that we were about to slip over the edge, that a day's depression could turn quickly into a suicide attempt or a hospitalization,
or a violent interchange between my parents. What might have
seemed only a messy kitchen seemed to me a symbol for what
lurked beneath the surface: a lack of control that could spin without warning into insanity. In this way I learned to become obsessive
about small things: I wanted to control the disorder of our home
because I could not control the disorder of our lives.

Secretly I craved my best friend's house, where her mother often
was ironing when we came through the door, filling the air with the
scent of hot steam and starch. A mother who drove the car pool,
hosted sleepovers, played bridge, and joined the PTA; perhaps to

counteract these shameful longings came my equally intense disdain for this same woman, who had "nothing better" than housework and family to fill her days. My mother, I told myself, was a *poet*.

How lucky our family was to have Me-me, who came twice a week to wash and iron, vacuum, and clean around the piles of mess. A brusque, abrupt woman in a stained housedress, chain-smoking Camels even as she shoved the vacuum back and forth, she showed her love for us in rough ways: yelling at Joy, shaking her head at Mother — whom she still treated as a child — and chiding me for the soup I spilled down the front of my clothes because I insisted on reading and eating at the same time.

Me-me had worked for Mother's family since Mother herself was a child, and then had come to our house when Joy was born, sent over by Mary Gray and Ralph to help Anne with the housework. She had been with us as long as I could remember, Mondays and Thursdays, straightening up and filling the kitchen with the smell of buttery slow-roasting chicken, turkey soup with rice, roast beef hash. Me-me was the voice of reason, a steady solid presence like Nana.

On Thursdays when I was young, the basement windows steamed up and the harsh smell of drying cotton filled my nose as Me-me fed the clean, damp linen through the old-fashioned mangle. Those sheets and pillowcases, tablecloths, and bureau scarves emerged miraculously sleek and crisp; in later years the sheets went to the laundry, and Me-me only ironed the clothing, as more time had to be devoted to "straightening up." But however you looked at it, twice a week Me-me took what was wrinkled and made it smooth.

By the time we got to Weston, Daddy had taken over cooking dinner when he got home from work and doing the marketing on Saturdays. While the marketing was a chore, the cooking tapped a creative streak in him, and he discovered himself enjoying it a bit, especially on the weekends, when he wasn't so tired. I was growing up in a home where the husband did more of the housekeeping than the wife. Not yet a feminist, I pitied my father for having to go off to work early in the morning and then return home late to do the cooking.

Since going into therapy himself in the early sixties, he had come to cope with Mother's needs in new ways, trying to be supportive: despite his desperation and frustration with her illness, despite the violence that still plagued their marriage, he loved her very much. Each night at bedtime he stroked her head gently, over and over, until she fell asleep, intoning the chant she so needed to hear: "Anne, you are a good girl." As a Christmas gift one year he bought her large notebooks in which to transcribe her therapy notes — despite his resentment of the therapy itself. He bought her filing cabinets and pencils — tools with which to ply and organize her trade. Knowing her fear of shopping, he purchased her stamps so she could avoid the trip to the post office when she needed to submit poems or send out correspondence.

Mother's agoraphobia prevented her from entering any kind of store — not for food or prescriptions, not for clothing — and to compensate, she became the catalog queen, the delivery junkie. Agoraphobia: fear of the market place, fear of open spaces. We did not know the word for this mental disease, but we certainly knew the symptoms. For Joy and me, Mother's agoraphobia meant that we, too, were housebound. We did not "go shopping." Nana hunted the bargain racks and brought home the sort of clothes she thought we ought to have, in styles completely out-of-date; hand-me-downs that came from Maxine's daughters turned out to be my favorites as they were still more or less in fashion. By the time I got to high school other girls were taken by their mothers for new hairstyles, manicures, and leg waxes. Joy and I relied on Nana to give us home perms and advice on our pimples, and Joanie taught us how to file our fingernails.

Mother didn't seem to care how we dressed or how kempt our hair was. "You are beautiful," she said to me often. "I love your soulful eyes." Her own childhood had been filled with shopping sprees for beautiful clothes, weekly visits to the hairdresser for a wash and set, and her parents' constant entreaties to improve her outward appearance. All this attention to her exterior and none to her interior — as a little girl she had been typically messy, infuriating both Harveys — now made her blind to our growing needs as young women.

In later years I would come to resent her inattention to matters of beauty — wishing for the kind of mother who would show me how to put on eye makeup and get me a manicure for the fingernails I bit with such fury, wishing that someone would help me do something with my long, lank hair, my blotchy skin, my skinny figure. I had two handsome parents and yet I was homely and flatchested. Intensifying the situation were the boys calling for Joy, two years my junior, who had inherited Nana's beautiful high bosom and lustrous chestnut hair.

Inside me, resentment grew. My friends went to each other's homes for the afternoons and sometimes stayed to dinner: I was afraid to have other girls over to our house because I could never be certain that Mother would be acting normally, or that she and Daddy would not drink too much and start a fight. But while I feared my father's anger and hated the circumstances that aroused it, by this time I didn't really resent Mother's absorption in her work itself, because when she was submerged in the world of words she was happy.

I was increasingly proud of my mother's writing and also beginning to understand that while the way she looked when she was writing might remind me unconsciously of her sickness — like a secret tide that tugged at memory — in fact, she was rarely crazy when she was writing. What took her away from us was not her desire to write, but her depression: when depression descended, she did not — could not — write much. Depression led to suicide attempts, and nothing was worse than that. And so, even when I was young, I intuitively understood the magic creating a poem brought to her. While I disliked the concentration it required of her, I could nevertheless relax: on the days poems were being written, Mother was not going to the hospital.

Years later, in a letter she wrote to me on my twenty-first birthday, she said,

You and Joy always said, while growing up, "Well, if I had a normal mother . . . !" meaning the apron and the cookies and none of this typewriting stuff that was shocking the hell out of friends' mothers . . . But I say to myself better I was mucking around looking for truth.

Yes, better indeed, I would have said to her then; yes, better indeed, I say to her now. My desire for a "normal" mother was really just a craving for a *healthy* mother — one who did not take rainbow assortments of sleeping pills every night or go to a psychiatrist four days a week, the kind of mother who did not disappear for two weeks into the mental ward at Massachusetts General Hospital, where the nurse locked the door behind me as I came in to visit my mother and behind me as I went out.

Sometime during these years, I became aware that when Mother wrote at such a high level of concentration, she induced in herself a trancelike behavior similar to that which preceded a hospitalization. If I called her name she often did not respond, as if she were drugged, or, if she were able to respond, it might only be to scream with fury: "Don't interrupt me!" Or, equally unpredictably, she might reach out and take my hand, show me what she was working on. I never knew what to expect.

Nothing was sacred when the call hit Mother: her Muse did not hesitate to interrupt either dinnertime or sleep. The stereo played the same record again and again, she shut the study door, and Joy and I tiptoed from kitchen to bedroom because the slightest noise brought shouts of frustration from the vicinity of Mother's typewriter. Even the Dalmatians slunk silently from room to room, looking for a spot to sleep through the siege. This state of affairs often drove my father to angry invective. "For Chrissakes Anne," he would fume when she begged again for five minutes more and he resorted to basting one more time the leg of lamb that had gone from dried out to leathery two hours before.

As far back as May of 1957, she herself had remarked upon the similarity between the trances she used for writing and the trances that often appeared during her analysis, either of which could get out of control: "Only in that funny trance can I believe myself, or feel my feeling." The original diagnosis for my mother's mental illness was hysteria, but recently I have begun to wonder if the symptoms of depression and memory loss, on which the doctors usually seemed to focus, together with her incredible surges of energy while writing, on which they rarely seemed to comment, meant that she really suffered from manic depression — a disease that was much less understood thirty years ago than it is today. Inspired by moods I can easily describe as manic, she wrote her best poetry fueled with fever and fury; when her mood swing brought her back toward the center of the arc she was able to shape the abundance that had spilled forth earlier by weighing each word. When she was pathologically depressed, however, she became totally unable to work.*

When Mother was crazy she sat all day and twirled her hair, and the small amount of housework she was meant to take care of waited. Her typewriter was silent. When Mother was on a writing binge, she typed furiously, listened to the same record over and over for compulsive inspiration, and ignored the rest of the world. It might have looked somewhat the same, but the result was, of course, vastly different.

Between 1964, when Dr. Orne moved to Philadelphia and we moved to Weston, and 1969, Mother went through a period when her suicidal thoughts were under better control. Though she may have been hospitalized during these years to prevent suicide attempts, I believe she only had her stomach pumped twice, a triumph of sorts. Though this success was undoubtedly due to the calming effects of the newly prescribed Thorazine, I saw Mother's improved condition differently. I was now eleven, twelve, thirteen. I was her friend, and I saw myself taking care of her, guarding

---

*In the last years of her life, my mother would be given a short, unsuccessful trial of Lithium, the drug most often used to treat and diagnose manic-depressive illness. (If the patient improved during the course of the treatment then the diagnosis of manic-depression was considered confirmed.) However, heavy use of alcohol can interfere with Lithium's ability to improve the illness, and my mother's alcoholism at the time she tried the drug may have prevented it from being efficacious.

her, making sure her mood did not slide too far downhill before the family and her doctors intervened. My grandiose vision of myself as her lifeline placed upon me a heavy responsibility. What if I failed?

How I wanted to be in control, for in this way it seemed that I could keep her alive. I would be her companion, constantly pushing back the shadow that crouched at the edge of our vision, nursing, watching, keeping the vigil. I saw myself as the mediator between Mother and the rest of the family. Once Daddy had defended her to all her critics; now I took over.

And our attachment grew over the years as I, too, began to rouse myself in the middle of the night to type out an idea, an image, a series of lines. As I began to write I discovered what Mother had discovered: writing is magic because it harnesses the energy generated by the chaos within. Writing works better at cleaning up the mess than doing laundry or making beds. From the time I was eleven years old, I began to write poetry, mostly as a way of clarifying my feelings, but also as a way of sharing with Mother, of becoming a companion who could communicate about this passion.

Initially I typed my poems on the portable manual typewriter she had taken on her trip to Europe in 1963, but when I started high school I received an electric Smith-Corona as my big Christmas present, along with a ream of manila paper and a slim box of bond — this part of the gift set forth the proper ratio of worksheets to final drafts. "Under every word written are ten that didn't need to be said," she once commented. This method of writing and rewriting ad infinitum stays with me even now, when I create drafts on my computer instead of on the typewriter.

I wanted to be part of my mother's world, and writing poems was a sure path to membership. I shared every draft as it emerged, and Mother began to show her work to me in return. While she was happy that I was writing — choosing to express my deepest feelings and questions in her medium — she warned me off as well: "Don't be a writer, Linda." I could see the pitfalls: the days when she was "blocked," when neither word nor idea found its way out through her fingers. The politics of poetry began to stand out clearly as I grew old enough to intuit its presence: I watched her "make nice" to magazine editors she disliked, write blurbs for fellow poets whose work she didn't respect.

The struggle to make a living was even more obvious: she gave readings of her poetry to support us when my father's business performed poorly. "I hate it," she said. "I hate standing up there on the stage like some kind of a freak with everyone staring." Nevertheless, I saw something else as well: success. My mother was a success in ways my father and my grandmother could never have begun to imagine. She was a success in ways my best friend's mother, who loved to iron, would never be. She earned a lot of money; sometimes she could pay our bills all on her own. People respected her. My mother had power beyond the home. I wanted that, too.

I didn't, however, want the pain I sometimes saw: a reading during which a few members of the audience in the front row stood up and walked out after she had read "Her Kind"; a reading where people came up to her afterwards to say they found poetry like "The Fury of Cocks" or "The Ballad of the Lonely Masturbator" obscene and pornographic; the family chain reaction of fury at certain poems; the savage reviews by poets or editors she respected. The most poignant image I have of the difficulties she endured as an artist was my discovery, on the evening of her suicide, that she still carried in her wallet a clipping of the ax-job James Dickey had done on *All My Pretty Ones* in the *New York Times*.

"For you to be a poet will be too difficult," she said to me. "I'll always be hanging over your head like some old gray ghost." Was this a challenge? A dare? A good piece of advice? I was only sixteen.

I decided she was right, and so for a time I shared her fantasy that I would train to be either a social worker, like her friend Lois Ames, or a psychiatrist. In these roles, I could go on caring for her and never have to compete. In the end, however, it was Joy who elected to become the nurse.

Nevertheless, Mother was generous in teaching me everything she knew about writing, going over each line in detail, sharing what she knew or felt instinctively. She also began to ask me for my opinion of her poems as they emerged from her typewriter and

thoughtfully considered whatever reaction I could muster. We were
continuing the lesson begun so long ago that Thanksgiving afternoon on Nana's bed: where once she had taught me how to see,
now she taught me how to express. And perhaps, despite her advice
to me, she just couldn't help herself: what simple enjoyment came
from this sharing.

Mother's years of "workshopping" over the telephone with
Maxine Kumin had given her the gift of immediacy: in a second she
was able to put her finger on the innards of a poem and judge what
did and did not work. Watching her grow excited when one of my
lines or metaphors pleased her filled me with a shy ecstasy. She was
gentle — kind, really — with the lines that did not work, and
never embarrassed me, even when I had written something truly
terrible. Never once did she laugh at my naïveté, my clichés, the
melodrama of my adolescent yearnings.

I loved these workshop sessions, usually held at the kitchen
table, where we drank cups of tea as we laughed. She liked to sit in
her chair in the corner, her feet up on the opposite seat, a cigarette
spiraling smoke into the air. She read the poem aloud, just as dramatically as if she were performing it. I had to guard against getting
caught up in the sound of her voice, for her low throatiness and
sense of timing could sometimes make a bad line sound like a good
line.

"What do you think?" she would ask, looking up with those
eyes whose blue-green depths held so much beauty for me. Her lipstick had usually worn off by this time in the afternoon and as she
frowned with concentration I could see how the grooves in her face
had deepened.

"That line — I don't understand what you are trying to get at
there," I would say, tentatively at first, chewing on my fingernail.
"The metaphors are so . . . mixed up." In the beginning I had worried that admitting I didn't understand something would surely
brand me as an ignorant child, not worthy of her attention. Gradually, however, I grew secure enough to venture forth with my opinion, which she greeted with respect — a respect that made me glow
with pleasure.

"Hmm." She would tap her pencil on the kitchen table. "I guess it doesn't work." She would scribble something across the paper and I would get up to make us more tea. Over the years, as I watched her trust and rely upon my reactions, I began to understand that my life would always be involved with writing, even if I did not write for a living.

I had always expected to go to college and then begin work at some kind of career; both my parents repeatedly underscored the mistake they had made in dropping out of school and marrying too young. I had seen my mother struggle for years to try and give herself the education she had missed. These were powerful precedents.

Though Mother never applied the word "feminist" to herself, when I was fifteen she gave me her copy of Betty Friedan's *The Feminine Mystique*, complete with her scribbled notes across the pages — notes that showed her identification with the problems Friedan described. At seventeen I joined a group of older feminists who met weekly in Cambridge; Mother was curious about it and asked for an update each week. I think she would have liked to come with me, but felt shy. She encouraged me to think broadly, read broadly, develop my own ideas and search out the world in ways she was not able to. She provided me a powerful — if flawed — role model of all a gifted woman could stretch for and achieve.

As I moved from junior to senior high school, Mother started to teach poetry to a class of seniors at nearby Wayland High. She began to develop as a teacher with students who often had the same perspectives I did. I returned home from school every day eager to report on my activities, eager to share with her, eager to be with her. At last she seemed to like me and to look forward to being with me. After the early years of separation and striving to be good and worthy enough to remain at her side, acceptance was mine. We were, quite suddenly, friends.

When I came home from school, she was always on the phone, her legs propped high against the bookshelf in her writing room, tilted backward in her desk chair, smoking. She dressed casually, in knit slacks and Oxford cotton shirts, her black hair cut short and set in a stiff teased hairdo around her face, emphasizing her enormous eyes with their exotic fringe of lashes. By this time in her life she wore no makeup at all, save for bright red lipstick.

She waved at me and indicated she was about to hang up, because she knew I was eager to have her to myself for a little while. Joy, the social butterfly of the family, would have disappeared to a friend's house. We talked, she drank tea while I ate canned vegetable soup, we laughed. These are some of the happiest memories I have of my mother. How far I had come from those early uncertain days when I did not know whether my mother would allow me to stay with her. Suddenly I was safe: there was friendship between us, and that friendship ran deep and strong — unequaled by any I had with my peers. I gave her the nickname Muggy, and she created several for me: Bobolink, Chickenbiddy, Linda Pie, Stringbean, and, of course, Linda Gray.

I could talk to her about any subject without embarrassment and be guaranteed an empathetic response: about the boys I liked and wished would like me back; about my shyness and my anxieties; about my love of English class and the reading assignments; about my wish to be a pretty girl instead of a gangly thirteen-year-old whose pimples had arrived but whose breasts and period hadn't. When my period finally did begin, Mother was the one who stood on the other side of the bathroom door, coaching me on how to insert a tampon. What I could not understand then was that though my mother now made a wonderful and devoted friend, she still could not draw the line and be a *mother:* a guide, a teacher, a loving adult who could keep a certain amount of distance so that I could learn to live and think on my own. At a time when most adolescents move away from their parents in a step toward independence, my mother drew me tight in an unhealthy embrace that ensured we would be as intimate as sisters.

In 1964, the winter before I turned twelve, I decided I wanted to learn to ride horseback, and I went with Maxine Kumin and her daughters to the home they owned in the New Hampshire mountains. There I learned to ignore my frozen toes, my numb fingers, and my own clumsiness as, determined, I learned how to post and sit to a canter.

That summer I went back to the riding stables near Maxine's, which ran a small sleep-away camp for girls. The camp at High-lawn Farm was no Teelawooket, the elite summer institution to which Mother's parents had sent her, where the mounts were led out complete with gleaming tack and where the girls never had to do an ounce of grooming work. Highlawn was a working farm, where cows were slaughtered for winter meat and hay was mowed and baled, where riding lessons and trail rides for the public dur-ing the warm months provided a year's worth of income to the owners. A small cohort of twelve girls provided the summer help under the guise of being campers. It cost only two hundred dollars a month but offered the intense experience with horses that I craved.

That first summer, when I turned eleven, I was desperately homesick for the first week and then wrote to beg to be allowed to stay for August. Mother said she would think about it, and con-sulted with all her support systems, including Dr. Frederick Duhl, who had replaced Dr. Orne that same spring, when Orne moved his practice to Philadelphia. Dr. Duhl would be going on vacation in August, and Mother was already worried about the anx-iety his departure would create for her. She wrote me her answer in a letter.

> You must come home in August. We have thought it over thor-oughly and at some length. Daddy and I have talked. Dr. Duhl and I have talked. Maxine and I have talked. . . . Honey, at Highlawn Farm you are learning lots about freedom and lots about responsi-bility. Here, at home, you must learn these things too. I need you home. That is a responsibility but it is also a freedom. Freedom, because now you know that you're not just the baby needing the mother — but also the friend of mother, who needs you . . . Linda, you are almost twelve. Please give me another year to grow

up myself so that I can let you go longer. Meanwhile try to put up with me the way I am.

Hating every minute of the day camp to which I was relegated the second month of that summer, angry that I had been made to come home from sleep-away camp because my mother needed me to play mother again, I spent all my time fantasizing about going back to Highlawn Farm next summer; that winter I did nothing except return in my memory to the small tents set up under the pines and the barn full of horses.

Eventually, I spent five summers at Highlawn Farm, each one an oasis of peace: no fighting between my parents; no worrying about Mother. These summers went one of two ways: either wet, in which case we lived in mud, slopped through ankle-deep puddles with top-heavy wheelbarrows, and prayed we would not sink before reaching the steaming manure pile; or hot, in which case the mud turned to dust so thick we wore it like a tan. Either way, Mother did not really enjoy visiting and came only because she missed me so much.

In 1969, for my sixteenth birthday, Mother and Dad came up to camp for the weekend. They brought me a transistor radio and took me out to dinner. As we said good-bye in the back of the car that evening, I quietly lifted a pack of cigarettes from the carton lying on the back seat. I was a counselor in training at Highlawn Farm that year, able to have more control over what I did, and how I loved that, so different from the claustrophobia I felt at home. That night, I took the pack of cigarettes with me and went to my favorite place, a large tree-fringed pasture with a broad face that sloped sharply downward. At the top of the slope stood an old metal barrel, the sort that once held oil and was usually painted red with white stripes to create jumps in the ring.

I walked out in the dark without even a flashlight, finding my way by instinct, and climbed up on that barrel to watch the stars. Without the glow of a city nearby, the sky seemed pregnant and low-bellied with light. Above my head, the thick net of stars seemed so close I could have touched it. The smell of the damp green pasture enfolded me like a mother's arms. The horses moved around me, heads down, grazing and nickering, mares making small night noises to their foals, an occasional thump and squeal as someone got kicked. On the face of this pasture I found peace.

I mused on all that Mother was missing. A ride, for instance, just before sunset. Every day with a friend I took Bay Lady onto the trail at that magical hour Mother had dubbed "the long green." As the sun began to fade west, it cast its light on a slant; viewed through the trees, the light acquired a particular tone and color: golden green, long, low, and lovely through the foliage. Mother had seen the long green only from the windows of her house and car; she had never ridden the woods at that time, never seen them fill with the amber light, never heard the birds respond to this clock of illumination with their last songs of the day; she had never known this poetry. How I wished I could have taken her, just once.

No saddle or blanket lay between my bare thighs and the horse's sleek damp sides, and only a snaffle guided the head of an animal who willingly merged with me in both enjoyment and intent: free from the tyranny of the ring, of formal etiquette and precise moves, we were free to move at last.

I grew into my horse, became more than myself, an imagined centaur. When we reached the open field, its back rippling under the wind, I stretched my body deep into the length of Bay Lady's, and we galloped through the field of long grasses. I thought momentarily of the risk of rabbit holes but gave myself over to the joy of pure sinewy movement instead, her effort and mine, hers to run and mine to become one with a motion I could only borrow for that moment. We moved with the wind, on the wind, in the wind, over the field of light.

That night, sitting in the dark on the barrel I had come to think of as my own, I pulled out one of the cigarettes I had stolen from the carton in the car and puffed at it awkwardly. The coal at the end made a red star in the darkness, marking the movement of my hands. It tasted as bad as I had remembered, and I put it out in the small puddle of rainwater that had collected in the top against the rim of the barrel. I could learn to smoke later. I had plenty of time. I put my face back up to the stars and when I had drunk enough of their pure white light, I said good-night to the horses and went to bed.

Animals had become my perfect companions. You could talk to them, tell them your secrets, stroke them, love them, nurture them. They asked for little in return, made no intrusions into your privacy. They did not push you too far. Caring for an animal was basic, simple, and natural. It made me feel capable rather than overwhelmed.

Animals. Precious and fragile. Sturdy and loving. Animals that drank the air, moved through water, slept, ate, and died. The tanks of salt-water fish Daddy and I nurtured, in colors so vibrant and shapes so other-worldly. The felines we had, beginning with Joy's rescue of a stray she named Violet; Violet shortly gave birth to Rosy; later, when I was sixteen, Joy gave me a gray kitten named Roo, whom Mother "gave away" without asking me during my first year at Harvard.

We had dogs, too — a parade of Dalmatians that moved non-stop. First there was Clover, run over by a truck on Route 128; then came Angel, who drove Mother to distraction by puddling on the floor continually, untrainable, deaf, and eventually placed on a farm (did this really mean euthanized?); then Penny, who had lived the first six months of her life in someone else's home, where beatings had made her head-shy, but who spent the rest of her life in the midst of our turbulence quite happily; her daughter Gidget, who died young of a heritable skin condition; and finally Daisy, who stole all our hearts, especially Mother's, killed the year after Mother's suicide while chasing a car.

꒳

Time at Highlawn Farm passed all too quickly: summers left me longing for the next spring to arrive. At home, Mother grew more excited with the opportunities my adolescence provided her, caught up on the wave of her own memories. She remembered the thrill of her own wild and daring adolescence, and recounted the story of losing her virginity, on a blanket in the woods, under the stars. She told me too of the men who approached her now as she traveled around the country giving poetry readings.

One night we sat in the kitchen after dinner, the lights turned off, dark moving in, but still I could see her face, illuminated from the lamp over the stove. We were side by side, turned toward each other; she had her feet up on my chair, her toes nudging the side of my thigh. I sipped a Tab and lifted my long brown hair off my back. Mother was still drinking, the ice clinking in her glass in the dark.

"With men," she shrugged, "it doesn't seem to matter how long they've known you. This one, I'd only known him a few days when I was down in New York writing my play at the Algonquin." She drank again and lit a new cigarette, the ember glowing red as she dragged in. "'Let's go up to my room and fuck,' he says to me."

I was glad for the dark. Anxiety whined in my ears like the drone of rising hornets as I thought of my father. I had read *Madame Bovary* and *Ethan Frome*; I knew about married people having affairs, but still — I was shocked. At fifteen, it was the first time I had heard the word *fuck* used to describe sexual intercourse rather than used just as a curse word. It made having sex with a man seem just as coarse as I had feared, worse even than the first word she had taught me for making love: *mating*, as if we were animals. And the revelation hurt me, too, for my father's sake. As a teenager, I adored him, even with his shortcomings — his temper and his violence, his lack of love for the written word — and I wanted desperately to protect him.

Sex had seemed a painful, frightening subject for as far back as I could remember. When Joy and I were young Mother had insisted that Daddy walk around without clothes so that we could get used to seeing a man. Unfortunately, my father's penis looked nothing like the little wieners the boys liked to wave behind the bushes at school, so what we got used to was seeing how immense a penis could be.

But my troubles had really begun in earnest sometime when I was nearly nine years old. One afternoon, upon returning from the beach, I had a bathing suit and a bottom full of sand and tried to enlist Mother's help in wiping it out. She handed me a towel, and as I struggled to free myself from the grit that had worked its way between the lips of my vulva, I told her that my friend Nancy had told me that the little bump in the middle of me was just like a boy's penis and would grow bigger. Was it true? Mother shook her head and said that was my clitoris. "But when you mate," she went on, "it will feel good there." And then she touched me, showing me what she meant.

Over the years, this kind of inappropriate behavior continued, making me cringe. Under the guise of educating both Joy and me, Mother explained the smaller details of sex. Position. Orgasm. Masturbation. "Do you masturbate a lot?" she asked when I was thirteen or so.

I was embarrassed. Mortified. "Not at all," I whispered.

"Don't be ridiculous." She dismissed me with a wave of her hand. "Everyone masturbates. Why lie about it?"

Ashamed, I tried to think of something else, fast. "What about tomorrow night?" I asked. "Can I sleep over at the Gardiners'?"

"Why are you changing the subject?" She was twirling her hair around her finger and having an early drink before my father came home. "You *have* to masturbate — why are you acting so embarrassed about it? I didn't raise you to be guilty about sex!" Her voice had a rising tone now and I stared at her.

"I don't!" I finally cried, goaded. "Not after that baby-sitter!"

"What baby-sitter?"

"When we were little in Newton. The one who used to do that in front of me. She was disgusting."

Mother dropped her head. "Oh, God!"

My accusation about the "baby-sitter" that day was the closest I ever came to confronting Mother about her own uncontrolled sexual behavior in front of me. It was not a mere baby-sitter who had deliberately masturbated in front of me, but the most important caretaker of my life. Living with Mother, I had seen enough sexual acting out to last me a lifetime, and the images of her fingers moving over her vulva had remained with me, horrifying and unexplained, triggering in my mind nausea and fear every time I felt the merest glimmer of sexual sensation myself. When Mother had exhibited herself like that she must have been dissociated, crazy. I was not about to allow myself to lose control that way.

My accusation about the baby-sitter was a reprimand encoded, a metaphor: as a child I trusted the person taking care of me and she had betrayed me. As a result, I had no desire to touch myself "there," nor any desire to allow anyone else to do so. The only orgasms I had ever experienced by the time I was eighteen were those that came to me in dreams — when my conscious shame could not control me.

In contrast, it seemed Mother had never had good control over herself. Her inability to set limits for herself, to refrain from acting out nearly every impulse, often led us into difficult, traumatic situations. Thus, it is not surprising that her psychological intimacy with me on the subject of sexual matters, her pressure for me to have sex and then report back on it, her curiosity about my body and the ways it was changing as I moved into adolescence, were mirrored by a disturbing physical intimacy.

As upsetting as the times she masturbated in front of me — or one other memory that I cauterized deep inside a dark well, unremembered until many years later — was another moment that, like an epiphany, became emblematic of the way in which she possessed my body. When I was in fourth grade I longed for a bra as the girls all around me began to develop breasts and sport lacy scraps that gave minimal support, but that, along with nylon stockings and white gloves for dancing school, symbolized the move from childhood into womanhood. Mother refused me such a purchase every time I asked, though she would not only admit to, but immortalize, the changes my body was undergoing in her famous poem "Little Girl, My Stringbean, My Lovely Woman."

By sixth grade my friends began to remark, slyly, on the way my small breasts bounced under my undershirt as I walked down the hallway and across the playground. At home I put in one last desperate plea. We were standing in the hallway outside her writing room when I popped the question, my heart thumping with anxiety. She looked at me thoughtfully and then reached out and slipped her hand down the front of my yellow bathing suit, cupping my breast to weigh it in her palm. "They are getting pretty big," she agreed. "Maybe Maxine and I will take you."

Overjoyed at the positive response, I shrugged off my embarrassment at her fingers grasping my breast: didn't all mothers touch their daughters' bodies this way? Wasn't ownership a mother's right?

So it seemed to me. I remember the seventh grade, my first year of junior high, when I had to get up earlier than either Joy or Daddy to catch my bus. That spring Mother was not sleeping well, and she often crept into my room just as the sun came around the corner of my window. Sliding between the covers, she pressed her long body against mine and I would wake to find her curled around me. Under the warm heap of covers, her naked belly and thighs pressed against my back and bare buttocks, my nightgown having bunched up around my waist during the night. As she rocked herself back and forth against me, her flesh damp and sticky, I closed my eyes and lay still, choking with disgust, my throat clenched against a scream I tamped down inside. I wanted to shove her away, but instead I waited for her to finish. The sound of that unvoiced scream echoes still inside my body.

With time I learned to set my alarm earlier. When she came in I would be sitting at my makeup table, stroking on layers of mascara and blush. I loved it then, how we could talk while she lay in my bed, smoking.

But soon the pressure began to build in a new, more subtle way; she introduced deeper subjects into our early morning talks, into our afternoons over the kitchen table, topics like the loss of my virginity. Virginity seemed to me then a handicap I needed to get rid of if I wanted to be part of the woman's world in which Mother lived. I wanted to bring stories of sexual conquest home to her as if I were making an offering, but was repulsed by the idea of surrendering my body that way. Still, as a teenager, I submitted to gropings

and graspings in the backseats of cars, or in the bedrooms of
houses where parents were out for the evening. The inexpert touch
of young boys in the dark, the choked breathing, the damp urgency,
sticky flesh, wet mouths, reminded me unconsciously of other inva-
sions I had also tolerated with disgust. To say no felt more risky to
me than to say yes, but I did not question why.

I was a moody teenager, prone to hanging around the house on
the weekends. Often I was depressed, and the world seemed overwhelmingly gray. I listened to Mother's Frank Sinatra and Judy
Garland records — not the Beatles or the Stones until much later. I
was caught in a different era, Mother's era. Unlike my friends at
fifteen, I didn't worry about kissing and dating — I worried about
whether or not I had to sleep with someone to live up to Mother's
expectations. I worried about why I felt numb and anxious so much
of the time.

To Mother, the sexual freedom available to me as a teenager in
the sixties seemed like heaven. When she was an adolescent, her
sexual behavior was inhibited largely by a fear of pregnancy. In fact,
she and my father had eloped because she was worried that she was
pregnant from their single sexual escapade, fueled by Singapore
Slings — though this turned out not to be the case. She therefore
imagined that obtaining birth control for me at the earliest possible
age was imperative. And so, at fifteen, she took me to see her gynecologist and arranged for me to get a prescription for birth control
pills. As it turned out, I had no need of the birth control prescription until I was on my way out her door, college-bound.

During my freshman year at Harvard, while back home for
Thanksgiving, Mother and I had a strange conversation, one that
left me feeling breathless and vaguely repulsed, though I didn't understand why. I had encountered my very first gay women on campus, and this led to a discussion of homosexuality.

"What do you think lesbians do with each other in bed?"
Mother asked dreamily, watching the rings of smoke curl up toward
the ceiling.

My stomach turned over. I had had crushes on other girls at
camp, and I had wondered if I might be sexually "perverse," a les-

bian. Though I did not want to get into specific sexual details, I answered her nevertheless, knowing full well that if my best friend had asked the question I wouldn't have felt so weird about answering. "I think they sixty-nine," I said matter-of-factly, drawing mostly on pornography I had seen or read.

"The women I know just masturbate each other." More smoke. "And kiss."

Her words had a startling effect: my fear evaporated in a sizzle of anger. Her words were a tease: she wanted me to ask of whom she was speaking, and eagerness steamed off her skin. I was damned if I'd give her the satisfaction of dumping yet another sexual revelation in my lap. I didn't want to know who was sleeping with whom. Perhaps the thought went even deeper, subconscious but present: I didn't want to know with which woman *she'd* been sleeping. I stretched casually, then got up and left the room. Four years later I would read in her letters of her affair with her friend Anne Wilder.

↜

It was not only her sexual life about which she was frank: Mother discussed every aspect of her life — from the details of her flirtations, to which publications had accepted new poems, to gossip about friends, to news of Maxine and her daughters, to what Daddy had said or done on a variety of issues, complete with a rehash of the recent arguments between them. She expected me to side with her, and at first I did, for my father's violence was horrible and traumatic to watch. How many nights did Joy and I freeze in fear as we heard their voices escalate during cocktail hour, anger seeping upward through the floorboards like invisible, combustible gas, until the whole house lit up with the explosion of their words and the fists that inevitably followed. I wanted to run away from the anger and the hitting and the hate. But I stayed, ear pressed to the door, ready to leap in to help Mother if she should call me. Which, often, she did.

Over time the pattern of these fights became visible to me. They always began with the lubrication of alcohol, and a little bickering, not even an argument at first. My parents' disagreement could center upon something halfway significant, such as finances or politics, but as often as not could take root in something completely trivial — like which brand of soap to buy or how long to cook the stew. It was almost as if the tension in them built to an unmanageable level and they sought a release for it. They both had another drink, and Mother's words got hotter and sharper; Daddy grew more and more silent; she layered on the sarcasm, provoking her opponent with a stream of well-chosen words. She kept at it until he responded, which didn't take long once another martini — or, in later years, Scotch — had been consumed. *Thud-thud.* But perhaps the strangest of all: that vision of Mother hitting herself.

Each had his or her chosen weapon: he his fist, she her words. She relied on my father to help her act out the punishment she craved, the pain that seemed, like a shock treatment, to lift her depression. When Daddy's control of his temper improved, the situation became simultaneously more healthy and less satisfying. "When I feel depressed I keep wanting to hurt myself, but he no longer [hurts me]: I need to be punished, then forgiven, [I] never realized he was actually doing this for me," she once explained to Dr. Orne. "No one would believe what goes on: he starts choking me and I start yelling 'Go on, kill me' then he really starts to hit me and I hit myself."

Though there were respites from the physical violence between my parents, sooner or later they always reverted to this old pattern. As my understanding of these duels grew, it became harder and harder to sympathize with either of them. The struggles satisfied some need, or inner tension, or perhaps even sexual frustration. They were created by my parents as a couple, and I saw neither of them as victims. As Dr. Orne had once pointed out to Mother, she used my father as a weapon with which to punish herself: his violence was not simply a volcano that erupted without warning, but instead one that erupted under the pressure of her verbal prodding.

For Joy and me the anxiety surrounding cocktail hour became a permanent scar on these nights of our adolescence. Mealtimes themselves were no better in terms of anxiety: if there had not been an argument at cocktail hour, yet another hurdle was to be faced over food. As sisters, we tried to do everything the same way every day, hoping to stave off whatever might attack next, from whatever flank. Some nights nothing transpired. Then others, Mother would be tearful, or argumentative, or depressed, or just plain crazy.

One Saturday Daddy didn't get dinner on the table until eight or nine o'clock. My parents were very high and so the scene around the table became edged with tension. Joy was out that night, staying over at a friend's house.

Mother picked up her drumstick and eyed it just the way she always eyed the roast beef on her plate at Nana's: by the time I was a teenager, she was unable to swallow most meats. This night she tried, gagging on it. Sitting tensely in my chair, I watched her out the corner of my eye.

Suddenly she clapped her hand over her mouth and shoved herself back from the table. Running from the room she began to vomit into her hand. Daddy sighed and shut his eyes for a minute. We could hear her at the toilet, making awful straining sounds, because she had not closed the door. She never did. Daddy went back to eating with a certain stoicism. I couldn't possibly eat while Mother was throwing up. After a few minutes the water in the guest bath ran and she came back. No one said anything.

She sat down, taking several large gulps of her drink. By now she drank only vodka, because even alcohol could make her gag, and sipping vodka was like sipping water. I looked over at her and saw that her eyes had begun to flick mechanically up and down, focused on the wall behind my father's head. This aspect of her illness — which Joy and I had nicknamed "headlighting" — was always a sign of impending disaster.

Daddy and I pretended nothing was happening: if we pretended maybe we could make it so. Her eyes traveled faster and faster and she started speaking. "They're too tight! I can't breathe with them on!" I froze and studied my plate. *Please, God, don't let her fall apart!* I stared so hard at my chicken wings that my eyes started to water. "You have to take them off or I'll suffocate!"

"What's on TV tonight, Daddy?" I choked out.

"Take them off," Mother commanded, her eyes rolling back into her head as her arms crossed dramatically over her breast.

"Take off what, Anne?" Daddy's voice was irritated — but underneath the irritation lay a dark vein of fear.

"The chains!" Her voice sounded slurry and drugged. She had gone deep into a trance. "Unbind my chains!"

I looked at Daddy, my heart banging away inside my chest.

"Unbind my chains!" she shouted, one last time, before heaving herself forward into the table. Her head landed right in the middle of the mashed potatoes on her plate.

"Mommy!" I started to cry and shake her by the shoulder. "Mommy, wake up!"

Daddy came around the edge of the table and lifted her face out of the plate, gently wiped the potatoes from her face. "Anne, stop it," he said firmly. "You're scaring Linda."

"The chains, take off my chains."

I began to cry and we took her upstairs, stripped off her clothes, and slid her red satin nightgown over her head. Once settled in bed, she turned on her side and seemed to sleep.

"Will she be all right?" I asked tremulously.

"Don't worry," he said. "It's going to be fine."

The man who had tucked her in so tenderly was the same man who sometimes punched her in a fit of rage. Just as my mother could be both generous and greedy, my father could be a fury with rock-hard fists, or the tender husband who stroked his wife's face for several hours each night as she fell asleep.

Later that evening, as I tried to fall asleep in the dark of my own bedroom, I left my door open, perhaps the better to guard my mother from herself. Their bedroom door was wide open, and a while later Mother's voice roused me from the drowsy state I had entered around midnight. It grew louder, and I awoke all the way, swinging my feet to the floor in case she should call for me. I waited on the edge of the bed, shivering. I heard her say something about being pregnant, laughing now, a little wildness in her voice. My heart sank as I realized she was obviously having another one of the trances I had witnessed at the dinner table. Then, as if my own body and heart could not tolerate any more emotional up-heaval, nausea broke across me in a wave, bringing with it a cold sweat. I ran for the bathroom, arriving over the toilet bowl just in time. When I finished vomiting, I lay for a while on the cool tile floor.

I looked up to see Mother standing in the doorway, still dressed in her beautiful red satin nightgown. "Bobolink, are you all right?" she asked, bending to feel my forehead.

"I just felt sick," I said. "I heard you having another one of those fits, saying you were pregnant. I had to throw up."

The light from the hall caught her face and its smile. "Oh, no, honey," she said. "That was just Daddy and me having sex. He took me by surprise and I didn't have my diaphragm in and I was worried I might get pregnant."

I stared up at her. *Unbind my chains,* she had said. *I'll get pregnant,* she had said. Was there some distinction here that I did not per-ceive? Where did insanity stop and sex begin?

ॐ

We set up strict boundaries around our family as if we were behind a fence, as if gates and posts could keep us safe. I did not invite friends to spend the night unless my parents were having a good stretch, unless Mother seemed "all right" on Saturday afternoon. If their friends stopped by for a drink without calling first, Mother and Dad would wait them out rather than asking if they would like to join us for dinner — even when ample food cooked in the oven, grow-ing more well done by the minute. This lack of hospitality was a by-product of our desire to guard Mother, like Rapunzel in her tower, so that nothing would upset her equilibrium. Our need to protect her often embarrassed both Joy and me. We were not like other families: we couldn't bring our friends home to stay for supper; we couldn't reciprocate the generosity other mothers offered. We loved Mother, yet we didn't want her to be different in this way. No day went by that we did not remember the many times insanity had come to the door uninvited, and then sat down to dinner. Who could forget her crazy eyes or her head in the mashed potatoes?

Her mental instability was a terminal illness; our family stood by as helplessly as that of a cancer patient, trying to keep her comfortable, trying to beat back death for just one more year. Trying not to say good-bye. Trying to say good-bye. Though we never spoke of it openly, we knew with our collective consciousness that one day my mother would kill herself. There was neither escape nor alternative, and so we resigned ourselves. This awareness, however unconscious, gave the family a purpose around which to unite, and we allowed ourselves no room for divisiveness. Even my sister's and my own teenage rebellions muted according to Mother's needs. In a tight cordon we surrounded her, as if she were a stream of water spouting from a hose and we were children trying to catch with our hands her quicksilver light.

Acting in counterpoint to the tension were the long, delightful afternoons during which Mother and I talked, looking over drafts of her poems, afternoons when she recommended new books for me to tackle: *Madame Bovary, Catcher in the Rye, Henderson the Rain King, One Flew Over the Cuckoo's Nest, Ethan Frome, Sister Carrie, The Age of Innocence,* and a variety of Kafka works. On my own I began to read Arthur Rimbaud in the original as part of an independent study I designed for French class. This led me to begin writing poetry in French as well. Mother loved discussing books with me. Our companionship took a literary turn. In a rare outing, she drove me to the Hathaway House Bookshop in Wellesley (her agoraphobia was somewhat selective — bookstores were not so intimidating), where she had worked as a salesclerk during the early years of her marriage. Together we browsed. She told me she would buy me any book I wanted. "There's always money for books, Linda." I was at my happiest amid shelves of books, as was she.

At home the books piled themselves into stacks, growing out of every corner, a hodgepodge of printed wealth. By the time I was nine I had discovered Nancy Drew, then Trixie Belden and Cherry Ames. I kept my library card in my jewelry box and spent long afternoons in the steamy warmth of the small, dimly lit local branch. In the children's section, I read from one end of women's biography to the other, feasting on stories of Clara Barton and pioneer women. I liked reading of strong women in control of their lives, their loves, their world. I envied them this quality and desperately wanted to be one of them — in control of my destiny in ways my mother never would be, in ways I could not then be because I was a child subject to the whims of irrational adults. Each book brought a lasting pleasure: I spent hours reading during the day, and under the covers with a flashlight at night.

Mother steered me to *Gone with the Wind*, and I was enraptured, for the first time, by a novel of great length, history as its backbone, by titillating romance. I read the book so many times that eventually its cover fell off. One spring afternoon, Mother and I ventured together into Boston, a place I had been only a few times, though it was only a half hour's drive away. Mother had never taken either Joy or me for lunch or to the theater because of her agoraphobia, but when the movie *Gone with the Wind* was rereleased that year, she steeled herself and took me to see Vivien Leigh cast her spell. Enthralled, I whispered the lines before the actors could until Mother had to tell me to be quiet.

Mother had many friends, and they all fit particular needs. Rita Ernst and Sandy Robart lived on our street in Newton Lower Falls and passed many afternoons sitting around our kitchen table, laughing with Mother raucously. Maxine was the affectionate big sister Mother felt she never had, a calming influence with whom she could share everything from craft to love affairs and from whom she could learn about poetry until she felt powerful enough to sally forth on her own. She also had an ever-increasing cohort of poetry pals. In the middle sixties, playing out her attraction to "doctor types," she attached herself to the psychiatrist Anne Wilder, and pursued her passionately; eventually the two had a tempestuous love affair. Lois Ames, a social worker, also fit in well, providing Mother with a wonderful traveling companion for readings and the like; sometime in the late sixties Mother would ask Lois to be her biographer.

Mother could be a wonderful friend: excitable, magnetic, and loyal. The intensity with which she approached her friendships set an important model for me, but it was one I would have to "un-learn" later in life: for Mother you were either one of her closest friends or you were no friend at all. She had neither time nor energy for the casual acquaintanceship, except where her fans were concerned. She craved the hard lock: two minds, hearts, and souls as one, nothing unsaid, nothing untold, nothing unsung. If you didn't meet her standards she didn't hold it against you — she just dismissed you from her mind. She made no friends with the parents of my friends and once in Weston distanced herself from all neighbors save those few she and Daddy occasionally saw as a couple.

As I grew older I became Mother's live-in best friend, an enthralled and adoring little sister. She needed look no further than my room down the hall when she sought companionship. I provided for her an intimacy unequaled by anyone else in our home, including my father, with whom she felt, progressively, that she could share little. "I am married to a very intense, practical SQUARE," she said in a letter to a young poet. "He is good for me for he has complete plans on how to run each day. He is with the world. I am not of it whatsoever."

In a therapy session the year I turned nine, she had explained to Dr. Orne: "Talking to Linda is like talking to my own soul." Later she wrote to Anne Wilder of the discovery that I, too, like Maxine, could speak and understand what she called "Language," the name she gave to the power of words to communicate a wealth of nuance and meaning, to encompass a scope greater than could be achieved by using any single or literal point of view. When she wrote "The Fortress," the lengthy poem addressed to me after we had taken that nap together on Thanksgiving afternoon, she described certain inheritances:

> the brown mole
> under your left eye, inherited
> from my right cheek: a spot of danger
> where a bewitched worm ate its way through our soul.

Already we were linked, from her cheek to mine; already we were joined by the bewitched worm and the dangerous trail it leaves; by the mole, evidence of the worm's passage into our collective soul.

Mother believed, as did her family, that the curative magic of language passes between generations, hand to hand, a "gray" chain of talent weaving down through time: from the essayist Arthur Gray Staples to his letter- and poetry-writing daughter, Mary Gray Harvey; from Mary Gray to her daughter Anne Gray Harvey Sexton, the poet; and so from Anne Gray to Linda Gray, novelist.

Mother's appropriation of my memories — the wolves under my bed in "The Fortress," for example — set an important standard for me at an impressionable age: any detail, any emotion, could be used when you were writing. The poet built a poem on personal experiences, enlarged and enhanced. She deemed nothing too minor nor too inconsequential nor too private — neither her own passions, adulteries, womanly crises, nor her daughter's nightmares, shy questions, changing body. Reach out and grab what you see and hear, said her example: be greedy with life, and for God's sake don't ask permission.

As I grew up I observed that while writers might hold magic in their hands, they lived in ordinary ways — in houses such as mine. They came to visit, they ate and drank and talked with us. Visitors in those years included Tillie Olson, George Starbuck, Tony Hecht, the artist Barbara Swan, James Wright, W. D. Snodgrass, and, of course, Maxine Kumin. Sometimes Mother's poetry workshop with John Holmes was held in the living room under my bedroom, and from the dark cocoon of my blankets I listened to their spirited discussion over lines and words and ideas. Words, words, words. Words were more important than people.

In the spring of 1966, when I was in junior high school, our companionship in reading and in writing gave her an idea: she had scheduled a reading tour and wanted me to accompany her. As she observed to Anne Wilder, "Linda's never flown, stayed at a hotel or a motel or ridden in a taxi. It's about time she got a ride somewhere except in my VW or Kayo's Batman Buick or on a horse. Besides, we could talk and girl talk it up." Of course, Mother had always taken some kind of nursemaid with her on her reading trips, as she was terrified of being on her own. Oftentimes it was another poet, sometimes a friend. Now I was old enough to stand in.

And so we packed our suitcases — hers with the tailored reading dresses she favored at that time, mine with hand-me-down suits from Joanie — and set off for Pennsylvania and Maryland and, finally, the Virginia colleges of Sweetbriar and William and Mary. At cocktail parties, pretending a maturity I didn't feel and dressed with more sophistication than my gawky adolescent figure could support, I nevertheless held my own by discussing Kafka's "Metamorphosis" with faculty members. The sensation of being an interesting person was a novelty for me.

Delighted by my success, Mother even took me along when she met the famous James Dickey — whose tour intersected hers in Baltimore — for lunch in an airport lounge before we caught our flight into another state. She and he sat on one side of the booth and I across the way. They ordered sandwiches they never touched and drinks they never set down. Heads together, their bodies bumping in a teasing sort of intimacy, they gossiped about writers and mutual friends. Mother was in one of her gay moods, tossing her hair back, her voice growing louder, her laughter more intense, as they whaled down another drink. An uncomfortable observer, I realized I had become quite nearly invisible, intimidated by Dickey and his reputation and by my mother's flirtatious attitude — she appeared to have forgotten she was married to my father. What might have been the sort of ordinary verbal foreplay in which many monogamous adults engage seemed to me a threat, and I reacted with anxiety: by now I suspected my mother had had affairs, and she didn't seem to care whether or not my father found out. No flirtation seemed without consequence in my mother's hands.

I found that trip south taxing. I was not a good traveler; since childhood, I experienced leaving home not as an adventure, but as a trauma during which I relived, unconsciously, that separation from my mother when I was three. To accompany Mother this time engendered both excitement and fear, as she cast me in the role of an adult and caretaker as well. While I was to accompany her everywhere — to every cocktail party and dinner — I was also responsible for her. And I got used, fast, to being ignored while Mother went about her business. Later I would look back on this trip and realize that I had been there for one purpose: keeping things straight and cleaning up the mess.

I perceived that if I were careful enough, I might be able to control the unpredictable nature of our trip simply by taking good care of Mother. And so once again I became the gatekeeper, carrying the plane tickets, preventing her from leaving her purse in the terminal, getting us to the gate on time, making sure she didn't drink so much she couldn't get off the airplane, remembering everyone's name so that I could prompt her when she forgot.

Readings themselves brought out the worst in Mother. Desperate to have the audience love her, she drank a great deal, urgently, to bolster herself before going on stage. She envisioned herself as Judy Garland, one of her favorite singers, and wanted listening to Anne read to be as much of a high as listening to Judy sing. I had never been solely responsible for Mother when she was drinking and I, not quite thirteen, was unprepared.

At the party following the Sweetbriar reading, what had been a threat that day in the lounge with Dickey escalated into a nightmare: Mother resumed drinking after the reading ended and began to drape herself all over Philip Legler, a young poet and married Sweetbriar faculty member. Her arms around his neck, her head on his shoulder, she took one drink after another, three drinks, four drinks. Her obvious sexual invitation and her inebriation brought me deep shame. I tried to hide my distress and wondered with a pounding heart how I would ever get her out of this place before she did something disastrous. I remembered all too well a party at our neighbor's home where she had taken off her blouse at the dinner table, determined to prove that a brassiere was no more revealing than a bikini top. I had been hired as kitchen help that night, but this evening at Sweetbriar I was on the front lines. I tugged on her arm and suggested we leave — only to be ignored.

At last I managed to persuade Legler to drive us back to our seedy motel room (it was on this trip that I learned the meaning of her favorite expression, "This is the pits") but not before she had passed out from the combination of alcohol and the slug of sleeping pills she had insisted on taking while still at the party despite my pleas that she wait. Legler carried her from car to bed, and after I locked the door behind him, I undressed her.

I lay awake that night, worrying that she had taken too much medication, tossing and turning on my bed with sagging springs, holding my breath to see if I could still hear hers. The night passed slowly, and I lay there wondering: "How many did she take? What will I do if I don't hear her breathing anymore? How will I get her to the hospital — I don't even know where it is!" When dawn finally flicked its pink tongue around the corners of our windows, I was too exhausted to worry further. In the daylight I could tell she was still alive. We'd made it through the long night.

Later she would apologize to Legler in a letter: "I feel kind of awful the way I acted at Sweetbriar taking my pills. I mean, I waited too long to get to that motel. The pills aren't kidding, or rather I'm not, they just knock me out." It obviously never occurred to her to apologize to me.

Thinking of my father as we drove on to Williamsburg, I tried to silence a persistent question: What would have happened between her and Legler had I not been there to chaperone? As I would shortly come to know when she could no longer resist the temptation to share her illicit news, she did indeed have a number of extramarital affairs; her affair with Legler, however, did not begin until after she had divorced my father — although Legler was still married at the time.

When we arrived in Williamsburg, Mother got her period and became rapidly obsessed about whether her pads and tampons would be sufficient to stanch the flow. The room in which we were staying was spacious, in keeping with the colonial taste of the town, and had a bathroom as big as my bedroom back home. Sitting on the toilet, she called me in and asked me to hand her a new pad from the box at her feet. Her legs were spread and the toilet bowl was red with blood. "Look how much there is," she said. My stomach churned. I myself had not yet begun to menstruate, and the amount of blood alarmed me. "Bleeding like this is sometimes cancer," she whispered, her blue eyes filled with fear. "Cancer," I echoed, thinking of my grandmother Ga-ga and the rot that had overtaken her body when I was six. I gave Mother the pad and she swaddled herself up like a newborn in a raft of diapers.

Nevertheless, as Mother liked to say, "the show must go on," and so she appeared that night before a packed audience to great applause. My mood improved, and I relaxed a little: there was no repeat of the excesses of Sweetbriar. As if understanding that she needed to make some effort on my behalf, Mother arranged for us to have lunch on the terrace at the Williamsburg Inn the following day. The meal remains memorable: a tender, flavorful pot roast, the best I'd ever eaten. We walked through streets overflowing with spring flowers and cool sunshine. I had borrowed one of Joanie's chic coats, complete with three-quarter-length sleeves and a pair of long gloves. Mother and I held hands as we strolled: mother, daughter; partners, friends.

Back in Weston, I resumed worrying about her health. As she recounted in an inimitably dramatic letter to Philip Legler following our return home, she was worried too:

> If I don't die tonight there is always tomorrow when I have an apt. with my O.B. because Linda took the pamphlet from the cancer collecting lady this Sunday and immediately read my symptom at William and Mary and the month before, namely I almost bled to death. Not usual for me so in I go to be checked over like a piece of meat. I would have forgotten it but Linda reminds me I don't want to die. She also underlined HOARSENESS, as I almost lost my voice completely on this last trip . . . Linda, the dear, knows [the seven Cancer danger signals] by heart. She has a cold. She is upstairs reciting [them] and waiting, oh longing, to menstruate and be a woman and meanwhile please god don't let mummy die of too much of it.

My new role: to protect, to worry, to nurse, to care for her as a parent would have. Now I had three words in my worry vocabulary:

cancer, depression, and suicide. In these years, her depression was often a daily fact, even though the suicide threats had diminished somewhat due to the Thorazine. And, as I identified with her, so did I identify with her symptoms, like an expectant father with sympathetic pregnancy ailments: depression and anxiety had become antagonists in my life too.

When her gynecologist put Mother on bed rest, I emptied her bloody bedpans and wondered if, after all her testing of Death, he would come to get her on his own terms, and possibly, before she was ready. In May of that year she finally had a D & C. Later she began to take the birth control pill — whose chemistry, ironically, had been synthesized by her future biographer's husband, Carl Djerassi. The pill temporarily cured the problem.

I didn't stop worrying.

Live or Die

Turn, my hungers!
For once make a deliberate decision.
There are brains that rot here
like black bananas.
Hearts have grown as flat as dinner plates.
Anne, Anne,
flee on your donkey,
flee this sad hotel,
ride out on some hairy beast . . .
any old way you please.

— Anne Sexton
"Flee on Your Donkey"

*D*EATH LIVED at our house: lurking in the quart-sized pharmaceutical jugs of Thorazine, chloral hydrate, Nembutal, and Deprol on Mother's dresser; in the crystal decanters of booze; on the tip of my mother's tongue or clenched between my father's fists; patiently waiting in the car parked in the large garage; behind the bars of the mental hospital. Even as a small child I pictured death not as a tall stranger riding a dark horse, nor as a monster with three heads, but as an event of perfect and dreadful simplicity — final separation. Not a myth, but instead reality. On May 8, 1969, when I was almost sixteen, death visited us again, this time slithering into our lives over the telephone.

In the dark, from the cocoon of sleep and warm sheets, the ringing was shrill and persistent enough to set even the most inexperienced heart racing. My mother — on whose bedside table rested the phone — was in New York, living in the Algonquin Hotel for long periods as she worked with the director and producer on the final version of her play *Mercy Street*.

That night the ringing continued till Joy answered and summoned my father. He stumbled to the phone on the empty side of
the bed, alarm singing through his blood. From my bedroom I
heard all sound stop except for his sleepy, confused voice as he
spoke. The night hugged my face, black and still.

Illumination pierced my room: Joy had switched on the overhead light in the hall. She cried out the words that would so mark
us all: "Joanie's dead!" Quick as lightning, a thought seared my
mind: *Thank God it's not Mother.*

Joanie — killed, like her father, in a car accident. My mind repeated it numbly: Joanie is dead; my friend, my friend is dead. I
could not even cry, for to cry would make it true.

Only five days before, Joy and I had been bridesmaids at Joanie's
wedding. We had all gone to the hairdresser's together, and then
Joanie herself had helped us with our makeup. She had been thirty-
five years old, beautiful, laughing, happy at last. Then, the honeymoon. The drunk driver hit her car head on.

The coroner theorized that her neck had snapped instantly. She
had not a mark on her, except for a tiny scratch above her right
knee. As if in reflex to keep the pain of my loss away from my
heart, I wondered about this theory of instant, painless death.
Though both my mother's parents had died when I was six, and my
father's father when I was seven, my understanding of death came
from the miasma of fear that seemed to hover over us whenever
Mother's mood took a nosedive. You waited for death; like a train
far down the track, it took a long time coming, its trail of smoke
marking the backdrop of blue sky, barely but indeed visible in the
distance.

We grieved for Joanie, each locked into his or her own little
world. Mother came home from New York, reluctantly, it seemed
to me; her relationship with Joanie had not been unlike her relationship with her own sisters — fraught with ambivalence. As for
my father, who could say? His grief seemed deep but silent. For Joy
and me, however, a light had been doused, an adult forever gone
upon whom we had been able to depend — not only for guidance,

but for fun. She had been stability in my world of chaos, the bearer of picnics and small spur-of-the-moment gifts, my companion at the movies, fellow Audrey Hepburn fan, pal of summers in Maine, sand castle builder extraordinaire. My friend.

By the time we got to the funeral home I thought I had control of myself. There were many people there, many I knew, many who hugged me in consolation. I felt disconnected and blank. At the far end of the room lay Joanie's coffin, surrounded by banks of gladiolas. Slowly I walked forward and knelt down on the small stool by her side.

I ran my fingers along the edge of the polished wood. I wished I could hold her hand just one more time. No more picnics, I thought then. No more silver polishing on rainy Saturdays. No more Christmas shopping. No more laughter. No more laughter. The giddy way Joanie and I could spiral up into the emotional stratosphere together, everything riding on that soar of pleasure, giggling till we wanted to wet our pants and had to cross our legs, as if nothing else in the world existed except this one hysterical thing right here and right now. These small joys were gone forever.

I started to shake. Tears poured from me at last, rage at the damage I felt. The pain would not leave. I cried harder, unable to stop, my sobs tearing down my last defenses, until, like the tide rolling in over the ramparts we had once built around our sand castles, a sea of grief flooded me. Someone from the funeral home helped me up from the kneeler and out of the room. Back at Nana's house, I passed tea sandwiches to guests. Later I would help my grandmother pack the cartons full of wedding gifts that had to be returned to their senders.

Nana was devastated; this last blow seemed more than she could bear. My father remembers that morning in May when he arrived at Nana's house to tell her of Joanie's death. "Oh, my God," she said with horror, "the wrong one died." He never really recovered from this remark any more than Nana ever recovered from the tragic death of the daughter she loved beyond anyone else.

Despite the passage of years, the mere mention of Joanie's name brought Nana to tears until her own death nearly twenty years later, in 1986. She left Joanie's bedroom undisturbed, the face powders and lipsticks still in the dressing table drawers, the shoes and dresses in the closet. Mother came, over time, to nickname this room "the shrine Billie built to Joanie." Gradually Nana began to call Joy "Joanie," in an attempt to reverse the past, in unconscious acknowledgment of the mother-daughter bond they had shared in those early years when Joy had lived with her. It drove my mother nuts.

꒛

In a house so obsessed with death, where babies were too needy and difficult to be kept at home, where older daughters were needed so intensely that they could not be lived without for a second month away at camp, what room could there ever have been for a litter of squirming, nursing puppies? In January of 1966, however, despite Mother's perpetual depression, our Dalmatian Penny gave birth. Thus was life imported into our house as one by one the puppies arrived the way crocuses do in springtime: insistently, pushing their heads up despite the blanket of sterile white snow.

My parents had neglected to have Penny spayed before she came into heat for the first time, and when she escaped over the six-foot backyard fence to couple with some neighborhood lothario, they had imported Maxine Kumin's Dalmatian, Caesar, in hopes of salvaging a few purebred pups.

As Penny swelled so did the discussion that would later give rise to a poem, which poem would, in turn, give rise to a myth. If, my parents speculated, the puppies turned out to be mutts, we would have trouble finding homes for them. Me-me instructed us that we could simply have a pail of water ready at their birth and solve the problem by submerging them. She promised my mother that she — a breeder of champion Old English sheepdogs, three of whom slept on her bed every night — would even take care of it if we called her as Penny began to whelp.

Naturally, Joy and I — then thirteen and eleven — protested. Even Daddy protested after a while. All three of us liked animals, and why should the puppies be killed if they were not purebred?

Surely they would be cute? Surely someone would want them?

Mother tolerated the two cats and the dog, the tank full of fish that Dad and I tended, but she really had no interest in most animals. Dad was the one who built the barn out behind the house, hammering his thumbs and swearing, who hung over the fence at the dusty arenas of our horse shows and puffed up with pride at our blue ribbons and trophies. Mother came and smoked, making small talk with Maxine, her dislike of large, smelly animals evident even as she supported us with her unwilling presence. As a child she had been forced to ride and had hated it, developing a fear that stayed with her into adulthood. Only once did we coax her up onto a horse; on a summer Sunday she sat nervously astride Maxine's mare, Xantippe, stiffly perched in her sunglasses, sweater, and straw hat.

But even Mother did not really entertain any notion of killing Penny's puppies. The idea of waiting pails of water became a private joke, an option discarded as soon as it had been conceived. One January morning I arose at my usual six o'clock, the house around me silent and cold. Always the first to rise, because my bus came before anyone else's, I got dressed and went downstairs, turning the thermostat up as I passed it. A strange chirping and mewling caught my ear as I walked by the basement door. Mice, I thought, recoiling. Then, in a flash, I knew. Puppies! Upstairs I ran, broadcasting the news as if I were Paul Revere.

In the pen my father had built scrambled a heap of white fur, blind faces crying out for the mother they could neither see nor find. Joy and Daddy appeared and then, after a while, even Mother stumbled downstairs in a medicated haze to light up a cigarette and watch the last two pups be whelped. Though he had never witnessed a single human birth in his life, my father was midwife to the exhausted Penny, gently tearing open the sacs, rubbing the puppies clean. A miracle had happened in the night: life, tumbling in our laps and on our floors. Life, squirming its way into all our hearts. An abundance of life — not death.

Mother loved those puppies, cuddled them, fed them, and returned their kisses with rapture. Still, it was in her nature to seek the dramatic. And so, engaged at that time in a struggle to finish her book *Live or Die* with an upbeat ending, she wrote a poem called "Live" to honor the occasion:

> *So I say Live*
> *and turn my shadow three times round*
> *to feed our puppies as they come,*
> *the eight Dalmatians we didn't drown*
> *despite the warning: The abort! The destroy!*
> *Despite the pails of water that waited*
> *to drown them, to pull them down like stones,*
> *they came, each one headfirst,*
> *blowing bubbles the color of cataract-blue*
> *and fumbling for the tiny tits.*
> *Just last week, eight Dalmatians,*
> *¾ of a lb., lined up like cord wood*
> *each*
> *like a*
> *birch tree.*
> *I promise to love more if they come,*
> *because in spite of cruelty*
> *and the stuffed railroad cars for the ovens,*
> *I am not what I expected. Not an Eichmann.*
> *The poison just didn't take.*
> *So I won't hang around in my hospital shift,*
> *repeating the Black Mass and all of it.*
> *I say Live, Live, because of the sun,*
> *the dream, the excitable gift.*

In 1988, on reading a first draft of Mother's biography, which included an account of the creation of the poem and the near rescue of the puppies from drowning at birth, I realized that once again Mother's literary license had created a fiction that had survived for the more than twenty years since the poem's publication. Eventually Mother's biographer, Diane Middlebrook, would revise the version recounted in her original draft. Mother had never had any real intention of drowning the puppies — much less if they were purebred Dals that we could sell for a reasonable sum. There were no pails of water waiting, and we slept through the vigil of death she painted. Literary license also gave Mother the metaphor about "birch trees," for — as anyone familiar with Disney knows — Dals are born without any spots showing through their temporarily snow-white coats.

What would it have meant to my mother to kill Penny's eight puppies? Perhaps it would have served to confirm that she did indeed carry a "death baby" inside her. Perhaps the myth she created out of the situation was not solely commercial in its purpose, but also provided her with the hope that some small part of her was not a killer, "not an Eichmann." Certainly, to me, the poem's expressed desire to live was paramount, a jet trail of hope in the black sky of her depression.

After Mother's death, an interviewer for a PBS station asked me which of her poems was my favorite. "'Live,'" I answered without a pause. Surely this poem embodied my greatest fantasy: there, on that page, my mother chose life over death. I could not perceive the formulaic aspects of the poem at that time, nor quite appreciate the canny search she had made, looking for an upbeat ending for the book called *Live or Die*. Who would buy such a book if the final poem were entitled "Die," even if, for the poet, "Die" suited her better?

The next spring another telephone call echoed through our house: Mother had been awarded the Pulitzer Prize. She went dancing from room to room, whooping and hollering. My proud father left work early, bringing home with him a case of excellent champagne and flowers: this sort of notice was the kind he understood. Maxine drove right over, along with several other close friends, and an instant party was created. Even Mother's sister Jane sent a telegram congratulating her and noting that "it is great to be related to a celebrity." A single phone call had catapulted her into the mainstream she so craved.

Life magazine ran a long story on her; her popularity swelled; the fee she could command for a reading escalated sharply. She became known outside poetry circles by a far greater audience. Over the years there would be more prizes, more honorary doctorates, more acclaim. "I have to be great, that's the entire problem — I want to leave the impact of my personality carved in marble," she had said to Dr. Orne back in 1961 in one of her more grandiose moods. His response, which expressed concern over her destructive need to become a star, was a sad prediction of the years to come.

Independence

I'm here, that somebody else,
an old tree in the background.

Darling,
stand still at your door,
sure of yourself, a white stone, a good stone —
as exceptional as laughter
you will strike fire,
that new thing!

— Anne Sexton
"Little Girl, My Stringbean, My
Lovely Woman"

LIKE THE WIND eroding the shape of the dunes on the beach, my adolescent intimacy with Mother began to change. While she loved the young adult I was in the midst of becoming — an interesting person with whom she could talk over complicated matters of adulthood and someone who spoke "Language" — she simultaneously missed the cheek-to-cheek companionship that had marked my ninth through sixteenth years. During high school, I began the slow and painful process of putting some distance between us. Because our relationship had been so tight, even the smallest change seemed drastic to us both. Gradually I stopped confiding in her and stopped listening to her secrets in exchange. I began to resist her intrusive questions. Without warning, aspects of my life existed to which she no longer had access. This loss shocked her, and she fought it.

The separation was painful for me too, and I was only able to accomplish it gradually by transferring many of my emotions onto the safe harbor of another woman, a psychiatrist who was paid to listen and who had no personal investment in anything I said. I began to see her once a week in the autumn of 1968, during my sophomore year in high school. The summer before that school year began, I wrote a poem called "The Rabbit Hole" that described the numb depression I felt increasingly, my bleak outlook. The occasional blue Saturdays when I mooned around listening to Frank Sinatra and Judy Garland records had extended themselves into a sadness and desperation that recurred more and more frequently.

Depression constituted a main ingredient of the atmospheric mix in the Sexton home, and it didn't seem in the least bit strange that I, too, should suffer its effects. I didn't allow myself to worry about what such depression meant for my future, or whether over time I would become as dysfunctional as my mother, because I didn't think much about the future at all. To maintain my balance each day on the rickety bridge spanning our own personal abyss felt difficult enough. I found I could pay little attention to the outside world. My vision was peculiarly limited, aimed inward in unhealthy ways. The global struggles being played out in Vietnam seemed distant to me, a mere mirror: of the war my mother fought daily with her insanity; of the battles my parents pitched against each other; of the constant protest for freedom in which I marched now against Mother herself.

When I asked my mother if I could see a therapist, she had responded nearly joyfully, seeing my request as an opportunity for reunion, something else we could share again. She made inquiries and took me for my first appointment to a respected psychiatrist, Dr. Adele Shambaugh, where the first blow was delivered to Mother when the doctor asked her to remain in the waiting room while she saw me alone.

Adele Shambaugh was blond, a woman who wore tailored, elegant clothing, expensive leather pumps, and she spoke with an accent, perhaps Austrian; she sat behind her desk while I occupied the wooden armchair in front of her. She was slender and quite handsome; caught in the grip of my first — but by no means my last — transference, I shyly grew to love her, and the more I loved her the more I resented my mother.

Dr. Shambaugh smoked constantly and kept her comments to a minimum. This didn't surprise me, as I knew the basic tenets of Freudian psychiatry with its necessary silences, and then, of course, Mother had spoken of her own psychiatric treatment often and in intimate detail. I liked reading about psychology — my goal was, at this point, to be a psychiatrist — and so I was struggling to understand Freud, Erik Erikson, and Simone de Beauvoir.

Dr. Shambaugh wasted no time in discouraging my dependence on Mother and my identification with her. In a private session with my parents, she addressed herself to these issues, pointing out to Mother that the "overabundance of love" she had thrust upon me was not a gift — but a burden that prevented me from growing up. Dr. Shambaugh encouraged me to think for myself, to stop telling Mother my secrets, to spend more of my time after school with my peers, to overcome my innate shyness and participate more in extracurricular activities. I tried out for and won a spot in the Girls Glee Club, the Mixed Chorus, and the Third Edition, an elite choral group, as well as publishing a few poems in our high school literary magazine. I began to get small singing roles in our school's musical comedies. Perhaps most important, I began to make new friends — ones my own age: Pedie and Priscilla and Susie now became the confidantes with whom I would spend hours on the phone, telling secrets and giggling. No, it didn't take long for Mother to resent Dr. Shambaugh's influence and begin to hate her.

At first Mother herself had driven me to these sessions, which were in Dr. Shambaugh's residential office on a side street of Cambridge, every Wednesday afternoon at four o'clock. We drove in together in her red Cougar, chatting the whole way, the car rapidly filling with smoke from Mother's cigarettes; she wore her camel hair coat and suede driving gloves to protect her from the cold New England weather.

Initially, as we drove home, she would ask me for details of my sessions. "What did you talk about?" she would inquire. "I'm paying for this, so I have a right to ask." With increasing unwillingness, I told her what she wanted to know: the recurring dreams about Joanie's death, my fantasies of suicide, my doctor's insistence that such fantasies were only manifestations of my over-identification with Mother.

This exchange of information quickly came to a halt when Dr. Shambaugh called Mother to discuss what she considered to be a breach of my privacy. After this, Mother stopped driving me to my sessions and had my grandmother take me instead.

This did not seem odd to me, as Nana had always been the general chauffeur, marshaling Joy and me from school to ballroom dancing lessons at Mrs. Ferguson's, to the dentist, orthodontist, and pediatrician, for new shoes and underwear. If anything it had seemed odd that Mother had driven me at all, a departure from habit that broke the pattern of Nana as mother-in-residence for all routine chores.

Later, Mother would tell me in detail about that call she received from Dr. Shambaugh, in which she insisted that Mother back off — not merely from asking about my appointments, but also from asking any personal questions at all. After Mother had hung up, she had gone upstairs to my room and cried on the bed; in my closet, she had held on to my clothes and sobbed her good-byes. She believed she was losing me, and she hated the woman she perceived as having replaced her. Every month when the bill came for my therapy she would complain bitterly: "I'm paying someone to take you away from me." Nevertheless, she did continue to fund my sessions and make it possible for me to achieve the necessary emotional separation from her — though she did pass on, in detail, all the gossip she could field about Dr. Shambaugh's private life. I was as miserable as a girl caught in a fight between her two best friends.

✣

In certain ways the separation I sought to achieve came as hard to me as it did to her, because separation itself had been my greatest fear ever since I was exiled to Mary Gray's and then to Blanche's. Most of me, even as a teenager, wanted to stay nestled right at my mother's feet. Conflicted about giving up the rich relationship we had — despite its inevitable price — I worried that she would fall apart if I did manage to achieve some measure of distance; I struggled to maintain that distance while simultaneously running back to her side — not unlike a toddler who is learning to walk. In these years Maxine often admonished me: "Stop taking the weight of the world on your shoulders, Linda. You're only a teenager." How I wished I could do so, as simply as she instructed.

If Mother couldn't have me for herself, the next best person to inherit guardianship was Maxine Kumin, her best friend of many years. Mother suggested to Maxine that I might benefit from a private poetry tutorial with her once a week and so, when I was in my junior year in high school, I began driving to Maxine's home after supper with my poems in hand. Modeling Mother's methods, I kept these typewritten drafts on manila paper in a black spring binder, revisions added in number one pencil. Maxine and I retired to her upstairs office, where, surrounded by books and the yellow light of a desk lamp, we sat and discussed everything from iambic pentameter and slant rhyme to birth control, oral sex, and the best method for shaving your legs. She was quite tender with me about my adolescent questions, and stern with me about my adolescent poetry. Perhaps having two daughters of her own, both older than I, had taught her how to counsel wisely without interfering or pressuring. In any case, during this time I felt that I had been adopted. Dr. Shambaugh was relieved that I was talking about these intimate issues to Maxine rather than to Mother, and Mother was relieved that I was talking to her alter ego, Maxine, instead of just to Shambaugh.

Concern about establishing individuality and independence is a natural adolescent preoccupation, but the intensity with which my mother and I experienced our separation, and the nature of the separation itself, marked the critical difference in our experiences. I didn't break curfew or joyride in cars — rather, I rebelled by refusing to listen to my mother's intense descriptions of her current love affair or to give her details of my own burgeoning sex life. I stayed after school for drama auditions rather than coming home to keep her company. I did not worry about getting grounded like most teenagers, but instead grew obsessed with the idea that she might kill herself in retaliation for all that I withheld. This dramatic concern was not so bizarre given the context of my situation: my mother had, at the simple introduction of a psychiatrist into my life, stood among my clothes and wept; during my first year at sleep-away camp, when I was ten, she had asked me to come home after the first month to watch over her.

꒜

In 1966, Mother took a bad fall down the staircase on her thirty-eighth birthday and broke her hip. Her fall, while looking like a mere accident, seemed to her fraught with Freudian meaning. She wrote a poem called "The Break" to express what had happened that night. "It was also my violent heart that broke, / falling down the front hall stairs," it began. Why a broken heart? Because shortly before she pitched forward into darkness and fell headlong down the carpeted risers, her lover had rejected her and told her he was returning to his wife.* Who was this man? Her psychiatrist, Dr. Frederick Duhl,† who charged Mother for their sessions, *à deux*, on the couch, so as not to arouse the suspicions of his wife, who handled his office billing.

Lying in bed while the hipbone knit and her heart smarted, she drank eggnogs and imported beer to bolster her energy and her spirits. She put on thirty pounds, becoming flabby through the stomach, face, and hips, ballooning to a size eighteen. Once up and around again, she didn't lose the weight: Thorazine, it seemed, had another side effect — weight gain.

Mother now became repugnant to me in a physical sense, too. Her nightly back rubs — supplied by Nurse Joy and Nurse Linda

---

*This sense of abandonment also precipitated her creation of the poem "For My Lover, Returning to His Wife."

†When editing *Anne Sexton: Self-Portrait in Letters* in 1975, I used a pseudonym to protect Dr. Frederick Duhl, as did Diane Middlebrook when she wrote her biography of my mother in 1991. However, since the *New York Times* named Duhl in their front-page story covering the variety of explosive issues raised by the biography, I no longer feel such compunction.

on an alternating basis — bared not only her back but her entire body, including her jellylike white buttocks, which she expected massaged as well. Touching her disgusted me, and increasingly I tried to be busy at "Mommy's massage time." Being near her uncovered body brought me an inexplicable shiver of revulsion.

She abandoned her weekly appointments at the hair salon and let her hair hang greasy and straight. The makeup in her dressing table dried up in its bottles. She wore two knit polyester pantsuits with elastic waistbands nearly continually: one prison gray, the other navy and covered with Dalmatian hairs. Where had Princess Anne gone? I wondered.

None of us could understand the metaphor Mother had painted before us because the metaphor revolved around the secret of her love affair: Mother had let herself "go" — originally down the stairs, and afterwards by letting her physical appearance deteriorate — because *Duhl* had let her go. My father, I later learned, was aware of this affair even as he wrote the checks for the appointments: he confronted neither Mother nor Duhl, hoping misguidedly that his wife's infidelity was only another symptom of her mental illness, and one that would be healed given time and patience.

Unfortunately, such a peaceful resolution never occurred, for after Duhl returned to his wife, he terminated his therapy with my mother. She found a new psychiatrist, Dr. Constance Chase,* but their relationship over the next six years was a rocky one. During these years her illness would grow markedly worse, and so it seems to me now that her fall down the long flight of stairs at 14 Black Oak Road was only the first misstep into darkness.

One night an argument between my parents began over cocktails. At the sound of their raised voices, Joy and I left our homework and went to keep a vigil on the staircase, peering through the banisters, anxiety and dread heavy in our chests. From our hiding place, we could just see Mother, where she sat tipping

*Constance Chase is a pseudonym.

back in her desk chair precariously, her feet up on the wall.

"I'm sick of it!" Mother said. "Not once in over a month! What's the matter with you?"

"Me!" Daddy paced back and forth with rage. "You're the one!"

"I *want* to have sex! You're the one who's rejecting me all the time!"

"Did it ever occur to you to ask yourself why? Your weight, your hair, your clothes — it's appalling. You've got to do something about it, Anne!"

"It wouldn't matter what I looked like! You have no libido!"

"Shut up," he said. His voice lowered. Joy and I exchanged a glance.

"It's the truth!"

He rushed at her, and she tipped over backward in her chair, crashing onto the floor.

"Linda!" she screamed. "Linda, help me!"

I raced down the stairs, heart thundering.

He was already helping her up. She was still screaming at him.

When she called, I still went running.

༉

The later years during high school had about them an air of relief, as — in addition to resenting her intrusive questions — I also began to refuse to answer them. When I allowed myself to fall back into our old ways I felt overwhelmed with a guilt that was stained with the secret pleasure of having satisfied her by giving her what she craved: intimacy on intimate subjects. At the same time, and for the first time, I began to fight with her, refusing her ideas and insisting on my own. And so, even as I began the process of putting distance between us, I remained irrevocably linked to her.

Years later, in 1991, I opened my mailbox to find an envelope of my mother's stationery, addressed to me in care of Maxine Kumin, without an address or a stamp or a postal cancelation. My heart knocked in my chest at the sight of this old ghost. I opened it slowly, feeling confused. It was a letter to me from Mother, written on October 30, 1969, a letter she had never given to me but had instead entrusted to Maxine, for possible delivery when I was older. From her farmhouse in New Hampshire, Maxine had sent it to me by way of Diane Middlebrook, who she knew would be seeing me shortly. Diane had attempted to deliver it to me, but when she discovered me away from home, she had attached a small handwritten explanation to the envelope. In a twist of fate worthy of a Hardy novel, Diane's note had dropped from the envelope onto the driveway, leaving the letter unexplained, unintroduced, a hole in the fabric of time that would whisk me back into the painful past.

Dearest Linda,

You are sixteen. I am forty, almost forty-one. I love you more than I love any human being, any anything. To lose you seems worse than death but that is what I must prepare to do. And I can't explain — maybe never can I explain. Maybe I can never hand you this letter. Maybe in two years or five years I'll tear it up. But I write to explain in case someday you want to know and I feel it is wise that you know — how we came to this place. This place where I must let you go — must even push you away, must stop being "your best friend" — your sister (they say I act like your sister not your mother. They say I try to be the "nice" friend who is never mean) . . .

The reason I was crying was not the reviews of MERCY STREET but about my meeting with Dr. Shabough (sp?) . . . She said I would destroy the therapy you need so much if I told you what she had said. When you asked I said I was too tired to re-member. I blamed the reviews. I lied. She was very worried about you going to Kenny's [my boyfriend] over Christmas and Daddy had never heard of the plan. You don't even know it yet but the plan is vetoed. And wisely too, I think. I know you'll be upset but you will get over it and there just isn't enough chaperoning at Ken-ny's as you well know. That isn't what upset me. She feels you are about fourteen emotionally and not, certainly not, ready for a sex life such as I have led you to think would be all right. She feels you are a long way from being ready. She feels it's my fault. And so does

Daddy. He wasn't too pleased with me, and I felt so guilty — so wrong, so much a bad mother. I feel I have failed you and yet I didn't mean to. And yet that isn't what upset the most. The hardest part was our closeness, our deep and lasting relationship, our bonds of confidences. They are, I am told, inhibiting your growth. We are like two children whispering together, two sisters. They say. I must be a mother and somehow push you away, somehow put a stop to our closeness, tell you not to talk about things with me; tell you to tell "those things" to your doctor. Further, I must stop depending on you for help, must stop leaning on you when I'm afraid. When Daddy and I have a fight I must not call for you. I must not ask you to go places with me when I'm afraid. And more, but I can't remember it all.

Yesterday I sobbed in your room, lying on your bed, asking, "Oh, Linda, forgive me!!" I opened your jewelry box just to look at your earrings because they reminded me of you. I opened your closet and told your clothes I was sorry. I cried and cried. It's true, when you are very upset you do make noise when you are crying. Then I went over to Maxine's and cried there. And when Daddy came home I cried before dinner. Daddy held out a pencil and said "See. This pencil has an eraser. We can erase the mistakes." I told him I couldn't trust my instinct anymore. I'd brought you up by instinct and I'd failed. Linda, I feel like I need a map to follow to tell me the way, to tell me how to act with you. Certainly I can't act like me. Acting like me got you in trouble. When you first learned to talk I talked to you as a friend. As you grew up I confided in you and talked to you as an adult. We have been close and true. But that is over. Somehow I must push you away so that you can stand straight and alone and firm and happy. I must do this so that you don't guess it would not be natural to push you away. I figure that you're supposed to push me away anyhow. That's what normally happens. Certainly you get cross with me. You have times you hate me. I value those times as it means you are growing up. However, it seems that I must hasten this process now. You no longer will confide in me. I won't be able to let you. I will have to say, over and over, discuss that with your doctor not me. I feel that there is no place for me now. I wonder what my role is. To be mean? I guess so. No longer the friendly sister. A cross mother with plenty of

discipline and lots of "no's." Oh little girl, my string bean, my
lovely woman — can I still say to you, "There is nothing in your
body that lies. All that is new is telling the truth." Yes! They won't
take that away. I may be guilty and feel full of holes but I can still
say a few things. I wonder if looking at *Ben Casey* with you is too
much like a child?

I wonder about your sexual self and if it will be happy. Dr. Duhl
always thought I did a wonderful job with you. He called yesterday
having read a review and then said, "What's wrong?" I told him. I
cried. He felt it had been handled incorrectly. He felt that to tell a
mother to push her daughter away was as bad as a mother telling
her daughter to take the pill. But last night after not eating dinner
I went upstairs and, crying, called Dr. Chase. She made some sense
out of it to me. She said I was probably unduly upset because my
relationship with you is like mine with my Nana. Friends. That I
was trying to do something different as just as I kissed a boy my
Nana didn't approve and she went crazy. So I never felt I had her
permission to be a sexual human being. I was trying to make that
different with you. Thus my great feeling of loss was akin to that
loss of Nana so many years ago. You can see what a mess people
can get in.

Linda, I don't know if I'll ever feel you should read this. I'm going to give it to Maxine to keep in case anything should happen to
me. It will take someone very sensitive and of great disgression [*sic*]
to decide if you should read it someday. If your eyes ever find this
page please know that I love you and that anything I do is motivated by love and concern and a desire for you to become your own
woman with your own words.

Mom

She was brave enough and strong enough not to give me the letter after she wrote it, and I can imagine how difficult it must have
been for her to restrain herself that way. I love her for that restraint,
because if this letter feels difficult to read now, I cannot imagine
what turmoil it would have brought to me at sixteen. Nevertheless,
Mother did make certain at the time that I knew all her feelings,
even if she never became quite as specific and detailed as she was in

this letter. I heard the story of her crying in my closet; her hatred of Shambaugh (whose name she could never bring herself to spell properly) grew more and more palpable as the months passed. In an increasingly strong undercurrent also ran her anger with me for having confided as much as I had in the doctor, and for having gotten her into trouble. I felt like a tattletale.

Now I also see how sharply the letter wields the threat of another suicide attempt ("in case anything should happen to me") or, at the least, the nasty promise that after my betrayal she will have to be — unwillingly of course — a mean mother who deals out discipline rather than love and companionship. From now on, in her mind, I would play the role of Snow White to her Queen, Rapunzel to her Mother Gothel. The letter implied that my desire to escape from childhood, to dissolve the bonds of the companionship that had once united us, might well spell death. If only she could have listened to her own words, expressed so movingly in her poem "Little Girl, My Stringbean, My Lovely Woman," and become, truly, "an old tree in the background" of my strike for independence.

I read this letter today and I want to cry: how sad was that time of our lives and how quickly it comes back at me, carried on the wind of her words. I am happy to know that I meant so much to her; nevertheless, I'm angry as well, angry that she had to make her feelings about our separation so plain at such a vulnerable time for me, angry that she ignored the cost of allowing me to see her distress, especially when it had been caused by my pitiful moves toward independence.

Why couldn't I have been the child and she the adult just once; why couldn't she have controlled her feelings for my sake; why didn't she love me enough? I wondered, as I sat there with that letter in my hand.

Though she did not show me the letter at that time, she played out her hand a few years later when I withheld from her a singularly important and intimate piece of information. In the spring of my senior year of high school I fell in love with a young man who was an accomplished pianist. He roused in me my first sexual feelings, totally unlike anything I had ever felt in those years when I let boys paw at my cold, unmoved body so that I would have a story to carry back to Mother.

I had almost given up hope that I would ever experience sexual pleasure. I still could not masturbate. I still had orgasms only in my sleep. Secretly I alternated between believing I was frigid, and worrying about whether I might be a lesbian. In the poem "Little Girl, My Stringbean, My Lovely Woman," Mother imagined, in a violent image, the young Romans initiating my body "with ladders and hammers," and then went on to admonish me:

> But before they enter
> I will have said,
> Your bones are lovely
> and before their strange hands
> there was this hand that formed.

Her hand had formed me, in oh, so many ways. Her hand — which I had now rejected. It infuriated her.

And then along came Ian.* My father didn't like him. My mother thought he was "dreamy." He had graduated from college, he was a pianist pursuing classical study at the graduate level. I was still a high school senior and I was totally swept away. So was Mother.

"Ian," she would say, coming to the entrance to our living room as he practiced, his strong broad hands pulling the magic of Chopin, Bach, and Wagner from the keys of our old baby grand. "Play that again. I love the emotion in your playing. How powerful." And she would stand and listen to him play, leaning against the doorjamb. She had lost a lot of her weight by then, and, as always, her looks were dramatic. She wanted him for herself, I could see — perhaps because through him she could replay her own youth, her own first time. I hated her. I wanted her to go away and leave us alone.

*Ian is a pseudonym.

I wasn't meant to have him, and perhaps that was the key. For the first time I *wanted* to go to bed with a man, though old fears held me back for at least two months. He was an expert at arousal. He knew how to play me; I was too young to know he knew how to play all women. All day long I daydreamed about having sex with him.

Mother, however, was enraged that I would not admit to her that I was sleeping with Ian. Initially this was not a lie, but she insisted that I was lying. "The smell of sex is all over you," she would hiss. What she scented, in fact, was not the sweetness of consummation, but the marvelously heady aroma of desire. For consummation I had to wait until she was not hanging over me like a vulture, waiting to check the sheets and authenticate the act with a poem. And so, one late Friday in July just after my eighteenth birthday, not three hours after Mother and Daddy had pulled out of the driveway for a weekend away, I lost my virginity, luxuriously and with pleasure, on the rose-covered bedspread of my childhood. When at last Ian entered me, it was unlike what she had promised: no searing pain but instead joy. I was totally, wildly, ready.

Later, Mother would secretly read my journal to discover what she wanted to know and then — what else? — write a poem about my sexual initiation as a way of showing me how she felt about my refusal to include her. Dr. Shambaugh had no sympathy for this breach of my privacy and suggested to me that I ought to have anticipated Mother's intrusion into my room and hidden the journal in a better spot than my desk drawer.

Mother called her poem "The Taker." It was a lyric of mournful, almost elegiac, tone — speaking not of celebration at my coming of age, but of abandonment and the passing by of the mother. The speaker of the poem uses the metaphor of the house, assuming for herself the role of the jilted nurturer:

> *While the house was away*
> *and the curtains were baby-sitting,*
> *you made your crossing over.*
> *The pitiless rugs had nothing to say,*

the grandfather clock went on with its knitting,
the disposal vomited up chives and clover . . .
Our song, Melancholy Baby, could not
be heard. Goodnight Moon was outgrown,
and two fireflies died unnoticed.
A moth lay down in the jelly pot.
The driveway waited. The grass was mown.
And string bean lay down in her wedding bed.
Her heart went out on a train to meet him
and her mother blessed her,
as best she could,
limb to limb.

When Mother came into my room one night and gave me the poem to read, I handed it back quite coolly. She'd been hammering away at it since sometime in the afternoon, but I was angry with her and I wasn't about to compliment a single line. "Too bad," I said, "that it's not true. You'll have to put it away until I'm not a virgin anymore." And with that I got up and left her sitting on the edge of my bed.

Ian took me from my mother with a finality no psychiatrist ever could have managed. The worst betrayal, of course, came because I had the audacity to take myself out of Mother's world of influence — and on a night when she was not present. The crossing over I had viewed with such celebration had now been painted as a transition brimming with sadness and rejection.

Another poem, "Mother and Daughter," would later catch the agony of our entire situation, filled with the confrontation of a daughter fighting to free herself from the influence of her omnipotent mother. When she showed it to me rolled fresh from her typewriter, she surely meant to shock me into acknowledging the pain I was bringing her:

Linda, you are leaving
your old body now.
You've picked my pocket clean
and you've racked up all my

poker chips and left me empty
and, as the river between us
narrows, you do calisthenics,
that womanly leggy semaphore.
Question you about this
and you will sew me a shroud . . .
Question you about this
and you will see my death
drooling at these gray lips
while you, my burglar, will eat
fruit and pass the time of day.

Her psychiatrist, Dr. Chase, rebuked her for having shown the poem to me. In a fury Mother wrote a letter back to her doctor, and in it she elucidated once again the covenant that had linked us in companionship and in pain since the time I was very small:

> I don't like you telling me what I can write poems about, what is a good subject. . . . Linda does not feel that way. She thinks of course I must write poems about her if I want to — just as she writes poems about me on occasions. She is a writer. She understands. I strongly resent the fact that you feel I am using Linda. . . . You so winningly said, "People come first" meaning before the writing. You forced me to say the truth. The writing comes first. . . . This is my way of mastering experience.

How guilty I felt at having left her behind me like some child abandoned on a distant shore. Perhaps unconsciously I was taking revenge for the way she had once abandoned me, however appropriate my action may have seemed on the surface. Even as I turned away, I missed her and wanted to return — despite the anger I felt at the poem, and its savagery. Even now as I type I hurt again, the pain sounding like a gong deep in the distance, its echo moving relentlessly toward me through the years as if it had been freshly struck today.

ᔓ

All these emotions tumble inside me even now. Part of what hurts most intensely are those positive feelings and the camaraderie I still felt about my mother during this war of increasing differences, for they created an intense ambivalence. Moments of poetry at our kitchen table; accompanying her to some of the classes she was teaching in creative writing as a newly appointed lecturer at Boston University; being a groupie with my friends for her emerging poetry rock group, Anne Sexton and Her Kind.

Her Kind, a group of musicians with an electric keyboard, an acoustic guitar, a flute, saxophone, bass, and drums, created original music to enhance Mother's poetry as she read it aloud. It was almost a rock group, more than a poetry reading. As she pointed out, the "poets" most listened to in America were in fact those who combined their poetry with music to create a lyric: "People flock to Bob Dylan, Janis Joplin, the Beatles — these are the popular poets of the English-speaking world."

My friends and I sat on the steps of our sunken living room, where the band often practiced on a Saturday or Sunday. We all had a crush on the guitarist, a high school senior who was also a football star, and we loved the music, the poetry, the beatnicky atmosphere. I held special status because I was the daughter of the star. When they went out for a concert, I got to tag along, providing a nursemaid for Mother as I had in the past on reading tours.

One afternoon Mother came into the kitchen and found me with my usual bowl of vegetable soup, and a book propped against the salt shaker.

"What are you reading, honey?"

I turned the blue book spine outward. "*Grimms'*," I replied, barely looking up.

"You never get tired of those stories, do you?" She sat down beside me, musing, cigarette smoke spiraling upward.

This was true, I thought. How often had I read and reread those fairy tales: I loved their dark, clever humor, the onionskin-thin pages, the fat binding falling apart from being so well loved. It was a gray day; the light coming through the window backlit her face. I had heard that tone in her voice before. A thinking tone. A little bit of excitement.

"Which are your favorites?" She picked up a paper napkin from the holder that stood next to the hand-painted china sugar bowl she had inherited from her Nana.

"'The Twelve Dancing Princesses,' 'The Little Peasant,' 'Godfather Death,' 'Rapunzel,' 'Briar Rose,' 'The White Snake,' 'Iron Hans.'" I was thinking aloud; as I spoke, she scribbled the titles on the napkin with a pencil. The napkin tore beneath the dull lead but that did not deter her. When I had finished she had quite a list and she disappeared back into her writing room. I returned to my book.

Shortly thereafter she showed me the poem "Iron Hans," and then "Snow White." I loved them all as they grew in her black binder like a tribe of children. They became the book *Transformations,* which she dedicated to me. I loved her for that, too.

But even as we shared the creation of *Transformations,* other difficulties brought us closer to the abyss of her despair again. Her psychiatrist, Dr. Chase, was not, in Mother's opinion, nearly sympathetic enough. There were increasing fights between them as Mother's demands grew more insistent: more love, more time, more midnight phone calls. Once again Mother began acting out with more suicide threats.

A spring afternoon at Nana's: my grandmother had just rolled my hair onto pink sponge rollers and doused it with evil-smelling permanent wave solution when the phone rang. It was Maxine, who had phoned our home only to discover Mother speaking gibberish and growing progressively more sleepy. Joy, the only one home, was unable to rouse her.

Nana left me sitting with the caustic solution on my hair and drove quickly to Black Oak Road. She was trying to drag Mother down the stairs and into the car to take her to the Emergency Room when Daddy came home. Together they got Mother to the hospital in time, but Mother didn't seem to take the cost of the episode too seriously, later writing of it to a friend as if it had

Mother and me in the
living room at our house
in Newton, 1953.

Nana helps me open a
Christmas present, c. 1955.
On my head is Joanie's
stewardess cap.

My aunt Joanie with me,
1953.

My maternal grand-
parents, Mary Gray and
Ralph Harvey, on the
ferry dock at Squirrel
Island, Maine.

Joy (right) and I show off our Halloween pumpkins in the living room at the Newton house, 1961. Behind us, Mother's writing room is visible.

George Sexton, my father's father, whom I called "Poppy," holding me in his lap in the den at my grandparents' home, c. 1956.

Mother and me, dressed up for a neighbor's wedding, c. 1961.

Joy (right) and me on our porch in Newton, summer 1957.

Daddy, Joy (seated), and me, tobogganing in January 1964.

My father, mid-1960s.

Mother in the kitchen in Newton, 1964.

The whole family, dressed up and on our way to Nana's for Christmas dinner, 1965.

Sitting with my best friend on the step into the living room, listening to a Saturday rehearsal of *Anne Sexton and Her Kind*. Left to right: Steve Rizzo, Mother, Theodore Casher, Bill Davies, Robert Clawson, me, Pedie Gardiner. (*Ted Polombaum/Photography Collection, Harry Ransom Humanities Research Center, University of Texas at Austin*)

With Mother, c. 1968.

Feeding one of Penny's puppies, 1966.

Reserve Champion at Highlawn Farm with "David," summer 1969.

Mother and Dad in the backyard after we moved to Weston, 1971.

Joy (right) and me as bridesmaids at Joanie's wedding, 1967.

Contact lenses, braces, and earrings, 1969.

John and me at the beach after our college graduation, 1975.

Daddy and me in the kitchen in Weston doing the Sunday crossword puzzle, about a year after Mother's death, 1976.

Mother in dress and hat she was married in, after eloping with Dad to Virginia Beach, 1948.

The hat I wore for my wedding was copied from Mother's wedding picture. Memorial Church, Harvard Yard, 1979.

Nana and me, spring 1981.

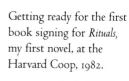

Getting ready for the first book signing for *Rituals,* my first novel, at the Harvard Coop, 1982.

Alexander "on safari" after his third birthday party, 1986.

Nicholas at six months, 1985.

Joy (right) and me, 1990.

Mother at her desk in
her red reading dress,
c. 1974. (*Arthur Furst*)

1994, forty years old.
(*Jim Fisk*)

John and me with
Rhiannon, March 1994.
(*Ed Forman*)

all been a lark, detailing in a proud tone how many pills she had taken, and the exact unfolding of events, right down to her shallow breathing. In the meanwhile, Joy — who was only fifteen years old — had been shell-shocked into dealing with a comatose mother, Nana and Daddy had once again gone through the hell of a trip to the Emergency Room, and my hair was frizzy from having been left too long in the chemical solution. I discovered a new emotion, bubbling up from underneath my fear: anger. I was getting very tired of it all. Very tired.

ॐ

College deepened the rift between us. I had arrived at Harvard an insecure eighteen-year-old, never having been away from home for any extended length of time except for camp. I was terrified, once again haunted by the specter of separation from my family — even though this time it was a separation that I chose. Arriving in Cambridge I set up my room with lots of familiar objects from home. I had been assigned no roommate, perhaps because I had indicated on my application that sometimes I got up in the middle of the night to work on a poem. Initially, having a single room seemed a luxury, but soon the drawback became apparent: it was a lot harder to make friends when you were on your own, and making friends had never come easily to me anyway.

The wealth of available courses intoxicated me. Expository writing was mandatory, but otherwise I had a lot of freedom. I signed up for a wonderful history course about Tudor England taught by the renowned Wilbur Jordan, and was pleased not to have anything to do with math or science my first semester. Gravitating toward the most familiar, I applied for a seminar in psychobiography, in which I was able to explore questions about the link between creativity and madness. Predictably enough, I initially chose Sylvia Plath as the writer I would study, but the professor suggested substituting Virginia Woolf instead; I became enthralled by Woolf's novels and essays, and eventually wrote my senior thesis on *To the Lighthouse*, the story of a family's reliance on and separation from a strong mother figure. In writing about Lily Briscoe, the young woman who struggles throughout Woolf's novel to paint her own vision and so escape the influence of Mrs. Ramsay's, I found my own voice, in prose, for the first time.

Naturally I also applied for a poetry writing workshop, one ordinarily limited to upperclassmen. Peter Klappert, a young poet who had won the Yale Series of Younger Poets several years before, had taken over from Robert Lowell, Harvard's man of literature and poetry; I, like others, was disappointed that Lowell, one of my mother's first mentors, was not teaching. Rumors about him and his mental health percolated through campus.

When I applied for the workshop, I submitted a manuscript of about thirty poems, many of which I had written during my private poetry tutorials with Maxine. Some of them sounded a good deal like Mother's poetry, but a few seemed more entirely my own. A phone call to my room in Daniels Hall informed me that I had made the first cut and summoned me for an interview in the basement of the freshmen's Union. I went filled with an odd mixture of emotion: shyness and boldness both — for as insecure as I was about myself as a person, I felt confident as a poet and critic. Mother and Maxine had taught me to believe in this part of myself.

Despite my self-confidence, however, I made sure that Peter Klappert knew my background: with little guile I asked if he thought it would be difficult for me to participate in a poetry seminar as the daughter of Anne Sexton. Unconsciously I wore her name around my neck like a good-luck charm: I envisioned for myself a future just like hers — hard work, admiration, respect, praise. I *could* be just like her, I told myself — surely I had inherited the talent and the determination.

I told Klappert that I had studied with Maxine Kumin the previous year. He was suitably impressed. Just as with my application to Harvard, I was never to know whether I had been admitted on my own strengths or on my mother's. Once a participant in the workshop, however, I learned humility: not everyone loved what I had written, including Peter Klappert. To be Mother's daughter posed no problem either, because not everyone loved *her* poetry. I listened and began to learn what it meant to be ordinary. I also began to learn about other kinds of poetry and poets, and this broadening made me realize what a small circle my mother actually occupied. Previously she had seemed like a giant; now, I saw her in context: Whitman, Yeats, Eliot, Moore, Bishop.

Mother complained that I did not call home very often, and as the years went by she became increasingly vocal in her protest. These years while I was away at college were marked by her increasing health problems — epileptic petit mal seizures, terrible sinus infections, and dental surgery — as well as by her withdrawal from her tranquilizer, Thorazine. In October of 1973, she made two back-to-back suicide attempts and was then hospitalized at the Human Resources Institute for a month, an institution she so much disliked that one night, when out on a dinner pass with a friend, she left the table on a pretext, grabbed a cab, and went home to Weston. Her need for more and more caretakers blossomed, and her generalized helplessness increased.

When I returned home for Christmas vacation that year, she seemed shakier than she had in a while. She was getting ready to phone the drugstore with a list of presents with which to stuff our stockings. I found the idea of ordering perfume by phone from a store one mile away preposterous. Just as I had refused, a few months earlier, to go by myself to return her bras that didn't fit — which she had also ordered over the phone — I now bundled her up in her winter coat and dragged her out with me.

"I'll help you," I said, as she protested. "We'll do this as a team, and it'll be fun." I felt determined that we would have a good time shopping together — an afternoon that strove toward health and normalcy rather than emphasizing sickness; now it seemed crucial that I take a stand against her illness — refuse to cater to it, refuse to be a facilitator of all its unreasonable demands. Instead, as the college girl now, I would outsmart it.

Standing in the middle of the drugstore selecting a lipstick for Joy, however, I turned to find Mother vomiting onto the floor. I put my arm around her and escorted her out into the parking lot, my face red with shame: shame that I had asked her to do something she plainly could not; shame that she had so embarrassed us in a public place; shame at the anger I felt about her condition.

Sometime that week, she and I argued. I don't remember the subject. I do remember coming into her writing room and finding her stretched out full length on the green couch. I called her name and she did not respond. I shook her shoulder and she did not respond. She was breathing normally, eyes open, but it appeared she could not hear or see me. At first I was sure she was ignoring me because we had argued. I got angry and shook her with more determination. Still no response. Puzzled, I soon realized that this was my first encounter with one of her fugue states, a behavior that bore a strong resemblance to her trances of those years she had been in treatment with Dr. Orne — except that a fugue was marked by lassitude while a trance could sometimes be accompanied by activity, such as masturbating or talking. I turned and walked from the room — frustrated, angry, and sad. After a while she awoke, and the evening proceeded as if nothing had occurred.

Despite the escalation of her illness, sometimes we could still recapture a little of the old intimacy that hadn't been inappropriate: often during this vacation we spent afternoons together at the kitchen table, drinking heavily sweetened and milked cups of tea, talking and reading aloud. In reverse from childhood years, I now read to her the poetry I was studying in my literature classes at Harvard. I had the strong desire to teach her everything I was learning, to share my education with her because she had had so little formal education herself. She listened raptly as I read aloud from Eliot — *The Wasteland* and *The Four Quartets*. She loved the thunder of his words, but said she missed the sort of imagery she herself used in such abundance. A poem wasn't really a poem, it seemed to her, unless it was full of metaphor; it took her a while to adjust to the prosody she heard in his work. She, in her turn, read her latest work to me for comment and listened to any "crit" I had to offer. Because I had become more widely read, I now made different kinds of comments on her work, and she accepted this change eagerly.

Also during that Christmas vacation she had agreed to write a eulogy for the poet Philip Rahv; when I came home from school I

found her staring with frustration at the piles of notes she had
made. That week I was able to help her turn those scattered
thoughts into an emotional memorial to a teacher she had loved. It
was difficult for her to communicate in prose, a medium that did
not come to her naturally. I loved being able to help her.

ᴈ

The autumn of my sophomore year at college Nana, widowed for
almost fifteen years, accepted a marriage proposal; in a small local
church in February of 1973 she married for the second time. I returned home for the weekend of the festivities to serve as her maid
of honor. A few hours before we were due to leave for the church,
Mother summoned me into the bathroom, where she was in the
tub.

I averted my eyes from her naked body. She pulled the washcloth up over her breasts, as if sensing my repugnance, and lit a cigarette. She had balanced the dark green ashtray from beside her bed
on the lip of the tub.

"I have to talk to you about Daddy and me," she began, inhaling
deeply.

I sat down on the toilet lid and waited.

"I'm going to ask Daddy for a divorce. Very soon."

"You're joking."

She shook her head, put the cigarette in the ashtray and began
to soap her armpits. "As soon as Nana's gone on her honeymoon."

"But why now?" I was incredulous, angry, upset, scared, and sad.
I couldn't believe this was happening and I felt like crying, or shaking her. "After all this time?"

"Because when I tell him that our marriage is in trouble he tells
me things like 'the ice maker needs to be fixed.'"

I understood what she meant: Daddy wasn't strong on talking
things over. "But he loves you."

"We don't have a sex life, Linda." She lay back and picked up
her cigarette. Her wet fingers made a translucent mark on the filter
paper.

I didn't answer. I didn't want to know anything about their sex
life, much less get dragged into a discussion about it.

"I made my mind up about a month ago," she went on, "but I didn't want to ruin Nana's wedding. I've got it all set up. I'll tell him at a friend's house, probably Fay and Bob Starmer's, and then he can stay here for a little while. Joy will go live with Loring and Louise, and I'll stay with friends until he can find a place of his own."

I just stared at her: she sounded like a teenager planning a mad-cap midnight escape from a dormitory. I didn't say anything but I thought to myself that she was getting crazy again. My mother needed my father. She needed the stability he provided and the freedom he gave her. Who else would put up with Mother? Who else would love her for her faults as well as her strengths? I had known for some time that she was dissatisfied with their sex life, but she'd always solved the problem before without resorting to losing her main caretaker. According to Joy, who was still living at home, the violence between my parents was as bad as ever, but somehow this didn't seem enough of a departure from the status quo to warrant a divorce. After all, they had been violent together for years. Perhaps I was willing to accept their marriage, with all its drawbacks, simply because to see my mother move forward into an uncertain future scared me so much.

Who would take care of her? This question consumed all my attention. She had stopped taking her Thorazine a month or so previously and had gotten quite manic — working with feverish intensity, speaking with agitation, pacing, and calling her friends at all hours of the day and night. Her hands shook, and her face even looked somehow palsied, lopsided. She had lost a lot of weight. The years of medication were taking their toll, I thought, or was it the sudden withdrawal that was causing all these symptoms?

The entire family — and Maxine — worried about her decision to withdraw from the drug. Even Dr. Chase had initially opposed it. Now it seemed to me that these ideas about divorce might be due in part to the lack of proper medication: without some kind of regulation, Mother tended to be like a car speeding along a windy road. I did not want to see her crash.

"Now, honey, I don't want you to think this is your fault, or

Joy's fault. I did stay with him because I thought you needed him when you were younger, but now you're old enough for me to be honest with you and to do what I need to do."

"It never occurred to me that it was my fault," I answered, even more totally astonished. Every time she opened her mouth that day she surprised me more.

"Oh, the children always think it's their fault," she said, dragging on her cigarette and sloshing the gray water over her body. "The parents stay together so the children won't be hurt and then the children blame themselves."

It seemed to me that she had just told me it was my fault, but I didn't say anything more. "I think you're making a big mistake." I stood up, feeling angry. "But it's really none of my business." With that I left her to her tepid water, her soap, and her betrayal. Would she really split apart the family that had held her together for so long?

Dr. Shambaugh assured me that my mother was not about to take such a precipitous step. She hypothesized that Mother felt anxious about dealing with Daddy now that Nana had remarried; would the anger he bore toward his mother be redirected into their marriage? This theory made sense to me in a psychological sort of way, and so I relaxed a little.

Until Sunday, when Mother called to tell me she had left my father. She had phoned him from the home of friends Bob and Fay Starmer and asked him to come over; there she had made her announcement in the presence of witnesses. He had thrown his wedding ring on the floor and stormed out, angry and hurt. Mother had gone to stay at Maxine's.

Night after night my parents called me that spring. "I love her so much," Daddy said, "but I don't understand what she's doing. She must be sick. It must be going off the Thorazine. Do you think she'll come home?" And Mother: "I went to the Smiths' for dinner last night and Lois's tonight. Everyone is so supportive. I'm so excited — Julie* has someone she wants me to meet."

*Julie is a pseudonym.

I got angry at Mother's insensitivity to my feelings for Daddy; his misery had become mine, and I didn't need her to tell me how great she felt. I was glad she was happy, but wished it didn't have to be at his expense. I worried about him and resented the ease with which she had flung herself into her new life. It was an exciting time for her, full of changes, and staying with friends made her feel like a royal visitor — the center of attention. Some of the dramatics she brought to the situation struck me as absurd, however, such as hiring a bodyguard to protect her from my father — a measure that ultimately proved paranoid, as he never once tried to approach her.

I worried, too, that the interest demonstrated by her friends would wear thin as the months progressed: no one, except the family, knew what it was like to deal with Mother full-time, year in and year out. Would these same people still be willing to be endlessly supportive five months from now? Joy, in the meantime, had been sent to live with Loring and Louise Conant, who were new friends of Mother's living in nearby Wellesley; ironically, Loring was also an internist at the Harvard University Health Services, and so he became my doctor and my friend during my parents' separation. Joy pleaded to attend a private boarding school in Maine the following autumn, and Mother acquiesced, finding a young couple to live with her as boarders in the house because she was afraid to be alone. In lieu of rent they cooked and mowed the grass.

One afternoon Mother called to tell me she expected me to testify against my father: "I need you to say that you witnessed him beating me up, that I was afraid for my life."

"No way," I said, furious.

"You have to," she insisted. "I need you to."

"I won't."

"You'll do it or you won't be staying at Harvard one minute longer."

"What do you mean?"

"Who do you think is paying your tuition? It sure isn't your father."

"So," I said slowly. "If I don't testify in court that he beat you up, then you'll stop paying my tuition."

"You have to do what's fair," she answered evasively. "I just want you to tell the truth."

"I'm happy to tell the truth," I said. "The whole truth — how he hit you after you'd provoked him again and again. I'd be happy to tell the entire story, Mom. Is that what you mean by 'the truth'?"

She never brought the subject up again, and she found a friend who was willing to testify under oath that she had seen my father hit my mother — a lie, I believe, because, with the exception of a night back in Newton when my parents had a fight in front of Carl and Rita Ernst, they never came to blows in situations where other people could see them or their complicated emotional dynamic. Mother's attempt to blackmail me into testifying against my father became a betrayal that split us apart and one from which our relationship never really recovered.

In the spring of my junior year, Mother made a direct frontal assault on my world. Or, at least, that was how it felt to me: she accepted an invitation to give a reading for the Harvard community at Sanders Theater. Everyone I knew on campus had been talking about the reading since the morning we opened our copies of the Harvard *Crimson* over breakfast to find a provocative ad featuring my mother. She herself had paid to have the ad designed and inserted into the newspaper because she worried that the organization sponsoring the reading was not doing an adequate job of publicizing her appearance. Believing that she was a second-rate professor from Boston University (comparisons of herself to Robert Lowell never ceased) brought to epic proportion her fear of playing to an empty hall. Drastic measures were called for and taken.

She also gave an interview to the *Crimson*, which ran before the reading, in which she expressed herself quite dramatically on a variety of issues, from teaching, to poetry, to food — and made no attempt to control the heavy spice of her language. I had just earned a spot on the editorial board of the *Crimson*, and the day after the article ran, one of my fellow editors approached me. "How does it feel to have your mother talk dirty in public?" he asked. I shrugged and asked when my next piece was due to run, pretending not to

care about Mother's vulgarity — but really I did, and I hated her
for having put me in such a position. Harvard had been my world
exclusively for these past three years: never once had she been there
to intrude. Never once had she come to visit, to take me out to
lunch, to sit in on a class with me. It was as if we lived on different
coasts: Cambridge seemed as far from Weston as from the moon,
even though it was only ten miles away. I wished I could call Dr.
Shambaugh, with whom I had terminated my therapy that fall, just
for advice or support, but somehow that seemed like admitting defeat and so I did not.

The result of all Mother's efforts: a packed house, SRO, with
students climbing up the outside walls to try and enter through the
balcony windows. I went early, anxiety filling me like poison, and
found a seat dead center, flanked by my roommates and friends, even
those who did not like poetry: Eric, Vicki, Ellen, Mary, Sarah, Jeff.

Mother had invited me to have dinner with her, the writer Dan
Wakefield, and her editor from Houghton Mifflin prior to the
reading, but I had declined. This excellent opportunity to make a
few publishing contacts went unrealized because I felt emotionally unable to deal with Mother in one of her frantic prereading
states — drinking heavily to escape her anxiety, somewhat hysterical, and always on the verge of last-minute collapse. I was done
being a nursemaid. I wasn't willing to deal with my anxiety that
in her desire to make the audience love her she would drink so
much that she would humiliate herself — and me — in front of all
my friends. I told her I had a late seminar, which was true, but my
refusal sounded thin, and I'm sure she felt hurt; in retrospect I can't
blame her. I wish I had gone, however horrible an experience it
might have been.

She had called me beforehand to ask if I would object if she
dedicated the Sanders reading to me. I was so thoroughly ambivalent about the entire matter that I told her I liked the idea of the
dedication but I wished she would not name me. Nevertheless, I
worried that she would go ahead and do it anyway.

Perhaps part of me, despite my proud stand, wished she would
defy me. As much as I did not wish to be recognized, I also craved

the honor. I did not want to be recognized as "Anne Sexton's daughter," and I was running from that label as hard as I could. And yet, there were the benefits: the extra attention, the second look an instructor might give my work, the small amount of notoriety among my peers that came from being the child of a famous person.

The crowd grew restless and impatient. The time for starting was past. I fingered my watch and wondered if something had happened to her. And then suddenly I saw her arrive at the back of the stage. The audience leaned forward in anticipation, hushed. Quickly, it seemed, Wakefield's introduction was over. I watched my mother cross the stage, as if she were a stranger, as if she were merely a performer I had paid to see. In her long, tight black-and-white dress she came to rest against the podium, gripping it tightly; six books and manuscript in hand, a glass of water on the lectern, her glasses, her cigarettes; she fumbled with the mike. I was sure her knees were shaking behind the skirt of that long dress.

She began to speak. "Only once in my life have I dedicated a reading," she began. Her words were slurred and furry, running into each other, nearly unintelligible. *Oh God,* I thought, *she's too drunk to read!* I closed my eyes, slid down in my seat, and tried to pray. "A short dedication," she went on, still sloppy, "however tonight I'm in a — one must be in a mood — for something and I was in a mood to give her a little longer dedication. I'd like to start it and then repeat with John F. Kennedy's unsaid — but of course the speech was passed on to the press — unsaid words in Dallas in 1963 . . ."

Suddenly, dramatically, she straightened up, squared her marvelous shoulders. Her voice caught hold and began to move in tandem with her brain. "'. . . Unless the Lord keepeth the city, the watchman guardeth in vain." In an instant, she was electric, radiant. She continued, stronger now.

> And with his words in mind I would like to dedicate this reading to a nameless woman. There are many kinds of love — woman to man, mother to child, woman to woman, man to man, God to us,

us to God, and friend to friend. Each love declares welcome. We give and we take. Love makes us at times the watchman. I think tonight of that woman who is very far away and somehow very near and speak not only to all of you but to name her without name. Once I gave her playing names like Bobolink or Pie or Stringbean.

I began to cry, tears running down my face.

And life passes on and the near become far and the watchman, ah, the watchman. Better said, "Unless the Lord keepeth the city, the watchman guardeth in vain." And I ask you to wonder with me tonight if this strange art, this writing, this reading of poems, this watchman here before you, this poet speaking in her assortment of souls, who guards poem by poem, but perhaps this, too . . . is in vain.

I bowed my head and let the tears fall like stones into my lap. She began reading "Her Kind," her signature poem, but I was trying to recover myself. I didn't know what the dedication meant, I couldn't begin to unravel it in the intensity of that moment. I only knew that the connection between us that night felt as strong as if it were twenty years before and we were still tied together, body to body.

Later she mailed me a copy of the dedication so that I could have it to keep. I studied it for a long time, still not certain of its meaning, ambivalent about it. Its melodrama — "but perhaps this too is in vain" — angered me even as I was moved by the honor she had done me in publicly acknowledging her love for me. Perhaps my confusion over the meaning of the dedication stemmed from the fact that after so many years of taking care of her, I saw myself as *her* watchman. I had now made it clear that I would not guard her city or her life anymore. I had drawn far away, and she had tried many times to summon me back, both with her own private voice and with that more public voice of her poetry as well. Today it seems to me that while I am the watchman, the gatekeeper — of both her life and her poetry — she, too, watched over me through her art, and that art was ultimately the most important love she was able to give.

Watching her read that night was a revelation to me. I had not been at one of her public performances in three or four years, and I looked upon her with wonder: how captivating she was, how slender, burning with excitement, her voice a drowsy rasp, her sexuality palpable in the way she draped herself against the podium, her arms bewitched sirens calling to us all.

She took that audience into her heart with her frankness, humor, and spontaneity. I watched the adulation and realized that the audience had become her family now — they were the ones who loved her without reservation. My friends, fellow students, teachers — all had expressions of awe on their faces. Rapture. And I was jealous, unspeakably jealous. In that moment I hated her and her power absolutely. In that moment I loved her and her power absolutely. She stood before us, her voice pure thunder.

By this point in her life, triumphs such as the Sanders Theater reading were often closely followed or preceded by failures or emotional crises. The morning of the reading she had fallen into a fugue state on the floor of her therapist's office, unable to be roused for two hours. A month before the reading, she had made another suicide attempt using her old stash of Thorazine. She had been trying to reach me for days, but I had successfully avoided her drunken calls. One Sunday the phone rang, and I decided to take the risk of answering it. To my surprise, it was Blanche, to whom I had not spoken in many years.

"What's going on?" she demanded. "I just called the house to talk to your mother and she sounds strange. I didn't even recognize her voice."

"I don't know," I said. "I'm here at school. I haven't seen her in a while."

"What kind of a daughter are you? Why aren't you taking care of her?"

I was silent, biting the inside of my cheek to keep from retorting, "What kind of a sister are you?"

"Well, you'd better get out there," she directed me. "Something's wrong."

I hung up the phone, feeling that she had chutzpah, telling me to "go out there." It would take me at least an hour and a half on the subway, and then there was the problem of getting from the station to the house. It would have been faster if Blanche herself had driven. I laughed without mirth. Angrily I paced.

I called the Conants, only to learn that Mother had been taken to the Emergency Room. Later I would discover that she had swallowed more than ninety pills over two days previously. She had slipped into a coma, and no one had found her until Blanche's call roused the couple who were living in the house with Mother at the time. It appeared it was harder to kill herself than she had anticipated because she had developed such a tolerance to all kinds of medication.

It seemed now that she needed nearly continual watching. Her friends were growing exhausted and burned out with the roller coaster of making sure Anne was not suicidal one day to the next. Maxine, Lois, Louise Conant, Patty Handloss, and a few others came up with the idea of establishing some kind of schedule so that one of them checked in with Mother every day. When Mother learned of this she was furious. "You're nothing but a witches' coven!" she told Louise suspiciously. "Stop talking about me behind my back!" More and more it seemed, she was arguing with one of them. With my father's departure, Mother had become a child in need of a parent, and no one was able to take on such a responsibility. Often she called me, drunk, and if my roommates said I was not home she accused them of lying. On a rampage, she then would phone my boyfriend's room looking for me and accuse *his* roommates of lying. It became more than embarrassing and I grew angrier. I resolved that — no matter how difficult it was — I would not allow her to draw me down into the quicksand of her disintegration.

Shortly after the Sanders reading, Mother had given a dual reading with Maxine in New Jersey, which had not gone well. She and

Maxine had exchanged bitter words over Mother's behavior both during and after the reading, and Maxine had made some kind of remark that Mother interpreted as an accusation that when she read her poetry the dramatic show she staged was "prostitution." Mother's feelings of betrayal were profound, perhaps magnified by my rejections at the time of the Sanders reading as well.

Though I knew nothing about it until after her death, when she and Maxine returned from New Jersey, Mother had gone home, slid into her most flamboyant reading dress — a long red one with gold buttons from throat to hem — and taken a cab to Cambridge. There she had the driver pull over on the bank of the Charles River directly opposite my Harvard dormitory. She danced her way along the embankment, wading in and out of the water, drinking milk from a thermos to wash down the handfuls of pills she had stashed in her pocketbook. A stranger stopped her and took her to the Mount Auburn Hospital Emergency Room. Later she would write "The Red Dance" to describe this suicide attempt made on the banks of the fortress into which I had fled from her "overabundance of love":

> . . . *Cars and trucks went by*
> *on Memorial Drive.*
> *And the Harvard students in the brick*
> *hallowed houses studied Sappho in cement rooms.*
> *And this Sappho danced on the grass*
> *and danced and danced and danced.*
> *It was a death dance.*

Sappho, a lesbian, was a lyric Greek poet ranked with Homer; Plato called her "the tenth muse." Spurned in love, she committed suicide by throwing herself into the sea.

Ironically, a month after the Sanders reading the release of a medical news story drew Mother and me close together again. With the publication of an article in *Ms.* magazine, a controversy erupted at Harvard around the drug diethylstilbestrol, or DES, a synthetic hormone resembling estrogen. Administered in the 1950s to prevent miscarriage, DES was often prescribed in 1974 for a different purpose — as a "morning after" pill for women who had had unprotected intercourse the night before. The Harvard University Health Services dispensed it. It was not until the early 1970s, however, that certain side effects of DES became clear, as young women who had been exposed while in utero began developing vaginal and cervical cancers never seen before in those so young.

Back in 1953, while my father was in the navy, Mother had been wintering out her first pregnancy in Florida, on a vacation trip with Mary Gray and Ralph. On the return train trip to Boston, she had begun to experience intermittent bleeding. Whisked by her father from the train station to the obstetrician's office, she was informed by Dr. May that there was a strong possibility she would lose the pregnancy; however, he said, a new remedy was now available. He prescribed a course of DES. Obeying her doctor — the times did not allow a woman to question her physician — Mother took the pills and stopped spotting. On July twenty-first, after a prolonged labor, she gave birth to a healthy, seven-pound baby whom she and my father named Linda Gray — Linda because it meant pretty in Spanish, my father's favorite foreign language; Gray after Mary Gray, her mother, and also after Arthur Gray Staples, Mother's favorite grandparent.

Now, twenty years later, Mother panicked. The prognosis for the women with vaginal cancer due to intra-uterine DES exposure was surgical mutilation and, sometimes, death. What had she done, so unwittingly and with the best of intentions? Had her desire to keep the pregnancy led her to deform me? The specter of thalidomide haunted her. She was furious with herself for not asking more questions of the fatherly Dr. May, and enraged that such medication could have been prescribed without adequate testing to determine its efficacy and safety. She raged. I was silent.

I was not angry with her. What could she have done? Why should she have even thought to question the recommendations made by her doctor, a man who had been delivering babies for years? Patient self-advocacy was a nonexistent concept in 1953. I vowed that if I were lucky enough to survive this experience intact I would never, but never, take more than a vitamin pill during my own pregnancies. I did not know then and could not imagine, however, how hard it could be to want a baby and to know that small life was slipping from you.

Scientists and physicians were conducting the leading research on DES right in Boston. Mother did not waste a minute, but called and managed to schedule an immediate appointment, despite a waiting list of over six months, by speaking to the physician directly and introducing herself as Dr. Sexton. (At this point she did hold several honorary doctorates of letters, so the ruse did not constitute a *complete* lie.) If she had been silent twenty years before, she was certainly using her voice now. Hysterical with fear, in private she kept admonishing me that my own calm was a defense against my natural emotions. I waited for the day of my examination with dread and tried to fend off as many of Mother's anxiety-inspiring phone calls as possible.

She took me herself for the examination at Beth Israel Hospital in Boston, and although I hated myself for needing her, I felt comforted by her presence and grateful that she had insisted on accompanying me. We sat in an enormous waiting room, a large open space with at least fifty chairs, a brown linoleum floor, and a long desk behind which nurses and clerks ran from one task to the next. The room's lack of boundaries increased my anxiety.

An hour passed. I had brought with me a paperback copy of Virginia Woolf's *The Waves*, and, too nervous to talk, I read aloud to Mother instead. The rhythm of Woolf's descriptions — the way the sea rolls its back toward the sky while dawn begins to stretch out its fingers — brought to us both images of the many hours we had each spent on beaches, soothed by the sound of the surf, rocked as if by a lullaby.

When the nurse finally summoned me, I discovered, once up on the table, that the "examination" more closely resembled minor surgery: a series of biopsies taken from my vagina and cervix in the pattern described by the face of a clock. The doctor administered no anesthesia of any kind because the vaginal walls and cervix were considered to be without nerve endings. Quickly I grew frightened by the pain and the blood-soaked swabs I could see passing between the doctor and his nurse. The chunks of tissue taken from my insides were set to float in little specimen jars on a table in plain view. I thought I was going to faint. I bit my hand, hard, and tried to hang on.

Mother did not hide from what was happening to me. She insisted on staying with me in that room, sitting on a chair on the other side of the curtain that enshrouded the exam table and its stirrups. I felt guilty at how much I needed her, but she rooted me to life, her presence a reassurance that I could endure this horrible experience, that eventually it would stop and she would take me home. Flat on my back and as helpless as an infant, I would have liked her to hold my hand, to smooth my hair off my sweaty forehead. I cried, my face averted in shame.

The doctor's verdict: I did show the signs of having been exposed to DES in utero, the so-called strawberry cervix. We would have to wait for the pathology on the biopsies to know whether the disturbed cells had mutated. He showed Mother slides of cancerous lesions, he discussed my odds. She nodded, listened, took it all in. I fled to the ladies' room where, despite a fresh tampon, blood ran down my thigh in a thick stream. Mother found me lying on the floor beside the toilet and brought me another tampon. Then she took me home.

Back at my dorm in Cambridge, I revived after a while and we went for lunch together in the cafeteria at my dormitory. It was the first time she had ever come to visit me at school, the first time I had ever welcomed her into my room or my life there. Neither of us was hungry, but it didn't matter: we were looking for other sorts of nourishment. This day my mother had taken care of *me*. We waited for the news of the biopsies and cheered when they came back normal. I would have to be checked every year, but at least I wouldn't lose my vagina or my uterus; most probably I would not die.

That day in the spring of 1974 remains my last positive recollection of my mother: marked in my memory, she stands by me tall and strong, a warrior who fights for her daughter. The next time Death appeared he did not come for me.

The Making of a Literary Executor

⟩⟩

The business of words keeps me awake.
I am drinking cocoa,
that warm brown mama.

I would like a simple life
yet all night I am laying
poems away in a long box.

It is my immortality box,
my lay-away plan,
my coffin.

— Anne Sexton
"The Ambition Bird"

*T*HE LAST YEARS of my mother's life were filled with a series of steadily escalating crises, increased suicide threats, and emotional losses. Much of this turmoil was precipitated, I believe, by
her divorce from my father. While severing the umbilical cord of
the marital bond had originally seemed to her a bid for independence and a stretch for a new life free from the tyranny of past
patterns, the rupture became the single element that ensured her
death. Freed from the stabilizing influence my father had exerted
on her and with no strong partner to replace him, Mother began to
spin out of control, faster and faster — a tornado in the making.
Dr. Chase, who had been feeling increasingly overwhelmed by my
mother's demands as a patient since the divorce, terminated their
therapy quite abruptly in late 1973, telling Mother that she felt her

love and transference had become as claustrophobic as a "straight-jacket." Joy and I both began to withdraw, as did many of her friends as well.

Having abandoned her medication just prior to the divorce, Mother began to replace its measured tranquilizing effects with self-administered doses of alcohol. She grew more shrill, more dramatic, more needy, more outrageous. She carried nips of vodka with her everywhere — even into faculty meetings at Boston University, where she passed them under the table to her colleague John Cheever.

Like a movie star, she demanded a particular seat on an airplane or in a restaurant. When dining out she ordered the most expensive items on the menu and often sent them back: caviar, champagne, tournedos à la Bernaise — and if there wasn't enough Bernaise for her filet she made a scene until they whipped up a whole new batch. (Interestingly enough, eating meat no longer seemed a problem.) To sign books after a reading she required a particular brand of pen. To endure her prereading anxiety she had to have a fried egg sandwich and several (four or five) double vodkas.

She argued with everyone, friends and family alike. Little by little she drove away many of those who had supported her for so long. By 1973, she had begun to drink around the clock, from rising to sleeping. In 1974 alone she made three suicide attempts. Time passed with the speed of a dream, all of us poised, waiting for the climax that would mean both disaster and freedom.

The last summer of her life I continued to flee from her dramatics, from her hysterics and her pain. I couldn't stand being around her. For the months of July and August 1974 I made my home in the heat of Inman Square: just as it had been throughout the school year, Cambridge yet again became my refuge. I shared an apartment — four rooms on the top floor of a ramshackle house — with two other women and a man. Antrim Street came directly off the Square, overlooking its busy traffic and catching the continuous shriek of the fire engines leaving the station nearby. I remember that summer as one of heat and noise, my window always open, the nights long and sweaty, my solitude self-imposed. I could have lived with her in Weston. I refused.

At school that year I had decided that a career as a writer was out of the question, and so I had turned instead to the idea of being an editor. I knew it would be difficult to break in initially, and that possibly I would have to work for several years as a "secretary" — which felt demeaning compared to the ambitions of my Harvard classmates, who were planning careers in law and medicine. However, in her inimitable fashion, Mother took my problem on herself, determined to solve it. She made inquiries at Houghton Mifflin to see if any summer work was available and wrangled me an interview in the production department. I managed to snag the job, which involved estimating the costs of reprinting trade books, but had they known my track record in math, they would never have hired me; still, calculator in hand, I managed not to make too many drastic mistakes.

Houghton Mifflin paid me just enough to carry my sixty-dollar share of the monthly rent, just enough to buy hot dogs and rice and quart bottles of pale American beer; just enough to bank some savings for books and living expenses to carry me through my upcoming senior year, as I had done other summers by working as a maid, a camp counselor, a secretary. As I commuted back and forth on the subway, I knew I ought to feel grateful to Mother for having made the proper introductions. No one else entering her senior year at Radcliffe was lucky enough to be working — in any capacity — at one of Boston's most prestigious publishers. I knew I ought to go and visit her. But I didn't.

I was tugged by a continual undertow of anger. When Mother and I talked over the phone, often as not we got into an argument. She wanted me to read her new manuscript, *The Awful Rowing Toward God*, and give her an opinion about a quarrel she was having with her new editor, Jonathan Galassi. I wanted nothing to do with any of it, but she called Galassi anyway and asked him to send the manuscript over to production so that I could read it. She would abide, she told him, by whatever I decided, because I was one of her "best critics." I gritted my teeth at the manipulation but read the manuscript and offered my opinion — which she took.

When she called at night her voice was now slurred by alcohol and a growing paranoia. "Louise and Maxine are talking behind my back," she would hiss. She was angry with all her friends — no one did anything right anymore. When she had first divorced my father, I had found myself fighting the anger that surged inside me when she described her excitement over dating again; I kept hearing my father as he wept over the phone, hoping she would still come home. Now I found it equally hard to be sympathetic to the all-consuming loneliness she felt and the lack of available men to date. She lived by the telephone, but increasingly her friends were too busy to talk for the hours her despair required. It did not make me happy to realize that what I had predicted when she first announced her intention to divorce had indeed come to pass: her friends had tired of dealing with her crises. Ready to return to their own lives, they just couldn't give often enough or in enough quantity. Sadly, we all knew that nothing would have been enough.

Often Mother begged me to come home for the weekend so we could spend time together — but I didn't want to go. Nothing at home was the same anymore. I didn't want to talk about the men she was dating — men she had often met by running advertisements in the personal columns. I couldn't laugh about her impulsive, upward mood swings either, because often as not they involved large sums of money: the hundred-dollar bill she lit with her lighter one night in a restaurant, the three cases of champagne she had just bought, the expensive generator she was having installed in the garage in case the power lines went out. Every month I watched my father scrape to pay his bills, sending Mother a monthly child-support check from which neither Joy nor I ever saw a dime. Nana paid for Joy's private school and living expenses, despite the hardship this expense imposed on her fixed income; the Conants paid for my tuition at Harvard, and I was saving every dollar I could from my summer job to go toward my expenses during the school year.

And so, I began to hate her. I hated her selfishness and her sickness, and I could no longer tell where one stopped and the other began. I pulled a shutter around my emotions, around my soul, and hibernated. I spent weekends with my father, who had settled into a small apartment in a newly built complex in Natick. Every Friday at five o'clock, I left Houghton Mifflin and took the subway down to South Station, near his office on Summer Street, so that we could drive out of town together. Those weekends spent with him became the mainstay of my summer, whose days were increasingly rocked by my constant awareness of Mother's disintegration.

The farther I moved away from her, however, the harder she pursued me. She called me at the office, she called me nights at my apartment — more and more depressed, sick, unhappy. Alone. Alone and getting desperate about being alone. Previously, she had always had companions with her in the house, young couples who rented a bedroom in exchange for cooking and yard duties. But that summer she had no other adult on whom to rely. She began looking for a replacement couple, although this process took several months. "I need you," she would say, pulling at me over the phone. She started to cry. "Oh, God, I'm so lonely," she sobbed. "Won't you come to see me?"

I went, consumed with guilt, pushing my anger into the background. I left feeling dirty and compromised because it was always as bad as I had anticipated: she was drunk, she was sorry for herself, she was deteriorating right in front me. I was angry with myself for having capitulated. I was terrified of what she had become.

I buried these times with Mother under the warm weekends I spent with Daddy. Without her around to soak up all the family energy, my father and I began to discover each other. Charming and handsome, he took me out to dinner at Ken's, a local steakhouse, and we drank martinis, very dry, very cold, straight up. He escorted me to Locke-Ober's — haute Boston — and taught me to eat little-neck clams on the half shell, while the waiters wondered in whispers if I was his young mistress. We laughed with delight about that and he tucked my arm into his as we walked back to his car through the warm Boston night. I was in the midst of a strong fantasy indulged:

finally I had Daddy all to myself, and there was never a time when he acted remotely violent with me. That part of him had been mothballed, put into deep storage. I knew there were ways to unlock the fury again, but I had no interest in trying.

Back in his apartment we cooked together; he taught me techniques he knew and then encouraged me to experiment on my own: complicated chicken concoctions perched on top of Holland rusks with hollandaise sauce; lobsters and steamed clams; long-marinated lamb shish kebab grilled on the barbecue he set up on his small balcony; sweet white corn on the cob, fresh from the farm stand, six ears apiece, soaked with butter; blenders of homemade whiskey sours, icy and smooth with Daddy's special trick — maple syrup as the sweetener. We sat by the pool and read junky paperbacks. We went to the movies. An intimacy grew between us, initially forged from his distress at being alone and my own loneliness, but growing into the pleasure that ran deep at discovering each other, peace in a summer of turmoil.

Frequently he asked how Mother was getting along. He, too, worried about her drinking. I could feel his fear for her, a strong lode of concern that ran right beneath his anger at her rejection. I could tell he still loved her. She had asked him out on a date, which he had accepted, but he felt offended by this sort of game. The divorce had wounded him, deep as a surgical cut, and he found such contradictory behavior confusing. He had only just begun to date, and he had sought the company of only one woman, a widow whom he would eventually marry four years after the divorce and three years after Mother's death.

Mother was wildly jealous of all the camaraderie. She hated the way I had allied myself with Daddy, while claiming merely to be hurt that I didn't want to spend time with her, at the spacious house in the cool, shaded suburbs. I didn't care what she thought anymore. I found it easier and easier to harden myself against her. Mother disgusted me now. How many weekends did she stay half drunk all day long? In the last year or two she had begun to substitute alcohol for food at nearly every turn. She lost a tremendous amount of weight with what she called her "liquid diet." Her metabolism seemed to be moving at a furious pace: she was so thin she seemed like a blowtorch at white heat; her hands shook with tremor; her face sometimes twitched. At the time of her death she weighed under 110 pounds, even though she was five foot eight. This weight loss contributed to the haggard, uneven look so characteristic of the time before her suicide.

She had found a new companion, one who could and would match her drink for drink, a nurse named Ziva;* often they spent weekends together in Weston. Ziva was an enormous woman whose ostensible purpose was to jolly Mother out of her depression, but much of the time they both spent the entire weekend lurching around the house, stumbling to the master bedroom to pass out. They slept in my parents' king-sized bed together, even though there were four other beds available; Mother insisted they had no sexual relationship, though during the week Ziva lived with her female lover and was quite frank about being a lesbian. I found it unspeakably repulsive that they slept in the same bed, and I resented her influence over my mother.

One night when I had reluctantly agreed to stay over in Weston for the night, I made a French chicken stew for Mother and Ziva that I had first created in my own kitchen on Antrim Street when I was learning to cook on a budget. The two of them didn't want to stop drinking to eat and were pursuing a lengthy cocktail hour while my meal dried out in the oven. I tried to get them to come to the table, but they procrastinated, punctuating the room with explosive laughter, knocking back drink after drink. Eventually Ziva manipulated the conversation around to the topic of Mother's suicide attempt the previous winter, the one wherein she had taken so much Thorazine that she had been comatose for several days.

"Why don't you tell Anne," Ziva suggested, "what you feel about that?"

I stared at her. "I don't know what you mean." My voice was stony.

"Linda, don't bullshit me!" She started to laugh. "You know

*Ziva is a pseudonym.

you had feelings about your mother's trying to kill herself then. Why don't you tell her?"

"Yes," Mother said, rising to the occasion. "Tell me."

"Why?"

"You'll both feel better," Ziva urged.

I shook my head. "No one would feel better."

"I'm sure I know it anyway," Mother declared, waving her glass around in the air.

"Really?" I was starting to feel angry at being pushed like this.

"Come on, don't be such a coward." Ziva was drinking, too, and suddenly I hated her: I hated her bulk, I hated her brashness, I hated the way she had invited herself into my family's life.

"Say it," Mother urged.

"Say it," Ziva bellowed.

"You really want to know?" I was losing control, responding to the jibe. "Fine!" Suddenly anger surged up hot and hard within me, making me reckless. "I hoped you would die! I wanted you to do it right this time! Is that what you want to hear?"

There was sudden silence in the room. Ziva looked over at Mother.

Mother looked stunned. She just sat there for a minute and then she started to cry. She rose from her chair with a lurch, smashed her glass against the fireplace, and threw herself face down on the ground. She beat her fists above her head and drummed her feet against the floor. "I hate you! I hate you!" she screamed. Ziva tried to stop her, but she pushed her away, ran upstairs, and slammed the bedroom door.

I just looked at Ziva, hate burning bright and clean in my heart. "Happy now?"

‰

As loneliness ate away at my mother's spirit those last few months of her life, she turned increasingly to God for succor: God did not chastise or criticize; God might even be a woman, "a consecrating mother"; God was as easily found in the leaves outside her window or in the voice of the radio that played incessantly beside her bed as in a church. The book that consumed her the last year of her life was about Anne finding God, Anne in her little rowboat calling God's bluff. She had entitled it *The Awful Rowing Toward God*:

> God was there like an island I had not rowed to,
> still ignorant of Him, my arms and my legs worked,
> and I grew, I grew,
> I wore rubies and bought tomatoes
> and now, in my middle age,
> about nineteen in the head I'd say,
> I am rowing, I am rowing
> though the oarlocks stick and are rusty
> and the sea blinks and rolls
> like a worried eyeball,
> but I am rowing, I am rowing,
> though the wind pushes me back
> and I know that that island will not be perfect,
> it will have the flaws of life,
> the absurdities of the dinner table,
> but there will be a door
> and I will open it
> and I will get rid of the rat inside of me,
> the gnawing pestilential rat.
> God will take it with his two hands
> and embrace it.
>
> — "Rowing"

Maxine had moved to New Hampshire, and she didn't call as much as Mother wanted her to. All Mother's other friends had set limits on what they would tolerate. Even Patty Handloss, Mother's minister, had told her she would not come to see her or speak to her on the telephone when she had been drinking. The "witches' coven" of friends had drawn back, and even the Conants had distanced themselves a little bit in self-defense. Mother hired her old friend, Joan Smith, who was also a registered nurse, to be with her full-time during the day, but even that did not provide her with the companionship she craved. Her new therapist — Barbara

Schwartz, who was a psychiatric social worker — would accept calls late at night, and many nights she talked Mother to sleep over the phone, lullabying her into dreamland just the way my father had once done by repeating "Anne, you are a good girl." Still, it wasn't the same as having a partner with her in bed, someone upon whom she could depend, someone who would stroke her head until she fell asleep.

The place we had once called home was home no more, and neither Joy nor I wanted any part of it. Mother had turned 14 Black Oak Road into a stage upon which she was the star, and increasingly sole, player; the rest of us were the supporting cast, but our lines played to the wind. Mother wrote the script, directed, and produced the drama. Nothing we felt, nothing we said or did, affected either action or denouement.

All the boundaries of decency had been permanently erased: my mother slept around; my mother drank as much as she wanted whenever she wanted; my mother did as she pleased regardless. It was, perhaps, hardest for Joy, who was living with her over the summer, having obtained Mother's promise that she would behave — a promise that Mother broke over and over again. When Mother's old friend Anne Wilder came to visit, she and Mother had sex in my parents' bed even though Joy was only a room away, well within earshot. "I really didn't care," Joy recollects now. "I was just too numb."

Somehow I did not fully understand my mother's increasing desperation, how her wild maneuvers must surely have been an attempt to feel *something, anything* — as she forced one sensation after another down her throat in an attempt to push back the black and numbing curtain of depression. Desperate, I shut her out because it all hurt so much. She was flailing wildly on that last slide down into death, but I, too much a child caught in my mother's maelstrom, could neither see nor comprehend it. Life inflicts this subtle cruelty: insight comes only with time.

By midsummer, Joy had moved from miserable to desperate, and she often called me at work for advice. I tried to help by encouraging her to resist Mother's demands. I empathized with her situation, yet I knew she had to make the break by herself. I was afraid that if I tried to intervene, both Joy and Mother would end up angry with me, for it was apparent to me that this time alone with Mother initially was as precious to Joy as it later became horrific. For the first time since she was the favorite daughter as a little girl she had Mother's undivided attention; and Mother was encouraging the creativity she saw in Joy — not with writing, but with photography. She bought Joy an expensive camera, and they spent a lot of time looking at the photos Joy took around the neighborhood or in the city. Now she and Joy shared an art form. I was jealous of their intimacy, but oddly relieved by it as well. No longer would I be the watchman, guarding the city.

But the peace between them couldn't last: Mother was growing progressively too ill. Joy was appalled by the obscenely revolving door into my mother's bedroom, at the intensity of the drinking and the temper outbursts; worse, she was overwhelmed by the impending threat of another suicide attempt.

As the situation grew more and more intense, I grew angrier and angrier with Mother. I'd been able to move into an apartment to escape her antics, but Joy was still in high school. I didn't want to watch Mother make my sister as guilt-ridden and responsible a caretaker as I had once been. At last, with a growing sense of urgency, I began to urge Joy to get out.

Midsummer. Mother began showing the usual signs of thinking about suicide. One night in particular, Joy felt worried about leaving the house to go out on the date she had planned. She went to check on Mother one last time before she left and discovered her lying in bed, asleep with the phone in her hand. She picked it up.

At the other end of the line was Barbara Schwartz.

"Did you know she had fallen asleep?" Joy inquired.

Schwartz reminded Joy that she often lullabied Anne to sleep and reassured her that she did not think Mother had taken an overdose.

Joy, however, couldn't rid herself of the eerie feeling that something was wrong. She sat and watched Mother sleep for a while and

THE MAKING OF A LITERARY EXECUTOR

then called Joan Smith. Joan, too, expressed concern, and told Joy to take Mother's pulse and respiration every fifteen minutes. Joy sat by the bed, waiting, and when Mother's breathing began to slow she called an ambulance.

My sister rode with Mother to Mount Auburn Hospital in Cambridge, where the Emergency Room doctors pumped Mother's stomach and began to examine her. Joy, coming back into the treatment room after signing the forms to commit her for a short period of observation, saw Mother spiral into an epileptic seizure, her face and body rigid, her tongue sticking from her mouth — a sight she has never been able to erase from memory.

Two nights later Mother put on her shoes, phoned a cab, and slipped out of her hospital room. Dr. Dinsmore, the physician who worked in tandem with Barbara Schwartz to regulate Mother's many medications, tracked her down at the house in Weston, examined her, and acceded to her demand that she be allowed to remain at home. Then he went downstairs and had a drink with Joy. Everyone was exhausted. Would the drama never end?

The next morning Joy was on her way out the door when Mother's voice commanded her to stop. "Don't go anywhere — I need you to drive me to Barbara Schwartz's office this morning."

Joy paused and looked at her. Mother was sitting at the kitchen table, sipping her coffee and working with her secretary, Jean Moulton. "If you're well enough to be home, Mother, you're well enough to drive."

Silence. And then the explosion. "Fuck you!" she screamed. "Fuck you!" She smashed her hands up and down on the kitchen table in the rhythm of a tantrum. "You think I'm going to put up with this shit? I hate you! Get the hell out of here! And don't come back!"

Joy turned coolly and left. She spent some time at a friend's house and then moved to Daddy's apartment.

A week later, Mother called her. "Come pick up your mail," she demanded, "but only between two and three o'clock. I may be entertaining a gentleman. I may be having sex all over the house. I don't want you bothering us."

❧

In July, my twenty-first birthday neared. Mother asked me out to the house for dinner. I went with ambivalence, for as much as I didn't want to see her, I also couldn't imagine having my birthday go by without spending some time together. Sitting in her writing room that afternoon she handed me my gift.

"What is it?" I asked, curious, fingering the thick envelope.

"Open it," she said, a bit smugly, swallowing from her glass of vodka.

I did. There was a check for a thousand dollars and a letter.

July 3, 1974

July 3rd — looking forward to that WONDEROUOUS [*sic*] DATE, July 21st when first child, a wonder of a daughter came bursting forth into the world. (In other words happy birthday, in other words, my God! That Linda Gray, that Linda Pie, that string-bean has become that surprising age 21!!!!!!!!! TWENTY-ONE! WOW! ZAP! YIKES! ZOOM! POW!

What does a mere mother do upon such an occasion? Aside from two pairs of very pretty panties (we Sextons always seem to find ours in rags and tatters it would seem). Well, my darling in her age of ages, what can I offer up to the gods in thanks for such a woman as you have become, true fighter, true to trust your instinct for right and wrong, a hard worker who can't even afford ketchup in her first apartment/work on her own?

I would tear down a star and put it into a smart jewelry box if I could. I would seal up love in a long thin bottle so that you could sip it whenever it was needed if I could. Instead I, who am lost in stores, and have further lost the Caedmon catalogue, give you bucks. I worked hard for them and I'm sure you realize what kind of work that is —

It would be nice to start them in your OWN saving account to withdraw at will for ketchup by the case or a diamond if it's your present wish, or any damn thing that Linda Gray Sexton who is twenty-one years old might want to do with them, dem bucks. I wish they were six million bucks — even more I wish they were stars that would buy you the world. But mothers can't give the world (nor fathers, nor even husbands, lovers or children) — the world sometimes just happens to us, or if we begin with more wisdom than your muggy had, we might help ourselves happen to the world. I feel that wisdom in you and I offer a prayer to it and to its growth.

Dearest pie, today nominated and legally named my literary executor (because I know you know the value, the potential of what I've tried in my small way to write, not only in financial potential for your future income, but maybe, just maybe — the spirit of the poems will go on past both of us, and one or two will be remembered in one hundred years. . . . And maybe not.).

You and Joy always said, while growing up, "Well, if I had a normal mother . . . !" meaning the apron and the cookies and none of this typewriting stuff that was shocking the hell out of friends' mothers . . . But I say to myself, better I was mucking around looking for truth, etc. . . . and after all we did have many "night-night time has come for Linda Gray" and "Goodnight moon" to read and "Melancholy baby" for your tears.

Forgive. Muggy gets sentimental at the thought of Linda pie, little girl, baby, growing and now grown (in a sense although we never stop growing and learning and most learning comes from the hard knocks). Could you possibly keep the amount of this million bucks titled stars to yourself? It is between you and me although the love with which it's given could be plain to a perceptive observer.

KETCHUP DIAMONDS RECORDS BOOKS? Who knows, only Linda.

I dried my eyes and hugged her, hard. Her generosity overwhelmed me. "But what do you mean, literary executor?" I asked then, puzzled.

She handed me a thick sheaf of documents.

I glanced at them. "Mom, this is your will!" I was shocked. It made me feel creepy. It seemed sacrilegious to look at a will before the person had died. Though we had always been forthright about the subject of death — Mother had given us her burial and funeral requests several years earlier — this seemed more official.

"Read it," she urged.

"Now?" I shook my head. I didn't want to.

"Now."

And so I skimmed it. A lot of it made no sense to me, but the one thing that stood out bright and clear was that she had appointed me her literary executor.

"But, Mom," I protested. "You never asked me about this."

"I knew you'd want to do it," she said airily, waving her hand through the smoke from her cigarette.

I looked down at the paperwork again. The dramatic way she had presented me with this fait accompli irritated me. I wasn't at all sure I wanted to join my life, myself, to her life in this way — even after death. Not at all.

"You should ask Maxine to do this," I pointed out. "She knows about these things as a writer. I'm just your daughter." Once again we were replaying the same old argument: *don't make me responsible for your life,* my reluctance said. *I don't want to be the gatekeeper anymore.*

Mother shook her head, both persuasive and tenacious. "Sometimes families and literary executors don't agree. It's better to have a family member if there's one you can trust. *No one* could be better than you. Do you remember Sandy McClatchy — he's that poet down at Yale?"

I nodded again.

"I did ask him if he'd do it — he knows a lot about this sort of thing — but he was the one who pointed out the benefits of having a family member. I need you to do this for me, Linda."

It seemed I did not have a choice, or perhaps I did not want to believe I did, for beneath my desire to refuse ran a strong fault line of vanity. She spun the story and made me believe: I was the one and only person who could do this job for her. I gave in at last, hesitant but flattered that she perceived me as special enough to oversee her work. The covenant of words would not be breached even by her death.

A few weeks later, Mother invited me out to dinner with Sandy McClatchy so that we could go over the details of the arrangement. She chose Ferdinand's Restaurant in Cambridge, one of her favorites, and over Veal Oscar and two pitchers of sangria, she explained, "It's a job, Linda. A serious job." She lit another cigarette. "You'll probably have to take time off from your own work — whatever that may be — to do it well and give it your full attention."

Her words brought me up short. I had never thought of it as anything other than a part-time exercise executed while I went on about my own life. "Then you'd better pay me," I responded, thinking about how I would support myself while I arranged her work and ignored my own. How had I gotten into this, I wondered resentfully. It felt as if I had just taken ten giant steps backward; I had fought so hard to make my life separate from hers, and here we were joined hip to hip again.

"Yes," McClatchy said. "That's a good idea. Like a salary."

"No," Mother disagreed, "not like a salary. More like a royalty, or — " she exclaimed with excitement, "a percentage, like an agent takes! That way you'll have an investment in the work as well!"

We all agreed that this approach would offer me a good incentive, and so I felt somewhat mollified. Besides, Mother's delight was infectious. And it was, after all, far off in the future. Mother had been living and dying for all of the twenty-one years I had known her.

Quickly she waved over a waiter, borrowed pen and paper, and on the spot drafted a codicil to her will that instructed I be paid a fee. I doubted it could hold up legally, although it did; somehow everything we discussed at the table that night seemed a giddy frolic — enhanced by the flickering candlelight and the heady, fruit-filled glasses of sangria. Mother's excitement, McClatchy's enthusiasm, and my own inclusion in this literary world seemed just one more wild ride with Anne.

As August waned toward September and I planned my return to school, Mother and I had one final talk. It was, I believe, the last time we ever spoke intimately. She was sitting in her study, drink in hand, talking to me as I stood ironing the clothes I would take back to Cambridge. She had recently asked my father out on a date, just to "see what it would be like."

"And what was it like?" I asked, trying to keep the edge of bitterness I felt out of my voice.

"Kind of sweet," she replied. "Like in my fantasy."

"What is your fantasy?"

"That he'll ask me to marry him again."

I stood stock still, the iron hot and steaming in my hand. "You've got to be kidding."

"No, really. I'd like to marry your father again."

I was almost speechless for a moment. "Why?"

"It's hard being forty-five and dating. You don't know what to do, what to expect. Everyone just wants to go to bed. There's no tenderness anymore."

I pushed my hot iron furiously into the creases of cotton, steaming, stamping out wrinkles. "Well," I said sarcastically. "That's all very nice, but it'll never happen."

"Why not? He kissed me on our date. Very tenderly. He still loves me."

"He's angry — that's why. You can't publicly humiliate him — and that *is* how he feels — and then just expect him to come running back when you say so." I shook the blouse out with a snap, thinking of the anguish my father had experienced when she'd kicked him out, of the twenty pounds he'd dropped, of Joy living in a home not her own, of the nights Daddy had called me in tears and I'd had to comfort him, of the pain we had all endured.

The ice in her glass chinked softly. "I want him back."

"For Chrissakes, why?" I asked, my anger truly showing at last.

"Because I found out that a little love is better than no love at all."

As far as I know, she never asked him. I had not been sympathetic to her plea of loneliness; I had not gone in and put my arms around her. Would I be so self-righteous now? I am nearly the same age she was when she discovered that divorce would not solve everything, that it was lonely to be single and forty-five. How I regret my own hardness.

Later, months after her funeral, I wanted my father to know she still loved him, and I told him about the conversation she and I had had that day. He started to sob. "Oh, God, if only I hadn't been so proud."

"What do you mean?"

"She wanted to start dating again and I was still too angry. I told her I wasn't interested in playing games. If only I hadn't been so angry — she'd be alive today."

I put my hand on his arm. "Daddy, she loved you, but even you couldn't have kept her alive any longer."

Only later would I be able to see with what determination Mother had planned her exit that summer. She had drawn up her will, appointed her literary and legal executors, put her manuscripts and correspondence in order. *The Awful Rowing Toward God* was well on its way toward publication. She was rowing toward Him hard now, every motion accelerating her small boat toward the arms she steadfastly believed would receive her in welcoming embrace once she had reached the lip of the waterfall.

The thunder from the approaching falls resounded throughout those last few months. How long had we been traveling on the swift river of her misery, anticipating the drop that would bring about the end of our family? How many years had we waited for her to die? Why was it then that we so stubbornly refused to look up and watch Mother row her little boat further and further into the distance?

Only now can I see how steadfastly we all refused to acknowledge her intent; only now can I admit that I had grown so tired of my mother's drama that I wished for the forbidden: that she would bring the curtain down and let us rest at last. That wish lay in my heart like a black stone, having been spoken of only once and then in anger, unadvisedly, to wound with terrible purpose.

Today I pull that stone from the pocket where I have stored it all these years to rub its smooth contours between my fingers. In the dark of my heart it lay forbidden; in the light of my day it remains shameful, but important to confront nevertheless.

I say these words to know them better: *I wished for my mother to die.* As much as I dreaded her suicide, I also craved it. I longed for freedom from the tyranny of her many neuroses that seemed, in that last year, to have overtaken her personality. By that last summer I did not like her anymore. Anne was her mental illness. Only once in a while did I see a glimmer of her shine through the demands of this noisy child dressed in adult's clothing. The woman I had loved was already gone.

I say these words to know them for the first time and to admit my greatest guilt: in the last months of my mother's life I chose to ignore her cry of loneliness. I refused to make her last days less painful. In the end, I left her to die alone.

The Rowing Endeth

I'm mooring my rowboat
at the dock of the island called God.

— Anne Sexton
"The Rowing Endeth"

THE PHONE RANG in my room on a Friday. I had spent the afternoon on my bed, reading *To the Lighthouse*, caught up in the rhythm of Virginia Woolf's vision of a daughter winning her independence, spiritual and artistic, from a powerful mother figure: Mary Gray and Anne Gray's story; Anne Gray and Linda Gray's story; every woman's story. The sun had not yet set, and the Charles River reflected its lazy gold light into the windows of my thirteenth-floor room in my Harvard dormitory. Down on the river the Harvard crews sculled, dipping the arms of their oars in rhythm, pulling through the water and the light. I looked at my watch when the phone rang and realized that I was going to be late to meet my boyfriend for dinner if I didn't hurry.

I almost didn't answer the phone. Then, at the last minute, I did, too curious to let it just ring.

"Hello, Linda?"

"Loring!" I was happy to hear Loring Conant's voice. He and his wife, Louise, were friends of mother's who had supported both Joy and me through the difficulties of my parents' divorce, and Loring was also my internist at the Harvard Health Services. "How are you?"

"Could you come by the office for a minute?"

I looked at my watch. Five o'clock. "On Monday? What time?"

"I need to talk to you now."

The "now" made his urgency apparent. Inside me, a small voice whispered: "No! Don't go!"

I put on my coat and locked the door.

The walk from my riverside dormitory up to Harvard Square was not a short one, and it held me, suspended, in the golden slant of the late day, kept me — for just a few minutes more — safe from the fear that had seized my body. *Please don't let it be Joy or Daddy.* The air was edged with a chill, the sky the clear dark blue that arrives at sunset in autumn.

Like the lens of a movie camera, my eyes recorded every detail of that walk with terrible accuracy: the yellow leaves in the gutter, the puddles around which I maneuvered, the muted colors of the houses I passed. *Please don't let it be Joy or Daddy.*

I stumbled over sidewalk curbs and found it nearly impossible to draw an adequate breath. I tried to run but the houses on the residential side streets passed in slow motion as I stuttered by. *Please don't let it be Joy or Daddy.*

The main clinic doors were locked. I went instead through the emergency entrance and up the stairs. Across the expanse of the dark waiting room and its empty chairs, Loring stood in the doorway to his office, silhouetted by the light behind him.

He drew me in and closed the door behind us. The overhead light made both of us look jaundiced. He still had on his white lab coat. He put his arm under my elbow to steady me. "Your mother killed herself this afternoon."

In a surge the current swept me downriver toward the waterfall that had been waiting for so many years. Over the edge I went, into the maw of churning water, free-fall, that long drop toward some rocky unknown place. In a hard jolt the bottom came up under me.

I sat, quickly, on the chair. "I knew that was it," I said, and then I laughed, a tinny unreal noise that came from somewhere outside my body. "I knew it." As if knowledge could protect me. As if knowledge could beat back impossible facts. *Thank you for not making it Joy or Daddy or Nana.* I laughed, one short despairing beat. *On October fourth my mother killed herself.* Suddenly my childhood nightmare had a name and a date. It was reality — not just some wolf under the bed.

"How?" I asked, after a minute had passed.

"In the car."

I looked up at him, startled. *In the car?* "You mean she drove off the road?"

He shook his head. "She closed the garage doors and started the car."

I saw her then, climbing behind the wheel of her red Cougar, her big pocketbook banging against her knees. Turning on the ignition and then the radio. Lighting a cigarette. Probably with a drink in her hand. Leaning her head back against the seat, chin up, to wait. Alone. While I had been reading, she had been dying. Alone. For once she had not called. That was when a little emotion began to trickle through: anger, bitterness, pain, sorrow. Relief. It was over.

Loring took me back to the dormitory to pack my suitcase. I wandered numbly in and out of my closet, looking for something dark and funereal. I couldn't organize my thoughts. I felt drunk, as if someone had stuck a needle of booze in my brain. In an ironic reversal of my walk to the Square an hour earlier, my body now functioned quite well while my mind had stopped. My roommate Vicki tried to help me pack, but I kept insisting I didn't need help: my mother had died, as expected; I was fine. Vicki started to cry.

Loring drove me to Nana's house. Although Nana had not set foot in my parents' home since my mother had ousted my father, the house-sitters sharing space with Mother at the time had nevertheless called Nana when they returned home from work to discover my mother in the front seat of the still-running car, with the garage door shut. Even in my state of shock, I could sense the irony of involving my grandmother. In all family crises, Nana had been the one everyone called, the one who would always take charge; how unsurprising that Nana should be the one to commandeer the site of the inevitable suicide.

With her death, Mother had reunited the family. The crisis of my parents' divorce ceased to exist; the new and uncomfortable rules to which we had never really gotten accustomed no longer applied. Nana had gone to the house and sat with my mother until the ambulance arrived, though when she returned home she broke down and cried at the horror of having spent that time next to my mother's body. The woman she had both loved and hated so intensely had finally died. I put my arms around her and we both cried together.

She had brought with her Mother's red phone book. "You've got to start making the calls," she said.

"Calls?" I repeated, taking the book from her in a daze.

"To tell people," she replied.

With this simple, fluid motion of her hand a fundamental relationship suddenly changed: I had fled to Nana's as a girl in need of succor, but I arrived to discover that I was the woman in charge.

The red loose-leaf notebook was my mother's Bible and I opened it reluctantly, as if I were invading her privacy: in it she kept the addresses and phone numbers of all her friends, all her literary contacts, old loves and new, psychiatrists current or recommended, suicide hot lines, hairdressers, ambulance services. Frequently she carried it with her in the car, and at home she kept it close at hand on top of the filing cabinet adjacent to her desk. Its yellow pages covered by her black felt-tip scrawl — decipherable only to those who knew the code — the book and its decreasing legibility in recent years mirrored her decline.

I began to make calls, hoping to give people the news before the reporters on the evening telecasts beat me to it. Whenever I took a break, the phone rang with press looking for comment. Many of Mother's friends had already heard from Louise Conant. I felt disappointed, a little cheated, at not being the bearer of such dramatic news. Perhaps selfishly, I believed that this story was mine to tell, and — to my chagrin — I realized how cathartic it was to relate it, to experience each time the shock of her death through my own words. I remembered Mother's angry letter to Dr. Chase in which she had said, "Writing about it is my way of mastering experience."

Nana made dinner. I sat staring into space, unable to eat, my eyes burning. The edges of the room seemed warped, as if the house itself had changed shape, rocked by the enormity of Mother's suicide.

I kept trying to get to my father, who was en route to a gathering of friends for a weekend on Cape Cod. Throughout the early evening, I phoned the house where they would be staying without success, beginning to feel panicky that he might inadvertently hear the news over the radio in his car. Beyond that, I needed him. I wanted all the family, closing in a circle to shut out the worst assault we had ever endured. Outwardly I stayed very calm, knowing that if I broke down and started to sob I might never stop.

Joy was also out of reach. What I would have given to hug her and have her hug me. What I would have given just to sit side by side on the couch in Nana's den and drink cocoa together — but Joy was in her last year at boarding school in Maine. After the divorce, my mother had named the Conants as Joy's guardians should Mother die, and so that night, in the absence of my father, they and I worried together over how best to tell my sister. They wanted to phone her, but I begged them to wait until I had spoken to my father. Wasn't he the one who really ought to make the decision?

At eleven o'clock Daddy finally arrived at his destination. I waited while they went to bring him to the phone.

"Linda Pie," he said. "Why are you calling so late? How'd you get the number?" His voice signaled his sense that something was wrong. I knew that he knew, without being told another word.

"Maybe you should sit down," I began, reverting to cliché in an attempt to prepare him.

"What's the matter?" There was open fear in his voice now.

"It's Mother," I said, stalling. That night I had told twenty to thirty people without any difficulty in expressing myself, but here I was, stammering in a desperate search for the right words. I was twenty-one and I had considered myself to have mastered the English language, but never before had I felt so inadequate. Never, in all my fantasies of this moment, had I imagined that I would be the one to bring him the news.

"What's wrong?" His voice had a high, tight edge to it now.

"It's Mother." More silence and then I plunged forward, not knowing what I would say until it came out of my mouth, ugly and bald. "She passed away this afternoon."

I cringed in the ensuing silence. Passed away! How could I have used such phony sugar-coated words? Even then, only eight hours after her death, I could already see her shaking her fist at me. Word-master, wordmonger: how pitiful did you find my attempt?

Perhaps with her death she had taken all language away from me. Perhaps I would never again be able to give voice to painful subjects with honesty — I worried about this later, when replaying that scene in my mind. What would the "right" words have been that lonely, difficult night? Mother herself had set the standard long ago: her brutally frank poetry spared no one in its effort to bring enlightenment about the most human of experiences. Today, I can admit to myself that I did not care about intellectual integrity or aesthetics during that phone call. I couldn't say, "Mother killed herself this afternoon," because I wanted to soften the story I had to tell. I wanted to comfort my father. If I couldn't give him a happy ending, my instinct told me to spare him the details. I wanted to insulate him from the blow. I was looking for a language of magic that could change our situation and make my mother's death not true.

"'How?'" His shock vibrated down the phone line. The woman whom he had kept alive for twenty-four years was dead. A fragile man beneath his bluster, he would experience this as his most deeply feared nightmare.

"She killed herself in the car." At last, the gritty facts. I felt cleaner.

"Oh, Linny Pie, no." His voice broke. I heard him begin to cry.

"I'm sorry, Daddy." Inadequate. A pitiful stretch across the distance.

He sobbed for a moment and then cleared his throat. "Tell me what I can do to help?"

His words now shocked me: wasn't it clear what he could do? He could come take over — in fact, I was counting on him to do just that.

"Can you come home?" I asked.

"Of course I can. If that's what you want."

"Only if you want." I felt confused. "I mean, I don't know how you feel about it."

His voice broke. "Of course I want to be there, but I don't want to intrude. I'm not really her husband anymore." He cleared his throat again.

"Daddy, of course you are!" I cried, my voice a tremolo in response to his. "Daddy, I need you."

"What about Joy?"

While waiting for my father to arrive at the Cape, I had come up with a plan for telling my sister and bringing her back to Weston. None of us thought it would be good for her to learn of Mother's suicide over the phone, so far from anyone who could comfort her. I hoped my father would come home and drive up to get her with his friend Bob Starmer, who had been supportive during his divorce from Mother. They could tell Joy when they arrived in Bethel. Loring and Louise were both worried that delaying so long to contact her risked the terrible consequence of her hearing about it some other way, but I had persuaded them to wait.

"I thought maybe you could drive up to tell her. I asked Bob Starmer if he would go with you."

"I'll start now," he said, "and be there in about three hours. If Bob and I leave right away we should get to Joy by seven tomorrow morning."

"I'll wait up for you."

After we hung up I looked at the clock that hung above the back door of my grandmother's kitchen. The lacy black hands stood at five past eleven. *I'll never forget this night,* I thought then. *I'll never forget this night, the time, the clock. This is the night I told my father that my mother was dead.*

🙠

Daddy did reach Joy by early Saturday morning, but not before the principal of the school took it upon himself to inform her. My father arrived only moments later to wrap her into his arms and bring her back to us.

While I waited for them to return, I kept calling Mother's close friends. Maxine felt we were all to blame for the tragedy and told me over and over that we had failed Anne. I closed my eyes and tried not to let the words hurt me, but they stayed heavy inside me. We all felt guilty, even as we knew we could not have kept her alive any longer.

Blanche phoned my grandmother's home early that Saturday morning in a state of shock, having learned of her sister's death in a news story. I don't remember whether Mother had listed either of her sisters' telephone numbers in her directory. Perhaps I had simply ignored the entries, not having had the courage to confront these two women with whom I felt so uncomfortable. Several days later, at the funeral home during visiting hours, a woman I did not recognize entered and I introduced myself to her. She looked at me oddly and said that she was Jane Jealous. I had seen neither Jane nor Blanche in at least ten years.

When Dad and Joy returned home we went together to Waterman's Funeral Home in Wellesley to arrange for the calling hours and memorial service. Again I expected my father to take the lead; again he did not. He clearly felt that the decisions belonged to me, the older of her two daughters.

Mother had left a folder with funeral instructions: in it she requested a plain pine box and a service held at home, with friends speaking and music performed by her poetry-rock group, Her Kind. She held no romantic notions about death and despised the mortuary trade. Though it only occurred to me later, requesting a service at home was a departure of sorts for her. A service at home meant no opportunity for drama, no room for the enormous audience she had so desperately sought in the later years of her life. She had always made death seem an intimate act: perhaps she wanted some small bit of privacy. She asked that her body be cremated and her ashes scattered over the ocean she so loved.

We wandered in the room full of coffins. The lights were low, the colors somber burgundy and navy. A room with thick, plush carpeting, the windows swagged with heavy draperies. Here there was no noise. This place existed apart from the street, the traffic, the staff of the funeral home, the rest of the living world. We walked there as if in a dream.

I looked for a plain pine box, but there were none. This room was full of Cadillacs, each model padded like a baby's bassinet, swathed in silks and satins, each displayed on its own pedestal and with its own price tag discreetly tucked under the bedding. Astonishingly beautiful with their wood of burnished mahogany, the caskets aroused in me the first sadness to rise above the shock of disbelief: my mother's body would lie, cold and final, here. My mother no more, in a box such as this — padded or plain, what did it matter? My mother would never again fill her lungs with the soft mild air of a March thaw, never camp out in her bikini with her lawn chair parked on top of a snowbank, using Mary Gray's old mink for a windscreen as she caught the early spring sun. My mother would never again revel in the daffodils pushing up through the New England mud.

Before they slid her into the oven, they would shut the lid of her coffin over her face. If she opened her eyes, she would see only total, airless black. The heat would fire up the sides of the box and parch her skin. Her broad and crooked smile, her long fingers, her quirky straight arrow eyebrows, her eyes, which once had colored from hazel to blue and back again — all this would char into ash. Never again would my mother put out her arms and hold me.

And because of all this, because of the pain that now flickered inside my gut like the flames to which I would shortly consign her, those gleaming coffins of hardwood tempted me. Permanent, they implied that whoever lay upon their satin cushions would live forever, protected from time and fire, or the wet earth, or the worms that feed in the dark of death.

Quickly, however, I led my family from the room, resolute about giving Mother what she had wanted. I asked about a plain pine box. Such an item, the funeral director informed me, had to be custom-crafted, consuming considerable time and money. While money was not at issue, time most certainly was a factor: we had set Sunday as the date for the visiting hours at Waterman's (in the end none of us could bear the thought of bringing her home for the visiting hours); on Monday there would be a memorial service in

St. Paul's Episcopal Church in Dedham, led by the rector there and Mother's minister, Patty Handloss.

The knowledge that Mother had not wanted her body enshrined kept me steady through this last difficult decision. Despite my fears of his disapproval, I saw that the funeral director nodded politely when I said we would take a crematorium box of gray pressed cardboard. My father remained silent. He would have bought her the biggest, deepest mahogany model available if it had been left to him.

To hide its ugly reality during visiting hours, we covered the casket in an enormous blanket woven of white and yellow daisies, Mother's favorite flower. This last detail was Nana's suggestion, for which she arranged and paid. Her ambivalent love for my mother survived even into her death.

Joy picked out the dress in which our mother would be cremated, the full-length flame of polyester knit with gold buttons running from floor to throat: her red reading dress. We packed a bra — but no jewelry. Underpants — but no shoes. From then on, the hours of every day blurred.

The visiting hours at the funeral home were the worst, a kaleidoscope of faces, well meaning, sodden with grief. I could hear my own bright chatter running like a brook over the rocks of my hysteria. I began to feel as if I were a hostess for a cocktail party to which we had invited too many guests. Most of the people I did not know or recognize. "Hello, I'm Linda Sexton, please come in and sign the guest book."

Daddy hung in the background, Mother's ex-husband, uncertain whether he had the right to be there. Some friends with whom he and Mother had had relationships as a couple for many years refused to speak to him even when he approached them and extended his hand.

Normally shy, I found playing hostess difficult. I stood in the arched entrance to the room in a daze, feeling like a wind-up doll with a one-track tape shoved into my mouth: "Hello, I'm Linda Sexton, please come in and sign the guest book." Behind me, on the other side of the room, I could feel the weight of Mother's body, hidden under its blanket of daisies. I did not have a tear to cry. My mouth was dry and gummy, my palms sweaty and cold.

"Hello, I'm Linda Sexton, please come in and sign the guest book." Everyone wanted to stand on the far side of the room, as far from the casket as possible. I began to feel dizzy, as if we were all on the deck of a large schooner, listing and taking on water. Soon we would capsize and sink. "Hello, I'm Linda Sexton, please come in and sign the guest book."

Somehow, at last, it was over. We went back to Nana's.

"You girls did a good job," Daddy said, as we stood, exhausted, in the dining room. His eyes were red, though he too had not cried in front of anyone all day. His voice rasped, worn down and without life.

"It was horrible," I said listlessly.

"When I went in early," he went on, sticking his hands in his pockets and fiddling with his key chain, "I asked them to open the casket so I could say good-bye." His voice faltered, and he began to weep, openly, head down, hands hanging by his sides. "She looked like a princess," he sobbed. "My Princess Anne." Joy and I ran to him and put our arms around him, buried our faces in his shoulders. Suddenly I found myself crying, a steady stream of tears that wet my chapped cheeks and lips. The pain rocked us in waves.

We decided not to advertise the time or date of the memorial service on Monday because of continuing pressure from the press. Instead, we passed the word to all her friends in a telephone chain, so that everyone knew the location. The church in Dedham was beautiful on that sunny autumn morning, and several of Mother's friends got up to read a variety of her poetry and to remember her with warmth. I sat in the pew next to my father and Joy and read from the prayer book in a daze. I kept my back very straight and wondered how I could be feeling so little, no tears, no reaction. I was drifting, cut loose from my mooring, the endless sea surrounding me. Mother had wanted tapes of Her Kind played, a more raucous celebration of her life with singing and dancing, but we were

still at the beginning of mourning her. It was too soon. Inside me
the numbness began to ache, like a tooth waking up from Novo-
cain.

A memorial service was also held at Boston University, given by
the faculty and her students, which neither Joy nor I attended. I felt
I would shatter if I had to keep up a strong front for even one more
day. *Time alone,* the voice inside my head kept saying over and over,
time alone. The days following the funeral were filled with silence —
and more time alone than I knew how to deal with. I kept trying to
wall off my feelings, but they were clever, they scaled the walls I
built and snuck up on me at night. I cried before sleeping. I cried in
the kitchen when I stirred a saucepan of soup. I cried when I
opened the front hall closet and saw a black hair on the collar of
her winter coat.

I may have been on the other side of the waterfall, but an immense stretch of white water lay before me.

Afterward

After the death,
after the black of black,
this lightness —
not to die, not to die —
that God begot.

— Anne Sexton
"The Fury of Sunrises"

*J*OY AND I began to clean out the clothes from Mother's closet. "Let's make this pile for charity," I suggested, "and this one for old friends."

"And this one for the things you and I want to keep," she said, shifting stacks of stockings and underwear on the king-sized bed in our parents' room. Louise Conant sat in the armchair and talked to us. Nana came and helped. "Linda," she said, "we could take that sundress and hem it for you."

In the bathroom, I opened the medicine cabinet and took out the aspirin bottle in which Mother had stored her jewelry. There, coated with white pill dust, lay her rings and a few pins, anything worth stealing. In her maroon velvet jewelry box were her earrings, her charm bracelets. The bracelets made us teary, as we looked at each charm and remembered the story that went along with its purchase. And then we divided up all the jewelry according to the typed list Mother had left for us in her desk. We blocked everything out and deadened ourselves to the pain. We didn't look at each other if either of us wished for something the other had. We were scared. We needed each other too much now to bicker about diamonds.

Joy opened Mother's dressing table drawers. They were stocked like a pharmacy with quart-sized jugs of the pills she used to get through the days: the tranquilizers that had been abandoned, the sleeping pills and barbiturates, the anti-seizure medication. We started to flush them down the toilet, hating them, the dissolving gelatin transforming the porcelain bowl into a circus of bright, ugly color. We cracked horrible jokes about the doctors who had allowed a suicidal woman the convenience of this death machine, putting such quantities at her disposal simply because they found it easier to write and she to fill single prescriptions several times a year rather than every two weeks. In the purses on top of the closet shelf we found more pills, in the pockets of her jackets, in the jewelry box, in the bedside table drawers. Her room, I saw then, had become an arsenal.

Joy went back to school the next week. Daddy returned to his apartment, and the couple who had been living with Mother in Weston gave me notice of their decision to move out of the house. I shrugged. I wanted them to stay, but I also wanted them to go because they reminded me: of her death, of her craziness in the last year, of all the anxiety I had borne since she and Daddy divorced. As if they were bad meat, I wanted to be rid of them. I cauterized my nerve endings and kept resolutely to my task of squaring away Mother's business. During the day, I had no trouble being as strong as was required. At night, though, alone in my childhood bed, I cried the sort of burning tears that bring no comfort. *She's gone, she's gone,* the wind sang now. *Mommy, come back,* I cried, limp with grief, burying my head beneath the pillow. Under my bed the wolves howled once more, and the dying woman rolled again in the tide.

Daytimes I spent sorting out all the urgent literary matters with Mother's secretary, Jean Moulton, who seemed to sense my fragility despite the facade I was so invested in presenting. She helped me take care of the enormous amount of correspondence, the readings that needed to be canceled, the details that still needed to be settled for the impending publication of *The Awful Rowing Toward God.* Mother had been editing the galleys with Maxine on the afternoon she killed herself. Quickly I learned how to dictate letters to Jean directly onto the typewriter. All this activity helped distract me from the palpable silence of the house, but each time I passed

Mother's desk with its empty chair her absence renewed itself. I sat in that chair a lot to make it seem less empty.

I began to understand how vast was the expanse of work that lay before me. It could not be dealt with in one week or two, not even in one year or two. It was now a permanent part of my life, just as was Mother's death. Eventually I had to go back to my dorm, to my other life, or else make a total break from everything I knew. And so I returned to college and tried to begin again where death had interrupted.

But I could not just go back and pick up my life again. I discovered, with a flicker of surprise, that I had been irrevocably altered. As soon as I entered my room, I began to feel strange and dislocated, a traveler returning from a long journey, unsure whether the space she used to inhabit still belonged to her. As the days went by, my anxiety did not dissipate. I found it hard to confide in my roommates. My boyfriend wanted me back the way I had been before and grew more and more impatient with my distraction and my depression. While continuing to be sympathetic, my roommates and friends were in too different a situation from me: their lives did continue as before, and my anxieties bewildered them.

Mourning my mother was a process that would engage me for years to come, and no two days during those first few months were the same. One day I blocked her from my mind, the next day I was tortured by loss, or guilt, or anger. Distance surrounded me now, from the young women and men who had been my tie to the present, from the woman who had been such a force in my past. Even my bids for independence from her had given me direction. Now I waited, becalmed, uncertain of what to do next. The only activities that made me feel better were working on my senior thesis on Virginia Woolf — plunging myself into a world of words — and taking care of Mother's work. Increasingly, for friendship, I relied on a few friends of Mother's: Lois Ames, Loring and Louise Conant, Patty Handloss. Now they were my friends as well, and we were bonded by her death.

I worried, too, about my father; Joy and I asked him if he wanted to move back into the home he had bought with Mother some seven years before. When he hired a truck and brought his apartment furnishings back to Weston, I sighed with relief: I had found a new watchdog for the house, that strongbox that held our memories. It was a talisman of our past, and neither Joy nor I nor Daddy was ready to let it go.

I thought more continually of Mother than I had when she was alive. I began to wear some of her clothes and jewelry; with these things on my body I felt safer. Stronger. Around my neck I hung her good-luck charm — a long gold chain and medallion that said, "Don't Let the Bastards Get You." I imported several bottles of her liquor from our home in Weston and set up a little bar in my room, to the horror of my roommates, so that I could entertain some of my friends. I liked a drink before dinner a lot. Or after dinner. I mixed stingers, one of Mother's favorite lethal postprandial libations. And then I liked a Scotch at bedtime — it helped me sleep. This ritual with alcohol, taken so directly from my own childhood, mirrored the landslide occurring inside me: who was I now? Linda alone? Linda taking care of Anne? Linda masquerading as Anne? Or — perhaps most horrible of all — Linda trying to keep Anne alive by *being* Anne?

ॐ

Once a week throughout that year, on Wednesday mornings, I started up Mother's red Cougar, the car in which she had died. In the car, feeling her presence there behind me, I drove from Cambridge to Weston to meet Jean Moulton. Leaving my classes and my work was neither convenient nor good for my grades; nevertheless, I found that the process of tending Mother's literary garden made the pain of losing her easier to bear: I had a constructive task and I helped myself by helping her.

During the month after her suicide, I started working with Mother's editors at Houghton Mifflin, Dick McAdoo and Jonathan Galassi. The jacket copy and press releases for *The Awful Rowing Toward God* all needed revision following her death, and slowly I began to learn, from the editorial viewpoint, how a book goes to press. Nothing I had done over the summer at Houghton Mifflin had prepared me for what I now faced. I flew on instinct alone. The feeling of competence I gained by making decisions — even inexperienced ones — allowed me to feel in control of my life, for just a few hours each week.

Jonathan and I would work together for the next several years on her posthumous poetry books *45 Mercy Street* (1976) and *Letters for Dr. Y* (1978), as well as on *Anne Sexton: A Self-Portrait in Letters* (1977). *45 Mercy Street* required a great deal of editing and restructuring, while *Letters for Dr. Y* was a collection that I assembled out of the various pieces of manuscript Mother had left in her desk. As I worked with Jonathan my confidence in my judgment grew, just as my confidence had once grown as a result of working with Mother.

But there was no way to crawl back into the skin of the Linda I had been before October 4th. Despite my fledgling confidence in the face of literary decisions, my personal life continued to disintegrate. On the day exams began in January, my boyfriend of four years left a "Dear John" letter under my door, afraid to face me. Later I would learn that he had been having an affair with another classmate since the month my mother died. I cried long and hard that morning, believing myself now totally alone. Then I got up and took my exam. The following week I went back into psychotherapy, with a gentle therapist at the Harvard University Health Services. I knew I had to try and slow down the emotions that were spiraling out of control. I was depressed. I was angry. And I was drinking too much.

Later in the year, a new friend brought me some stability. A young man with a wide grin, wild curling hair, broad shoulders, dark blue eyes. He was funny, he was compassionate. He was one of the smartest Harvard boys I knew. I had had a platonic relationship with John, who also lived in Mather House, since my sophomore year. That winter John and I began to talk more, to date a little, and somehow it seemed that he understood better than anyone the depth of the pain I felt but that I would not — could not — release.

Little by little he coaxed me out of my depression; sporadically

I came to the surface for a gulp of air before retreating, once again, to the depths. We went to the movies together; then we spent a weekend in New York at his parents', cramming three Broadway shows and two movies into a two-day visit. He held me tight. He let me rest against him. Time spent with John was time when I could put down the weight of Mother.

Love began like a catch in my throat, so small I hardly knew it was there. Holding hands and talking. Movies. Cheap dinners at the Wursthaus or Pizzeria Uno. Hours spent wandering through bookstores — a passion in common. More movies.

One day in the spring of senior year I received in the mail a book containing an article written by Sandy McClatchy, which bore the subtitle: *Anne Sexton, 1928–1974*. I stood there in my room, stunned. I kept looking at those dates, dates that made her life and death so real. They reminded me of the marker I had yet to set, above a grave I had yet to find. I tried to hold myself in check, but my horror grew, the pain spun through my body and heart, and at last the insubstantial walls I had built between me and my loss began to crack. *Mother*, I cried, throwing the book against the wall. John put his arms out and held me while I raged. *Where have you gone? Why have you left me again?*

҂

Where to bury her? How to bury her? Waterman's Funeral Home called me. They had apparently phoned the house in Weston several months ago and spoken with my father, but still no one had come to pick up the urn with my mother's ashes.

My father was having a very difficult time, alone in the house where he and my mother had once made a life together. Although his relationship with the woman he had begun dating the year before continued, he now seemed more haunted by my mother than ever before. His hearty forced cheer only thinly veiled his depression. It did not surprise me that he had avoided picking up Mother's ashes, nor that he had not asked me to do so.

At Waterman's, they handed me a box wrapped in plain brown paper, taller than it was wide, the shape perhaps of a small vase. It rattled when I shook it and was surprisingly heavy. It was winter now, too late for scattering ashes at sea because all the boats belonging to Daddy's friends were in dry dock until spring. Once home with the box, I debated where to store it. Eventually I slid it up onto a high shelf in my father's closet. Mother would have to wait.

Self-Portrait

A woman who writes feels too much.

— Anne Sexton,
"The Black Art"

THAT YEAR spring came heralded by the lilacs near my dorm: blooming lush and fragrant, purple and white, they defied the city's dirt. At my childhood home in the nearby suburb of Newton, a hedge of lilac had bordered our property just outside my bedroom window. Mother would cut the long, drooping clusters with her rusty green-handled kitchen scissors and bring them into the dining room, where they dispersed their scent throughout the house and signaled the start of gentle summer nights. Walking past those Cambridge lilacs at dusk, I thought of Mother and decided to call when I returned to the dorm to tell her that here in town the lilacs had begun. I picked a pale purple blossom and quickened my step, eager to get to the phone. As I turned the corner, memory spoke.

Gone, gone. She isn't coming back. There will be no more springs.

I ached with the illness of grief.

I walked slowly back to my room, scuffing my shoes over the sidewalk like a little girl. I sat and stared at the lilac. It stood in a water glass on my desk, beautiful but forlorn. What more perfect metaphor for loss than that elegant, drooping form, its heart-shaped leaf, its elegiac scent? Inside me I felt the shift that signaled a poem, but I repressed it. I didn't want to go so deep, take the risk, feel the blackness pull down over my head. I didn't want to "feel too much," or to hurt, ever again.

A facility with words and language was the only gift I ever believed I possessed, the only way I knew to control emotions, from depression to joy. But over the last few years of Mother's life, when my identification with her had become so dangerous, I had largely abandoned my writing. I had come to Harvard a poet, but I didn't want to leave as one. I hadn't written a poem in over two years, not since my parents' divorce, not since Mother began to spiral completely out of control.

The end of college, graduation, and care-taking Mother's literary estate consumed enough of my time to make it easy and yet difficult to sit around and brood: difficult because my time was full; easy because so much of my life centered around her death.

My senior year culminated with a surprise job offer that appealed to my interest in words. Houghton Mifflin asked me and Lois Ames — whom Mother had appointed her biographer sometime in the late sixties — if we would be interested in editing a volume of her letters. In 1977 this book was published as *Anne Sexton: A Self-Portrait in Letters*. Lois and I signed the contract as full collaborators, but she was also teaching full-time at Northeastern University, and it developed that her time was extremely limited; although we remained co-authors on the book, the bulk of sifting through the material and editing it fell to me.

And so I found myself alone each day in the reading room of the manuscripts library at Boston University, where Mother had placed the majority of her letters and manuscripts on loan. Sitting in that glass-walled room, I opened box after box. A meticulous saver and hoarder, my mother had kept letters from family, friends, and colleagues, as well as manuscript material and extensive notebooks that she had transcribed nearly verbatim from the many years of tape recordings of her sessions with Dr. Orne.

I did not in any way feel prepared to undertake this job by myself, and Lois's intermittent presence did not mitigate my initial loneliness as I sat at B.U. Just working on editing Mother's poetry with Jonathan Galassi had been hard enough. Now I was confronted by my mother's life — and this time without the buffer of another person to help me make painful discoveries. I tried to learn to accept that whenever Lois *was* able to participate, her contribution was valuable in terms of her wisdom and experience. Still, as the months slowly deepened toward the winter of 1975, and the work on the book grew more intense, I began to resent her for having left me alone with all this material; undoubtedly my emotions echoed the anger and vulnerability I had felt when my mother left me the year before.

Reading through Mother's life was like strapping myself onto a roller coaster every morning. When I sat down to each new file folder, I could not know whether I would be laughing or crying by noontime, giggling at her humor or disapproving of her naughtiness. The process of reading through all these documents taught me many lessons about the kind of *woman* she was, not just the kind of *mother* she was.

In one exchange with a publishing director at Houghton Mifflin she had told an outrageous lie: he had sent her uncorrected proofs of *The Death Notebooks*, asking her to autograph them for him; she, in turn, had written him a charming apology explaining that our Dalmatians had eaten them before she could return them. Yet I had seen those same signed galleys, just after her death, sitting high on the bookshelf above her desk.

When I reread her letters to me at camp, sorrow filled me like warm water in a vase. I cried, bowing my head and using Kleenex to keep my tears from falling on the felt-tip handwriting. When I read the letters Mother had written to the family on her one extended sojourn away from home — to Europe for a month — each one stimulated a new detail remembered from my childhood, this time viewed through the colored lens of her nostalgic words.

And I read in detail, for the first time, of her numerous extramarital affairs, those betrayals of my father. I learned what I had once only suspected: that she and her friend Anne Wilder had been lesbian lovers. This delight in erotic escapade resounded throughout the files: while in England with Lois Ames for a reading trip in 1967, she had had sex with another poet in the hotel room she was sharing with Lois, while Lois pretended to be asleep in the next bed; in Italy on her trip to Europe in 1963, she wrote passionate love letters to my father while having a torrid affair with a romantic Yugoslavian barber. The fear that she had gotten pregnant then necessitated many transatlantic calls to Dr. Orne.

There were materials that documented her depressions, her madness, her suicide attempts. One such was a letter to Dr. Orne, written in November of 1961, filled with a terrifying level of pain and desperation; one night she hung on to life by sheer willpower even though she had the "kill me" pills lined up beside her typewriter as she sat alone in the dark. "I'm in prison," she wrote. "Will no one help me it is dark stupid cant write in dark cant cant cant cant cant cant take pills, cant run, cantgo, cant move, cant scared xant [*sic*] move scream die run write shut up you."

Was any of this worse than that which I had witnessed? No. But here, despite my desire to remember my mother in a positive light, I had to confront every detail. Some of what I read hurt me.

Over the ensuing months of reading and taking notes for the book of letters, I also came to see my own early life replayed. There were things I had not known about our relationship, at least not in a factual sense. I had always perceived myself as the favorite daughter, the child with whom she had experienced the deepest bond. When I was a teenager she had dubbed me her "best critic" (flattery, perhaps, but an intelligent tactic that yielded her an attentive daily reader). What shock and fury then, to read what I had repressed in order to feel more comfortable: how she had spanked me with brushes and sneakers, slapped me, thrown me against a wall, repeatedly set me in front of a television set tuned to soap operas so that she could write poems. My younger sister was her favorite, she told her analyst, the only one she had the energy or inclination to love. "Something comes between me and Linda," she had confessed to Dr. Orne. "I hate her. I want her to go away and she knows it." She revealed to the doctor that she sometimes tried to choke me to stop my crying.

Sometimes the revelations I discovered jibed with my own memories, and sometimes they stood in direct contradiction to what I believed to have been true. Dueling perspectives: my mother's as a young mother, my own as a young child. I was learning how the human mind rewrites its own history when that history is too ugly to be embraced.

In the glass room at B.U., I hid my face in my hands and

cried — one of the few times I lost control in front of the ever-vigilant guards, who watched every minute and every move to make sure no one stole or destroyed the precious material in front of them. Was this a job? Was it a perverted sense of duty? What purpose did my torment serve?

How should a daughter feel when she learns her mother wanted to kill her, even if that emotion died as I grew older and less of a burden and was more able to take on the burden of caring for her? Outwardly, I remained rational and disengaged, sorting letters and rating them on a scale of one to five for use in the book, keeping neat files, drafting small bridges that would fit between the letters and shape the book into a narrative. Inwardly I was on fire with resentment and rejection, drinking my way to oblivion every night, an oblivion that shattered in dreams when she returned to harangue me. This separation of what I felt from what I acknowledged was a pattern long established. As a child I had learned to split off what I was feeling: when emotions overwhelmed, they had to be gotten rid of. It was only what I had been doing my whole life. No wonder I was so good at it.

I kept reading and I kept crying, and the only way I could not break apart was to tell myself I was creating something important. If I were able to keep the emotional devastation I felt out of the book, I reasoned, then I could not be accused of expurgating or sentimentalizing my mother's life. In those years, the Plath family had received much adverse publicity in the literary press for being unwilling to allow scholars access to the poet's notes, diaries, and early writings. It was rumored that Aurelia Plath had even taken a pair of nail scissors and cut out portions of Sylvia's diaries that she had not wanted anyone to see. I was determined to be different — frank and to the point — and to make my candor match that found in Mother's poetry.

If I had allowed myself to act like a daughter, I would have closed many of those boxes, taken them out of the library where they were on loan, and burned them. Then I would not have had to face the anger and accusations my own family would later make at the revelations I permitted. Then I would not have had to face my own anger or loss.

Mother, however, danced around that small glass room, reminding me of the job I had promised to do for her, as alive to me then as ever. When I closed the boxes at the end of the day it was like trying to force a genie back into the bottle. At night I went home to John, who was working in a biology lab that year, preparatory to entering Harvard Medical School the next autumn. He was living in a studio apartment, and I spent three nights a week there with him. The other nights I spent at home with my father and Joy, who was living at home while attending the Museum School of Fine Arts in Boston, studying photography.

Again and again now, I felt the internal pressure that signaled a poem was on the rise inside of me, a poem in response to the overwhelming emotions I now felt. But I hadn't been willing for several years to take the risk and dip down deep into the river where the emotions ran. Increasingly, though, I woke from a dream in the middle of the night and found myself thinking of the typewriter. On the nights I spent in the house in Weston with my father, I sometimes sat up in the dark and thought that I could hear Mother typing in the study below my bedroom in the early hours of the morning.

Eventually a poem erupted in me; it was a poem about the pain I still felt, the depth of despair. But it didn't take too long before I grew discouraged, once again, with poetry. For the time being at least I would never get *the sound of Mother* out of my head. Even today I sometimes sense beneath the layers of my prose a certain rhythm that takes me back to one of her rhythms. Mother's poetry is layered into my consciousness like geologic strata. I can hear her as clearly as any of those I studied: Eliot, Yeats, and Shakespeare. Or, perhaps, more so.

To shelter myself and find comfort, to escape from the loneliness of the day's work in that glass cubicle at Boston University, I began to drink heavily — over John's increasing protest. I was looking for anesthesia. Slowly during that year our relationship began to disintegrate. Still, I held tight. I didn't want to let go of the one sane person in the insane world I had created for myself by working on Mother's material. I hated that world, yet I took a perverse pleasure in it as well: I never once considered abandoning the project or turning it over to someone else. I wanted the praise when this job was completed, well done, for myself.

Nightly I dreamt that Mother returned: back to life she came, full force and furious that I was writing about her as if she were dead. I sat at her desk in her study, working on the book of letters. She sauntered in, expressing surprise to see me there. "What are you working on?" she inquired. "The book about your life," I answered. "You can't write about my life if I'm still alive," she retorted angrily. "It's mine, not yours, and I want it back." It seemed that every night brought a nightmare, and I tossed under the curse of her continued presence.

In one dream, I had at last nabbed Lois, and we were having lunch together in the main dining room at the Ritz-Carlton Hotel, overlooking the Public Garden. Spooning my vichyssoise from its iced silver cup, I looked up to see the captain roll the dessert cart by. He paused beside me, and asked if I would like to look at the pastries. I nodded and looked down into the cart, but saw that it had become an open coffin. I shoved myself back in my chair as Mother sat up, stretching out her arms, her face blue and contorted. "Bobolink, come take a nap with me," she entreated, her cold lips pursed for a kiss. "I'm waiting for you!" She caught hold of my arm and began to pull me toward her with awful strength.

I woke to my own noises of protest, as I struggled to escape from that downward suction into death. Sobs and sweat, heart jumping, fish on a line. John rolled away from me toward the wall. He was getting tired of my nightmares. I lay in the dark, tears rolling back into my ears. The worst separation of my life had really occurred: Mother was dead, and the only way I could rejoin her was too gruesome to contemplate. Yet I craved some kind of reunion,. some life after death — which kept me working on *Self-Portrait*, hammering away at the pain of this final loss with the only tool I knew how to heft.

The invasion of her death into my life continued daily throughout that first year and then into the second. The surge of events
that fell to me as her caretaker could not be stopped: in total ig-
norance I had accepted a job that would endure — without possibility of resignation — for the rest of my life. Emboldened by
Mother's death, fans came to knock at my door as if it were a
shrine; one wrote me letters promising that if only I would come to
Jesus I would be saved. The "Anne junkies" sent sheaves of poetry
for me to comment on, as she had often done, or file cards on
which they requested I write meaningful notes. One young woman
named Martha* — who had been institutionalized and who
identified heavily with Mother as a voice of the mentally ill —
haunted my days and nights by telephone; one morning as I spoke
on the phone with a friend, the operator cut in to ask me to hang
up because there was a family emergency. I dropped the phone
back into its cradle as if it were a bomb, heart racing. It rang nearly
immediately, and Martha's voice came down the line, telling me
she had gotten tired of hearing a busy signal. She wanted nothing
but to chat. The episode jolted me from the present back into that
nightmare slide of childhood when everything felt so out of control: who knew when or how the eerily skewed balance of mental
illness would intrude into my world, break open my privacy, cause
me anxiety — even it if was delivered from the voice of a near
stranger over the telephone?

꙳

Not until the summer of 1976, nearly two years after mother's suicide, when the work for *Self-Portrait* was nearing completion, did I
summon the strength to pull Mother's ashes off the top shelf of
Daddy's closet. I had recognized, at last, that in trying to scatter her
ashes over the sea we were actually just procrastinating about her final
resting spot. Finding a boat to take us had seemed insurmountable
because letting her go seemed insurmountable. Joy remembered
that Mother had once said she wouldn't mind being buried in the

---

*Martha is a pseudonym.

Sexton family plot in the Forest Hills Cemetery, next to Joanie and
my grandfather Poppy — whom she always spoke of with love, for
he had paid for a great deal of her early therapy and sat with her in
the hospital room after her first suicide attempt. I checked with the
office at the cemetery: there was plenty of space for a crematorium
urn beside Joanie's and over Poppy's deeper lying casket.

I took the box of ashes and placed it on the seat beside me in the
red Cougar that now belonged to me, strapping her in with the seat
belt. "Mom," I said, "we're off."

Having never driven to the cemetery before, I navigated our
course using a map, and when I reached the high iron gates it was
with a sense of triumph. The grounds were manicured sweeps of
lawn broken by the grace of weeping willows, pines, banks of
rhododendron. I set Mother down at the long counter in the
office and requested an interment a few days later. My voice trembled in my throat. I remember the people there and their kind
faces: they seemed to sense the pulse of the sadness running
through me.

The day of my mother's burial dawned sunny and hot, late August in New England. Joy, Nana, Daddy, and I stood on the small
hill in the cemetery, looking at each other with anxiety. Except for
the cardboard box, we were alone. The cemetery staff had dug a
small hole, set the earth discreetly to the side and covered the site
with artificial turf. They had left Mother to one side of the hole. It
had taken us nearly two years to force ourselves to this spot, and
now that we were here we did not know what to do. There was no
minister to aid us, no one to fill up the silence or wash away the
emotions with the comfort of words. Even worse, there was no one
to lift Mother and put her where she belonged. *What did you imagine
this would be like?* cried an angry voice inside me. *Did you think you could
escape the pain by waiting two years to bury her?*

The small box had assumed the weight of the body. I saw how
we all avoided looking at it, how we stepped past it as if it did not
exist to discuss on which panel Mother's inscription ought to be
engraved. We were procrastinating one last time. How much she

had meant to each one of us — how intense had been her beauty and her ugliness — to cause us such pain even now.

After a while, I went over to the box. "Should we do this?" I asked my sister. She nodded and we bent down together to pick up Mother. We set her, gently, into the damp dark hole in the earth. Joy scattered in the yellow pansies she had picked that morning from the garden in Weston, and their faces glowed up at us from out of the blackness, miniature reminders of the sun that Mother had loved so much. I grabbed for her hand and she grabbed for Daddy's, who caught Nana's. We all stood there and began to cry.

It had taken us two years, but finally we had buried her; laid her, as they say, to rest.

I ought to have known better.

Between Two Worlds

ॐ

Sew your lips shut
and let not a word or a deadstone sneak out.

— Anne Sexton
"Talking to Sheep"

*A*S THE MONTHS of editing *Self-Portrait* continued, I found
the work more wrenching and harder to bear. By the end of 1976 I
needed desperately to move on, to find some way out of the cave I
had created for myself, back into the gray daylight of my own
world. The book was nearly finished. Where was I to go now?

John and I were living together in Brookline, a small suburb of
Boston, while he worked toward his degree at Harvard Medical
School. Joy had moved into an apartment of her own and was now
working for an insurance company. Daddy still lived at the house in
Weston, but in 1977 he married the woman he had been dating
since the summer following his separation from Mother, and she
moved in with him there. Everyone seemed to be getting on with
his or her life except me. All around me were John's female classmates, bright young women pursuing medical careers with determination. I remembered my mother's wish that I become a
psychiatrist, and the idea that she might be disappointed at what I
had become lit up inside of me with a tiny but wicked flame.

I was still drinking too much, and John and I were still having
problems, but as I made the last marks on the page proofs for *Self-
Portrait*, it occurred to me that I was now in a position to choose a
new path for myself. A shift began inside of me. It was time to do
something more than merely tend Mother's garden. I needed to
find not just a room of my own, but work and a life of my own as
well. And so I sold Mother's red Cougar and began to drive John's

VW Rabbit. I stopped giving readings of her work. I stopped wearing her clothes.

And yes, finally, a glimmer of an idea did begin to shine inside of me. As I began the promotional tour for *Self-Portrait*, I began to wonder if I were not ready to write a book of my own.

Increasingly, the women my own age — particularly those from the Med. School, who were becoming my friends as well as John's — complained of a lack of balance in their lives. "How are we supposed to do all this?" they asked angrily, referring to their shifts of thirty-six straight hours at the hospital, with only twelve hours off before the revolving door began again. "How am I going to have any time for marriage or children or anything but career?" Becoming a professional was too important to compromise, but not one of these women was willing to be alone or childless either. For the first time we were beginning to question the promises the women's movement — and our mothers — had made about having a career and a family too.

By the spring, these questions had grown into an outline and a few sample chapters. I approached one of the agents in my mother's literary agency; she liked the concept and my writing and agreed to take on *Between Two Worlds: Young Women in Crisis*. By the fall I had signed a contract with William Morrow, filled with excitement. I worked hard through the winter, trudging up and down the snowy streets of Boston and Manhattan with my tape recorder and satchel, interviewing young women about their lives and their expectations for the future, their role models, their mothers and fathers, and their childhoods. If I didn't know what to do with my own life, I was keen to see and hear about the choices my peers were making. I began to see patterns: conflicting emotions among so many of us, caught off balance "between two worlds," in the battle between career and family.

I was particularly curious about these women's mothers: how they had influenced their daughters' self-image in both love and work. My own mother's example was so complicated by her mental illness that I was looking for answers in the lives of others. John read the manuscript weekly as it emerged from my typewriter and offered valuable insight. I found myself thinking of Mother and the way we had once "workshopped" at the kitchen table.

By the summer of 1978, I had taken control of my drinking — quite easily, as it developed. I was working full-time on my book now and only part-time on Mother's estate. I reached out more to friends my own age and joined a choir to which Joy belonged. One night a week we met in town for Szechuan food and gossip. Joy and I were becoming friends, different from the friends we had been when survival had tied us together. We were young women, and even though there still ran between us currents of jealousy and competition, there were also currents of warmth and enjoyment and laughter.

As the depression and grief began to lift, I felt happier. John and I grew happier as a couple, our love all the deeper from having weathered the aftershocks of Mother's death. We took a vacation together to a friend's house in the mountains and learned how to cross-country ski. We began to laugh at our financially restricted state; before ordering in the local Italian dive we would calculate our order to the nickel, including tax and tip, and then walk home via the bookstore, where an evening's entertainment of browsing came for free. John began to believe, at last, that he could trust me as much as I trusted him.

One night late in the winter of 1979, sitting on the floor of our bedroom and watching a movie while eating Chinese take-out, John asked me to marry him. With a gleam in my eye, I told him I'd have to think about it.

At last I would be able to build a real family, the family I had always dreamed of having when I was a child. My father seemed pleased — even taking in stride the news that we would be married by a rabbi rather than a minister — and opened a bottle of champagne. Mother, I felt certain, would have loved John: for his tenderness, love, and his respect for my writing — something she had never been able to share with my father. And I sensed her smiling at me, blessing us with her pleasure at our pleasure.

Though it caught me by surprise, the approach of my wedding day brought a new wave of sadness at Mother's absence. I reminded myself that if Mother had been with us she would surely have been doing something strange. My wedding day might well have belonged to her, Anne, the star.

But that was only a rationalization. However true, it didn't alleviate the sorrow one bit.

John and I were married by a rabbi in the nonsectarian Memorial Church in Harvard Yard. The August day was rainy, not the best for the outdoor reception I had planned in the garden at our home in Weston. My mother-in-law did not like my broad-brimmed picture hat and tried to convince me to remove it before I went down the aisle. I refused, for that hat was a talisman, hand-made and modeled on the hat my mother had worn on her wedding day; to the crown I had stitched a wreath of daisies, her favorite flower. God himself could not have persuaded me to take off this "something borrowed" from the one who could not be there to lend it herself.

The day passed in a blur, as all weddings do. After the reception John and I drove off in the blue Rabbit, trailing the caterer's dolly, adorned with a lot of shaving cream in obscene designs. We were to spend our honeymoon at the Conants' house on an island in Maine — a paradise of woodland quiet, and economical as well — but first we had an errand.

This time I had no map, but I remembered, guided by a memory that pulled at me like the long yellow finger that beckons from a lighthouse. Forest Hills. In our wedding-bedecked Volkswagen we wound through the drives studded with gray stones and granite monuments. Here: Ardisia Path, over the bridge, up by the stone angels.

We walked through the wet grass. *Mother, I've come to visit you because you can't come to me.*

John and I held hands as we stood there on the hillside. The rain had stopped now, and a late sun began to glimmer through the overcast.

I took my wedding bouquet and laid it on her foot-marker.

Daisies, Mom.

I miss you.

In Search of a Biographer

Jonah made his living inside the belly.
Mine comes from the exact same place.

— Anne Sexton
"Making a Living"

REQUESTS for the dramatic rights to Mother's life and access to her biographical material mushroomed after her death, so even while in the midst of wedding plans and finishing *Between Two Worlds*, I had to address the other issues a literary executor must: publication of the remaining poetry, requests to reprint or anthologize or to create dramatic productions based on her life and work, as well as beginning to think about the publication of a biography. The selection of a biographer and the complicated support this kind of intense project would require was the single task before me about which I worried the most.

I wanted to see a literary biography written that would focus on her life through the lens of her *work*. And I wanted to see it soon, for I felt anxious about all that explosive material locked up in her files — for now — but easily exploited if not handled carefully. As inquiries began to come in to Houghton Mifflin from journalists interested in writing about Mother's life, I realized that I would have to deal with the issue right away.

My mother's desire to have Lois Ames write her biography complicated the already difficult situation. Every day I wondered why I had allowed Mother to talk me into handling all this: what had once seemed glamorous had turned out to be painful. Sometimes I daydreamed about just having a job, a regular job like an editorial assistant or even a secretary in a publishing house; I longed to take the trolley into town at eight o'clock, come back out at six too tired to think or worry, fix supper, and then read until bedtime.

But that wasn't what I had chosen. I had chosen this work, this obligation to my mother and her poetry, and the freedom to pursue some kind of writer's life if I wanted it. Until my obligation to Mother was fulfilled and laid to rest, I couldn't allow myself the luxury of fantasizing about a new and different career.

First, I had to deal with Lois. When Lois and my mother first met, Lois was a psychiatric social worker living in the Chicago area, working on an "authorized" biography of Sylvia Plath with the cooperation of the ordinarily recalcitrant Plath estate. She and Mother soon became friends. Maybe Mother's motivations for offering Lois the job at that particular time were not entirely pure: she had been extremely jealous of Plath for quite a while, but especially since Plath's well-publicized suicide, a tragedy that had quickly reversed their positions on the visibility ladder in the contemporary poetry community. She had told Dr. Orne that Plath "took something that was mine — *that* death was mine!" Perhaps stealing the attention of her rival's sole "official" biographer was a metaphorical revenge for Plath's having stolen the "confessional" limelight.

Lois's decision to become Mother's biographer presaged the type of difficulties I would later encounter in collaborating with her on *Self-Portrait*. Confident that she could work on two biographies simultaneously while also pursuing her career as a practicing therapist and teacher, she began to accompany Mother on many of her reading trips, to tape her classroom sessions at Boston University, and to be a confidante for many secrets. By 1977 I believed that if I were to allow Lois to continue in her role as "designated" biographer, I would spend the next decade hounding her for pages she had not written; in the void created by this vain attempt, some determined journalist would come along and write a biography — perhaps of a sensational bent.

Despite Mother's expressed desire to have Lois as her biographer, I believed I had to find someone new, someone with whom I — and the rest of the family — could work. In addition, I had also concluded something important that Mother evidently had not recognized: needing to be as objective as possible, a biographer should *not* be a close friend of the subject. Friends — and family — were better suited to writing memoirs.

I appealed to Jonathan Galassi to begin a search with me for a new biographer. The idea of letting someone loose with all this incendiary material scared me, however, particularly as I knew that once the work began I would not have any kind of control or approval over the final manuscript. I liked being in control — I had craved it all my life, the perfect solution to those early years when the unpredictable elements of my parents' violence and my mother's mental illness could crash through the door at any time. Sometimes it still felt as if it were *my* life that was threatened with the exposure and examination of hers.

Perhaps even worse, I still felt confused, without even realizing it and despite years of therapy, about that deep connection that continued to exist between my mother and me: in my mind our faces still lived on as twins in the mirror; the mole on her cheek had become the mole on mine. Two anguished questions came to me, again and again: Could I really ever be more than Anne Sexton's literary executor? More than Anne Sexton's daughter? Would I be forever a thin, gray shadow?

I fought this battle with myself over and over through the years as, unwillingly, I loosened my hold on this peculiar connection between us — that connection that so interfered with my own ability to become a strong and independent person. And how it hurt. Ultimately, releasing control of her life and work became a metaphor for letting Mother herself go, for acknowledging that I hadn't been able to keep her alive then and I couldn't keep her alive now; to return to life myself I had better let the body drop and settle to the bottom of the pond.

꙳

As hard as it was for me to face, I knew the biography would require the same kind of honesty as had *Self-Portrait*. Her poetry demanded it. She demanded it, still waving at me from the sky. Confronted with the dilemma of family privacy versus truth, it did not take me long to reason my way to a solution: the best way to control the release of such explosive material and to protect the family — as well as Mother herself — lay in the selection of a discreet and sensitive writer with whom I could develop a solid working relationship. I knew my mother wanted a biography written and it was my job to make that happen. I did not ask my father or his mother, or my mother's sisters, for their opinions on the matter. I already knew their answer: they would wish to suppress any revelatory book on Mother's life — and their own — instead seeking a privacy my mother had never granted them in life and would not grant them with her death either.

When Mother had asked me to be her literary executor, I had not understood that this job would put me at odds with the rest of my family; I didn't look ahead to see that I would have to fight for Mother's point of view regardless of family feeling, even if that meant alienating myself from the others. I was only twenty-one: how could I really foresee that I would be responsible for publication decisions regarding family history, detail, and emotion that everyone else — and sometimes even I — would want kept private? In the end, only Joy would be there, standing close beside me, when the biography came out.

In the autumn of 1979 I began work on my first novel, *Rituals.* While I might fantasize about being a "regular working girl" I also was beginning to understand that I had before me a tremendous opportunity — provided by the very work that was so painful for me to do. Being literary executor paid me enough to get by, it gave me free time, and in that free time I found myself more and more driven to write. It seemed natural to begin my first novel — as Mother had her poetry — with a story I knew well: the struggle and pain of a young woman who has lost her mother to a sudden death, though not a suicide.

At this time our living expenses fell to me, as John's parents had cut him off financially just after we had married. They were enraged that John — who had repeatedly confided his dislike of medical school during his four-year stint — had at last decided to go on to business school rather than applying for an internship when he finished getting his M.D. later that year. He was able to obtain a student loan for the final year of medical school and for the two years of business school tuition, but we needed my advance for the novel to pay our rent, buy groceries, and keep the lights on. I felt proud to continue a tradition Mother had begun: we were both able to support ourselves — and, when money became tight, our husbands as well.

At Harvard Business School John was able to give full rein to the creative streak he had had to repress in medical school. With a friend, he started a small company, out of which they wrote *The Official M.B.A. Handbook: Or, How To Succeed in Business Without a Harvard M.B.A.*, which eventually spent sixteen weeks on the *New York Times* bestseller list. My own work was moving along well as I at last began to write about mourning for my mother through the voice of the novel. *Rituals* was published in the spring of 1982.

Even in the realm of handling Mother's work I seemed on the home stretch at last, although in addition to seeking a biographer, another major and daunting leg of the marathon still lay before me: placing Mother's archives permanently in a university library.

I had at last gathered up and inventoried all the written material pertaining to her life, including the contents of the filing cabinets and basement at 14 Black Oak Road, as well as the forty-odd boxes of manuscript and correspondence that had been on temporary loan to Boston University. Sometime in the autumn of 1978, Jonathan Galassi told me that the Harry Ransom Humanities Research Center at the University of Texas in Austin had expressed interest in purchasing Mother's papers. I was pleased to hear it, but I couldn't imagine sending Mother so far away. In my mind, her papers — those reams of yellow and white covered with her handwritten scrawl, her personal notes and postcards, all the intimate essence of her life — were what was left to me now. It would be very hard to let it go. And to Texas, a state I had never visited, but which I imagined barren and dusty — violently different from the "long green" of our late summer afternoons in New England.

Texas: too far away for a casual visit, too far for a knock-on-the-back-door, have-a-cup-of-tea.

Still, the "H.R.C.," as it is known, housed a bounty of distinguished modern collections — particularly of important women poets; among others who make their posthumous home there are Marianne Moore, Christina Rossetti, and Edith Sitwell. The university was eager to have Mother's work. More significantly, John was able to negotiate a favorable agreement with them that would enable me to continue controlling decisions regarding publication of the material. This sort of control over the way manuscript drafts and correspondence were used would become key in having leverage over the approach a biography would ultimately take.

I packed up forty boxes of letters and manuscripts. And then several special boxes, with personal items: I hoped the library might find the space to make an exhibition, let her readers know her through the objects with which she had surrounded herself. Her typewriter. Her eyeglasses and bankbook. The yellowed cartoons from the *New Yorker* that she had taped above her desk. Her calendar and her precious address book. I laid them in with tenderness, remembering the day Joy and I — too numb to feel, caught on the sharp hooks of shock — had packed her dresses, shoes, and pocketbooks. This time I was not too numb. This time I was alone, and the deep ache in my gut could be eased by nothing, not by the years that had passed, not by innumerable tears and rages and conversations with the dead.

I tried to focus on the more businesslike problems I faced as a way of wading through the renewed sadness: unique difficulties were posed by particular correspondences — especially those with her lovers — and early poems, as well as the notebooks Mother had made that transcribed audiotapes of her early psychiatric sessions. While she had included without restriction many of these "touchy" materials in the archive she had given on temporary loan to Boston University, I found this decision far too liberal. There was too much that I wasn't ready to have open to public view.

And then there was the mystery of the James Wright letters — a frustrating distraction, as this correspondence between my mother and the well-known poet appeared to be missing. I had first learned of her affair with Wright when her will directed me to find their love letters, stored for safekeeping in the home of a friend. Based on the content of the few letters I did find from Mother to Wright in her files, these letters undoubtedly contained many long critiques of the poetry both were writing at the time, and a variety of spirited debate over their own work and that of their peers. The correspondence between the two poets would have been a cornerstone of Mother's archive, but when I opened the suitcase that ought to have contained them, it had love letters to and from another man, not Wright.

And then, in the storage cabinet where Mother kept her stationery and supplies, I discovered a number of reels of audiotape tossed casually, their slick brown tape unwinding from the plastic spools. Because the reels bore no labels, at first I guessed they were recordings made by my father of our school plays as children. To check before I discarded them, I threaded them onto Mother's tape recorder. At first, the weaving voices, the long pauses, the conversations that followed no discernible track, made no sense to me: What was happening? Who was speaking? Gradually, and with shock, I realized that these were recordings of a few of Mother's psychiatric sessions with Dr. Orne, just a few of the many she had transcribed. Quickly, my hands shaking, I shut off the machine. I stared into space for a while. It had been quite some time since I'd heard her voice, and now to encounter it again so suddenly and in this way: a voice full of pain and fear, a voice tracing the "fever chart" of her own melancholy. Was there nothing I would not see or know before all this was finished? I cried for a while, but it didn't solve my problem. The tapes lay before me on the kitchen table, assuming more significance with each passing moment.

When I had been working on *Self-Portrait*, it had been hell to read the spiral-bound volumes at Boston University that contained her transcriptions of tapes just like the ones in front of me. I had had to confront her admissions in her own handwriting that she had hated and wanted to kill me. I had read her recountings of her sex life with my father — which was surprisingly passionate in the early years. "There wouldn't be anyone I'd rather have sex with [than Kayo]," she told Dr. Orne in 1964. "Even though everything is wrong with the marriage — a week ago we hated each other but in *this* area!" I read of her affairs — "[with] other men sex never meant anything to me" — which were surprisingly passionless until one at the very end of her life, with Philip Legler, the young poet she had met during that visit she and I made when I was thirteen to Sweetbriar College. The idea of having to look at or listen to any more seemed too much — I couldn't bear it. No daughter would ever want to know these intimate details about her mother's life.

Mother had placed her therapy notebooks in the archives at Boston University, a clear demonstration of her intent that they become part of her history. She had left the three tapes in front of me with other papers destined for her archive, and they bore no label instructing me to restrict access to them. Yet I certainly couldn't send these tapes off without listening to them first, any more than I had decided to allow the therapy notebooks to become part of her collection without reading them first.

Even having read the notebooks, however, I was simply not prepared to listen to the sound of Mother's voice speaking again, captured forever like a butterfly in a bottle — beautiful and yet horrifying because it was an artifact of something once living. Ghostlike she fluttered back into the room where I now sat bowed over the tape recorder, praying someone would tell me what to do.

The recordings were filled with the meander of her alternately drowsy and angry voice. I did not want the person on these tapes to have been my mother. They summoned to mind just what I had feared: Mother undone, Mother with her headlighting eyes, Mother having a tantrum, Mother sounding crazy.

I was just suddenly screaming and I couldn't stop.

I drink and drink as a way of hitting myself.

I started to spank Linda and Joan hit me in the face.

Three weeks ago I took matches and went into Linda's room.

> Writing is as important as my children.

> I hate Linda and slap her in the face.

Yet the tapes also contained the seeds of individual poems, and so they reminded me of the afternoons she and I "workshopped" her poetry and mine at the kitchen table. They reminded me of how much I missed her as well as how oppressive I found her illness. They caught the vitality of her voice, the richness and pain of her life. All here, unspooling into my lap.

Perhaps unlike therapy tapes from any other author — had such even existed — these between Mother and Dr. Orne were uniquely relevant to any searching analysis of her poetry. In her poems she wrote about her personal struggles, her mental illness, her life in its entirety; the psychiatrist operating the tape recorder to catch this waterfall of association was the one who had pushed her to begin writing poetry in the first place, the one who figured as inspiration for some of her earliest published poems. As Mother herself had said to Orne in a letter dated April 6, 1961, "Oh, God, therapy is a dirty mirror . . . If I am real, all I have done was born out of therapy, out of our souls and our heads."

At the point at which Mother had entered therapy with Orne, she had written only a few poems, during her high school years — and when her mother, Mary Gray, saw these, she had accused Anne of plagiarism.* Thus Mother carried each one of her new poems to the doctor like a pilgrim's gift to the shrine. The handwritten

---

*In the first edition of *Self-Portrait*, I included two poems, "On the Dunes" and "Spirit's House," which I discovered in a box of Mother's memorabilia from her teenage years, written in her hand. I had assumed that they represented early poetry she had written in high school, and so, along with a poem called "Cinquains," published in her high school literary magazine, I published these poems under her name. Shortly after publication, we received several letters suggesting that perhaps Mary Gray's accusations of plagiarism were not so far-fetched, as "On the Dunes" and "Spirit's House" had been written by Sara Teasdale. With horror I realized that Mother had merely copied out two favorite poems from her favorite poet. The error mine, I arranged for Houghton Mifflin to substitute other early poems of Mother's in the subsequent printings of *Self-Portrait*.

notes indicated her nascent creativity, as the tapes in Orne's possession would document when they came to light years later. Orne's suggestion to begin to put her emotions on paper had acted as the catalyst for the poet that had lived silently inside her for years.

In the long, rambling dialogues recorded by Mother and her doctor lay the seeds of her particular art: the unconscious associations engendered by the Freudian therapy she was undergoing would play out, nearly simultaneously, in another medium — her poetry. This associative process would later become the trademark of Anne Sexton. The therapy notebooks she had left would — together with the underlying tapes — demonstrate the twin processes of association and inspiration and how she made them work for her: the way in which a particular poem, or image, took root and grew, quite literally, in the mind. Those interested in titillating information would be disappointed; there was virtually nothing in the tapes or notebooks of which she had not already spoken openly in her poetry and her play.

Orne had insisted that Mother work hard, get to the root of her experience and her disturbances — no matter how painful. In this way, he was perhaps her first mentor. Her unconscious life was the stream that fed the poetry, and, as such, the links the tapes provided between the unconscious and the poetry would indeed prove fascinating.

Though I recognized the tapes' literary value, in my heart I wanted to burn them and the accompanying notebooks. I admitted this to no one, not even to John. The reasons were entirely selfish: I didn't want anyone else ever to read or hear about her habits of elimination and masturbation; I didn't want anyone to know how often she had cheated on my father. I wanted to lock up the madness, the violence, and the shame that spilled so abundantly into the rooms of her psychiatric treatment and were captured — with room for little interpretation — here, in her handwriting and in her voice.

Why didn't I burn the therapy notebooks and those tapes I

controlled? Some critics would later contend that a loving daughter would have protected her mother even from her own obsessive need to display herself through her poetry. I asked myself at that time, and at many points thereafter, whether my priority as a literary executor should be to protect and enhance the poet's *image* or her *work*. The tapes revealed important and formerly unknowable aspects of the manner in which she created, even as they exposed certain unattractive aspects of her life. As she said to Dr. Orne in 1961: "I can write, I don't have to come in here! I've already got something I can do with my unconscious with this same kind of material — introspection, catching on to something like we do in therapy. The last line of a poem is an insight." Was not her obsessive need to display her life the driving energy behind her poetry? And, as such, was it not as worthy of study as her use of meter and rhyme?

Ultimately, there was never any real question of destroying the tapes in my possession. I could not have done away with any poem, any letter, any object she had included in her archive any more than I was able to refuse her when she asked me to be her literary executor. I knew what *she* wanted; how ironic that with her death the complicated situation of satisfying her demands had altered so radically. In this matter, at least, I believed it entirely appropriate for me to put her wishes above my own. I asked myself this: had Mother won the Nobel Prize in biology, would we not have made her lab notebooks available to future generations of scientists? Burning the tapes, those lab notes full of inspiration, would have destroyed part of her gift to the world — and it would not have protected her privacy, for she had invaded it herself, long, long ago.

Though the conclusion that I should follow Mother's lead and include the three audiotapes and the therapy notebooks in the archive came hard, I had no idea of the enormous ethical issue I had unleashed with this comparatively small decision. It would not be much longer before I learned an astounding piece of news: Martin Orne still had in his possession the remaining three hundred hours of therapy tapes made during Mother's psychiatric sessions.

⟡

All those afternoons Mother and I had spent drinking tea and scrutinizing her poetry were an apprenticeship for the most controversial decision I had to face as her executor. However, once I had decided that I would not impose my own — or the family's — standards of privacy onto her life's work, what then was I to do with the tapes and notebooks? They could not be shoved, unattended, under a dusty attic rafter, as I had once let her ashes linger in my father's closet. I could not secret them away, for eventually my tenure as guardian would end. I was not willing to store them and ignore them, to let the burden and responsibility pass on to someone else. I decided the library at Texas could be a safe harbor where rules could be established regarding their care and usage. We needed a system for these items — the need was greater than for any other single piece of the archive — and a library would have just such a structure. John, who negotiated the contract with the H.R.C. for me, added a section that created a "Restricted Collection" within the archive, and so it was that the tapes and notebooks I had went into the boxes for Texas too, taped and sealed — restricted for now but some day available for posterity.

Mother had trusted me — and it was a trust I desperately wanted to uphold — to protect and manage her work. In the last letter I received from her written only three months before her death, she said, "I know you know the value, the potential of what I've tried in my small way to write . . . maybe, just maybe — the spirit of the poems will go on past both of us, and one or two will be remembered in one hundred years." Her ambition as a poet: to endure. My ambition as her literary executor: to ensure she did — and on her own terms. We were still a team.

And so I kept pushing along, checking off every task on my list. Once the archive was settled at the H.R.C. permanently I could turn my attention once again to my own work, and to the search for the biographer. In 1980, that quest came to an end. Sometime that year, Jonathan Galassi sent me a small paperbound volume written by a Stanford professor of women's literature, Dr. Diane Middlebrook. The idea of finding a biographer whose background was literary criticism, and who would approach the life through the poetry, both appealed to and reassured me. Jonathan arranged a meeting.

Breakfast. The Ritz-Carlton hotel, Boston, overlooking the Public Garden. It was winter. Dressed in a tight, fringed calf-skin pantsuit from North Beach Leathers in San Francisco, Diane Middlebrook was not at all what I expected. Her easy manner alarmed me. Still steeped in the Bostonian provincialism in which I had been raised, I had expected at least a briefcase. Later I would learn that Diane had been equally put off by my attire: I did not then have a winter coat other than my college parka, and so I had opted for Mother's old mink — a hand-me-down from her mother. In an unconscious sense this coat represented a last umbilical link to Mother: it had come from her mother to her, and she had donned it despite the warmth of the October day in 1974 before sitting down in the car to kill herself. It had become, for both of us, a macabre security blanket.

Although the mink was beginning to pull apart at the seams and had turned a brassy red, Diane saw only the fur and what it symbolized. I suppose I looked something like a debutante, decked out in Boston wealth and trying to act sophisticated as a way of hiding my not inconsiderable anxiety.

As soon as we began to talk, though, my anxiety dissipated. I became absorbed by her strong background of literary criticism, her ability to express herself, and her knowledge of the poetry scene in the 1960s into which my mother had made her entrance. Diane was also very concerned about how my father — and the rest of the entire family — would deal with the revelations included in this kind of biography. She seemed to have an implicit understanding of the difficulties the situation imposed: how to write something probing without hurting family members still alive. Her caution relaxed me. If I were able to find a writer whose goals for the book mirrored mine, I explained, I would relinquish control over the point of view of the final text. I believed that with sensitive handling, the truth could be written in spite of the family. I tried to sound confident, but underneath the linen napkin my knees trembled as Mother's had once trembled on the podium on the stage at readings. What if all this backfired?

As I had hoped, the proposal appeared to intrigue Diane, although she admitted to me that while she could well appreciate Mother's work, she was not entirely sympathetic to the dramatic, overblown style of her life. Her wariness regarding Mother's charisma seemed an asset, as I wasn't looking to engage an "Anne junkie." My mother's life story — viewed from certain stereotypical perspectives — could devolve into a flashy case history offering a variety of facile theses: art depends upon madness; suicide is a glamorous way to die; depression is a necessary prerequisite for creative writing and thinking. I did not want my mother offered up as a victim or dismissed as a mental case: she should be remembered for the strong and gifted poet she was, totally human, present in all her complicated faces.

Over the next few months we worked out an agreement that gave Diane full access to materials, implicit understanding that she would have permission to quote from published poetry and letters, as well as my help in making connections with the inner circle of Mother's family and friends. The unpublished material — of which there was so much — presented a more complicated issue, but over time an agreement for this too evolved. I retained control over publication of a small part of the unpublished material but relinquished control over the manuscript as a whole. We were committed.

♵

I waited a while after Diane had begun work to introduce her to my father and grandmother, hoping to persuade them to speak with her. In 1983, I wrote them both letters; with my father, I had often found it less threatening for him when I broached a new idea this way.

I didn't try to intercede directly on Diane's behalf with anyone else but wrote her a general letter of introduction instead. I was surprised but pleased to learn that even Mother's sister Blanche had given Diane an interview, who reported that Blanche was a born storyteller — a family trait, it appeared. But before Diane could interview my mother's oldest sister, Jane committed suicide.

At Diane's request I also wrote to the hospitals who had admitted my mother as a patient and asked them to release her medical and psychiatric records to Diane. All of them complied, although McLean Hospital initially resisted, requiring that I obtain a court order. I applied for one, and the court awarded it, upholding the precedent (now Massachusetts law) that the patient, or the patient's family, has the right to have copies of a medical record. The only hospital that did not produce the records was Massachusetts General, which maintained that Anne Sexton's records could not be found.

Diane copied all the records she received and sent them on to me, but I only skimmed them. I was sick of reading painful material, and for the first time — but not the last — I realized I was glad that the biography belonged to Diane and not to me. When she interviewed me for the first time, I cried and released into Diane's care all the ambivalence I felt at having been my mother's daughter. I was anxious to give it away — and naive enough to believe I could.

Over the years, though, I would read the drafts of Diane's book and be forced to return to my childhood with its moments of violence, insanity, and unpredictability. Back to my emotions. Gradually Diane's book became as much a part of my life as was my own work of writing fiction. Months would go by with no word from her, and then through my front door mail slot would slide a new draft of a chapter from Diane, which I picked up with excitement and dread.

At first, in my own interviews with her, I guarded and avoided certain topics; there was some terrain I was willing to hike across and some I was not. But as I watched the voice of the manuscript grow, I found it easier to confide in her. I could see that I might not like the story she was telling, but I could certainly respect it. The life of her book became my lifeline back to Mother, and Diane became the guardian of that link.

꒰꒱

I had never met Dr. Martin Orne, nor spoken with him on the phone. Early on, Diane had sent him the general letter of introduction I had written for her. However, despite this letter, Orne did not grant Diane an interview until 1985. And not until 1986 did he unleash the revelation that would lead to such controversy when the biography was published in 1991: the existence of the additional three hundred hours of therapy tapes, which it had never occurred to either Diane or me still existed. When Diane called to tell me the news, I was shocked. At first I could only remember my own experiences listening to the three tapes I had found in the stationery cabinet — I could not begin to imagine the pain contained in over three hundred hours of such tapes. But then it occurred to me: Diane would be the buffer; Diane would listen and transcribe. It wasn't my book, it wasn't my job. Within a short time I discovered I was glad that the tapes had survived. Their uniqueness for the purposes of the biography could not be contested.

I heard no more about the subject until late that year, in November of 1986, when Diane wrote to me again.

> BIG NEWS: Dr. Orne has just sent me three boxes, eighty pounds, of reel-to-reel tapes of therapy sessions . . . they are a true goldmine of the incidental stuff that makes biographies so good. She talks about phone calls, letters, prizes, being invited to submit poems to anthologies — all her poet stuff. And I've only heard six hours worth. . . . I'm telling you about this, but I'm not telling anyone else. I decided that the issue of release of psychiatric material is too touchy to crow about; so I made a policy of non-disclosure of what I'm doing until the book acknowledges it in print. . . . I don't want any leaks to get Orne in trouble with professional colleagues, so I decided to maintain complete silence even with people I'd normally share the information with. . . . This decision makes me rather uncomfortable, but seems to me the only way to exercise sufficient control to protect him. But I didn't want to withhold this information from you.

Because I had never spoken to Orne myself, I wrote him a letter to express my gratitude for his willingness to cooperate with Diane. At the same time, she and I quickly came to a private arrangement regarding her use of the tapes.

In a document both Diane and I had signed at the start of her work with the restricted part of the archive at Texas, we had agreed that she would show her notes from this material to no one and provide me with complete copies within two weeks of having made the notes; furthermore, when she began drafting the biography I would have the right to veto any usage of quotes or information derived from the tapes and notebooks. As she began her work with Orne's tapes, she knew that my agreement with her did not imply permission for her to quote from the material or to use information gleaned from it, even though it did give her access. I trusted her, as much as it was possible to trust, but I wasn't a fool.

The arrival of the tapes and Orne's accompanying notes brought about a delay in Diane's progress on the book. "I've only listened to about 75 hours out of 346," she wrote to me in July of 1987 from England, where she was spending the summer.

> Orne's material turned out to be a goldmine, once I figured out how to read his abbreviations; but the outcome has been to blow apart the part of the book I've already written, and of which I've felt so proud. I've had a clear(er), really heartbreaking view of 1956–7: I've seen the depth of her sickness in its earliest forms; and grasped for the first time what she meant about writing her poems for him (Orne). . . . The tapes really are in their way a setback. I haven't yet worked out an efficient way to listen to them — the time it takes is itself a frustration. . . . Sometimes I think back to the first months I spent on this project, when I thought it could be done — easily! — in two years: one for research, one for writing. And of course, it could have: a journalist working even with the unrestricted material would make short work of it, and a good story too. I'm afraid I frequently complain to sympathetic Carl and Leah that no one will ever know what labor it has taken to pull out and piece together the details in my long, long computer files labeled merely with the names of years — once I've done it, it will seem

that it was always there. So this morning I am making you my audience; but somewhere down the years — 1990? — there is a book
lying on a table with the title *Anne Sexton*. We open it and read the
story of her life. . . . Oh, it's a good story.

Still, she didn't regret the extra work:

> *I mean, there is nothing like this in the history of literary biography!* Braiding to-
> gether the doctor's notes gives glimpses of her development as a
> writer and as a person in those years, as she emerges from deeper
> despair than I ever realized before. Perhaps through a failure of
> imagination on my part, I didn't take in what she (and others)
> meant by "breakdown" — I saw her as more neurotic than pro-
> foundly sick.

Once Diane began sending me drafts of the chapters that did
quote from these sensitive sources I relaxed: the pieces of the taped
therapy sessions she chose to use did nothing more than eluci-
date text she had already established from other sources. Nothing
particularly new was revealed in this private dialogue between
doctor and patient, but it did illuminate, quite marvelously, the
burgeoning development of my mother's life as a poet. Never once
did I have to ask Diane to delete a quote from the restricted materials. Questions that arose were solely those of balance: *how much*
to include when making a painful point, but never *whether* to include.

When Diane came to town, we met at my kitchen table to review the progress she had made and the hurdles she still faced. As
always, she was dressed in some marvelously chic but offbeat style.
I came to admire the fluid motion and absolute organization with
which she dealt with her life — and the book. She was always re-
ceptive to a new idea, and she was punctual as well: each time
we met she provided me the comfort of knowing that the book
of my family's life was in control. I made us pot after pot of sharp
café filtre and often we didn't eat, but just sat, drinking and talking

about Mother and our own lives as well, for five or six hours.

Our fondness for each other grew, a respect and warmth that flowed beyond our working relationship. The strong bite of French roast had taken the place of sweet milky tea from the kitchen table of another time.

Call Me Mother

~

"And then she cried . . .
Oh my God, help me!
Where a child would have cried Mama!
Where a child would have believed Mama!
she bit the towel and called on God
and I saw her life stretch out . . .
I saw her torn in childbirth,
and I saw her, at that moment,
in her own death and I knew that she
knew."

— Anne Sexton
"Pain for a Daughter"

WHY DO YOU want to be a mother?" my new therapist had asked me, six months after my first pregnancy miscarried in 1981. At the time I was overwhelmed with grief for the baby I had lost, angry once again at the echoes: death had taken someone I loved with unpredictable swiftness.

"I have a lot of love to give."

"Don't you think that's a terrible burden to put on a child?" she had asked.

I burned with shame, caught on the truth of her observation. Didn't I know firsthand how hard it was to bear the weight of someone else's love? Still, I had no other answer to the question. I certainly didn't allow myself to remember — despite numerous hours spent baby-sitting as a teenager — that children made me anxious, especially small ones with lots of questions and an independent turn of mind, those whose continual "no"s made it seem the situation was slipping out of control. I would never have admitted, at that time, how much these emotions might make me a mother like my own had been, or admitted that my desire to have a child might have motivations beyond the obvious, unconscious urges that I did not then understand.

What I knew was simple: I craved another pregnancy. And so I rejoiced when my test was positive six months later. I stopped drinking alcohol, coffee, and diet soda, got plenty of rest, crossed my fingers through the first most dangerous weeks. As I started my second trimester, I donned maternity clothes and took out a baby-naming book, growing excited now that the stage when miscarriage was most likely had passed. But at fourteen weeks I started to bleed and we lost another baby. John and I wept, caught in a private grief.

Few of our friends understood what John and I experienced both times the tiny lives we had created lost their grip. There was no funeral, no gravestone to mark our mourning. As I had after Mother's death, I felt alienated from the rest of my world. To the storage closet went the maternity clothes, to the back of the book-shelf went the book of baby names. We didn't talk any more about Katherine and Anya, Zachary and Michael. A dark and panicky de-pression set in: were we doomed to be childless? Once again I felt alone: had I hoped the baby could fill the loss of companionship Mother's death had created?

Mother would have put her arms around me and let me cry. Good at comforting a hurt, especially one as deeply felt as this, she never tried to convince me to deny my feelings in order to cheer myself up. I could feel her hovering nearby, a good voice, a wise voice, trying to reach out. Once again I remembered the words of her letter written to me when I was sixteen: "Life is not easy. It is awfully lonely. *I* know that. Now you too know it — wherever you are, Linda, talking to me."

"Why aren't you here?" I shouted back in my mind. "I need you and you're *gone*."

After my third miscarriage in the spring of 1982, desperation at last forced John and me to the doorstep of a specialist in infertil-ity — the partner of the surgeon who had done much of the original research on the cancer-related problems of DES daughters and who had done my biopsies. He warned us that DES daughters were now experiencing a variety of infertility and pregnancy problems

and that we should prepare ourselves to discover the reasons behind the miscarriages. We didn't understand; wouldn't it be a relief
to know at last the reasons behind our losses? To find which treatment or medication to try next? It did not occur to either of us that
perhaps no treatment existed.

The infertility specialist prescribed a diagnostic hysterosalpingogram, a nasty X ray in which an opaque dye is injected into the
uterus and fallopian tubes to determine their structure. I approached the day of the procedure with anxiety over what we might
discover and fear of the pain. I remembered the day Mother had
stood by me when I had had my biopsies taken. I was still fighting
the DES battle, but now I did it without her.

As John held my hand while I waited for the test, I remembered
another hospital waiting room: perhaps fifteen years before,
Mother and I, on hard wooden seats, waiting. I don't remember
what symptom had brought her to the hospital for a barium X ray
that day; I remember only that I was once again the gatekeeper. The
technician gave her a tall glass of barium, thick as liquid clay;
Mother gagged as she tried to swallow it, a gray-green mustache
ringing her mouth as if she were a child drinking a cup of milk.
I panicked, holding her hand and praying she wouldn't vomit.
Somehow she got it all down. To pass the time she taught me gin
rummy — hand after hand, seeking the symmetry of three of a
kind, the well-ordered line of a single suit run. How I had wished
those cards could be the Tarot — predicting the outcome of barium swallows and suicide attempts. We had sat and played our
hands as if life itself depended on it. The tests came back more
normal than our lives would ever be.

Several weeks after my own tests, John and I returned to the infertility specialist's office, where he told us — with a great deal of
sympathy — that I would never be able to carry a pregnancy to
term. The odds: "a million to one." With the black film from my
hysterosalpingogram illuminated in front of us, he pointed out
how my uterus had been malformed by the DES Mother had taken
twenty-nine years before, when she was pregnant with me. Al-

though my uterus appeared normal in its exterior dimensions and on palpation, its interior cavity was severely distorted, appearing as a constricted T shape rather than the normal wide-open V, providing inadequate room for a fetus to grow and thrive. He urged us to stop trying to have a baby and begin looking to adopt one.

John and I left in a state of shock. Back in the Harvard dormitory where we were living then as dorm parents, we sank down on the edge of our bed to cry and hold each other tightly, as if we feared we might slip off into some terrible void. We had lost a part of ourselves and a part of our marriage: the hope to create a family.

Business school ended. My first novel, *Rituals*, was published to good reviews, and I began to work on a second. John took a job in investment banking, and we moved to Manhattan. We tried to put despair out of our hearts. After a lot of discussion, we registered with adoption agencies and private lawyers and began to investigate different ways to find a baby.

Throughout the month of June I felt sick and listless. I left restaurants mid-meal and woke mornings sunk in nausea. I ate a lot of saltines, just as I had when I was pregnant. We felt certain that I couldn't *be* pregnant because each previous pregnancy had been achieved only through the use of a fertility drug. It seemed a cruel joke. Perhaps time would cure me.

But time did not. Exasperated and convinced I was having a hysterical pregnancy, John went out one morning and bought a pregnancy home-test kit, believing that to see a negative result would jolt me back to reality. I gave him the urine sample, watched him measure it out with the eyedropper and went into the other room to work on *Mirror Images*, my new novel.

A few hours later, a whoop from the kitchen distracted me. I ran in to see John standing in front of the test tube, which rested in a stand mounted above a mirror. Reflecting up at us from the bottom of the tube was a small brown donut. Positive. I was pregnant for the fourth time.

I had, in fact, been pregnant that day six weeks before when I sat in the infertility specialist's office in Boston, listening to odds of a million to one. Momentarily I contemplated having an abortion just to save myself the emotional crisis of losing another baby, but naturally hope got the better of me. I found an obstetrician who specialized in high-risk pregnancies, and he put me on immediate bed rest for the remaining eight months. He suggested weekly injections of a hormone believed to help high-risk pregnancies go full-term. Initially I was horrified: my uterus had been deformed by my mother's use of a drug during her pregnancy with me, and now they wanted me to do the same?

I didn't discuss the decision with anyone other than John, humbled by the irony of being in exactly the same position as my mother years before. There was a drug available: it might or might not help. The doctors thought it was harmless, but how could anyone be sure?

I understood now how my mother must have felt when she took the tablets of DES, hoping to save a baby she very much wanted. I had lost three babies and grieved for every one of them. If I had been angry with her for my exposure to the drug or harbored any secret resentment, all of it now washed from me on the simple tide of empathy. I was in the same situation in which she had been, though my choice was complicated by the curse of more knowledge and awareness than had been available to her when she made her decision.

The obstetrician provided us with the pertinent literature on the drug, called Delalutin, a natural progesterone my body was already producing, though in smaller quantities. To use the drug carried a small risk of causing fetal heart abnormalities, cleft palate, and hand and foot deformity. The day we saw our baby's heartbeat on the ultrasound decided us.

Every week John injected me in the hip. I dreamt of giving birth to a child with cancer, whom, like a beloved pet, I had to put to sleep. I dreamt of miscarrying into the toilet, watching the small sac of membrane slide out of my body, lifting it from the blood-tinged water to see that in it sat a small boy in a rowboat, his hair dark brown, his ears the shape of perfect shells.

I lived in terror. I lived in a state of constant prayer. I would have given anything for this baby to be born whole and healthy. I looked everywhere for signs and portents. I stayed on my bed rest as rigidly as it had been prescribed for the remaining eight months of my pregnancy. During these months, typing in bed, I finished the first draft of *Mirror Images*, which gave me a creative outlet. Into this novel went all my emotions: I gave my voice to the heroine, Eve, who was also a "habitual aborter"; when Eve became pregnant for her third time I gave her Mother's voice too, let her binge on the midnight batches of butterscotch brownies my mother had baked and then eaten when she was pregnant with me. I remembered Mother's stories of her pregnancy cravings — ice cream sundaes, blond brownies, and more blond brownies — and compared them to my own — milk, cookies, and glazed doughnuts. And the one hunger we shared: fried-egg sandwiches, made just the way Mother had taught me when I was fifteen.

At the end of my novel, Eve lost her baby. Unconsciously I believed that if I created a story about miscarriage — if I lived it through Eve — perhaps it wouldn't have to happen to me again. Each month that passed, a little more hope grew inside of me.

I talked with Joy and my father several times a week. Daddy was surprisingly supportive about listening to both my fears and my fevered descriptions of every detail of the growing pregnancy. He wasn't ready to be a grandfather, he claimed, but he suddenly seemed ready to be a very supportive father. I depended on him for the emotional warmth I had once sought only from Mother.

When I felt the baby move inside me for the first time — a tiny tickle, a butterfly wing brushing my insides — I was stunned. Now he was no longer an image in a sonogram, a picture in a child development book, an idea, a series of possible names. He defined himself with that one motion and made himself heard, giving the first sign that he was a connected yet separate being: a voice spoke from within, and it did not belong to me.

In the bathtub at night, I talked to the baby through the wall of my belly, promising him that if he would just arrive safely, I would be the best possible mother. Never before had I felt such a fierce commitment. By now I was certain I was carrying a boy.

In the last two months of my pregnancy — when I began to truly believe that we might actually have this baby — I swamped myself with books on child development, looking for answers to all the questions other women might ask their mothers. *Where the hell are you when I need you?* I thought.

Mother hadn't really told me much about her own labor, and so her silence conferred upon this travail an aura of indescribable pain. She had promised me that she would be there for my labor, as her mother had been there for hers; she had promised me that she would rub my back to help with the pain, as Mary Gray had rubbed hers. My father had been in the navy at the time Mother went into labor; John would be by my side for the birth. She had had her mother; I did not. I was scared. *Where the hell are you when I need you?*

I did not know what kinds of drugs they had given her, or how long her labor had been. She had not called her breakdown after Joy's birth postpartum depression, but all my work in the archives of her life had led me to believe she had certainly experienced just this kind of depression. Perhaps what had only been postpartum blues had deepened into an even more acute illness — and that idea terrified me. What was going to happen to me? My desire to talk with her came over me like a fierce and unanticipated hunger, surprising me: why did I so crave her presence now when, as a mother, she had always seemed such a failure to me?

John's parents also lived in Manhattan, but his mother warned me in advance that she did not enjoy babies and advised us to get a nanny as she had done for her children. I smiled politely and told her I was going to handle it all myself. Perhaps, unconsciously, I expected that Nana would somehow miraculously appear as *my* mother-in-law — taking over and managing superbly. Or perhaps I expected that my children would shortly grow up to take care of me, as I had once taken care of my mother. Or perhaps I was just in a state of massive denial.

In February 1983, after thirty-six hours of intermittent, painful labor à la Lamaze, I gave birth to a healthy, seven-pound baby. "It's a boy!" said the obstetrician. "I know he's a boy," I said grouchily. "Does he have all his fingers and toes?" This was not an idle question, considering our fears about the drug I'd taken during the pregnancy, but in fact Alexander was whole, complete, and already crying. Alexander, the million to one. *I* was a mother at last.

How I wished Mother were there to hold him. She would have told me he was beautiful and written a poem for his birth. In the last few months before her suicide, she had bought two copies of the picture book *Goodnight Moon* — one for Joy and one for me — so that we would have them when our children were born. She was looking forward to being a grandmother, I think, even as she knew she would not be by my side to witness my crossing over to this new stage of my life. Holding the book on my lap, I showed Alexander the pictures even as tears made it difficult to see. *We're reading it, Mom.*

After Alexander was born, I relaxed a little. At first, being a mother to him was everything that I had dreamed and nothing that I had feared. The smell of his silky head, the clutch of minuscule fingers against my breast as he nursed. Cleaning him, caring for him, dressing him in soft cottons — doing a good job with my baby brought me free-floating joy. In that first month his world determined the parameters of mine. Inside me lay a deep pool of love; as with a new romance, every time he drank it brought me pleasure, and unconsciously I scoffed at Mother's difficulties and my own earlier fear.

However, as he woke more to life around him and his demands began to increase, and as I woke more to the responsibility he brought me, I began to feel anxious. Previously I had worried about losing him in a miscarriage, but now I worried about losing him through some obscure and hidden fault within my character. Was there lurking in me — as there had been in Mother — some hidden flaw that could be brought out through the stress of raising a child? Though I pretended to be in full control, diapering and nursing, stimulating and rocking, the isolation that surrounds caring for an infant wore on me, fraying my nerves. *Is this how it began for you?*

It was March in New York, windy and raw along the river our apartment overlooked. How long before I could take him to the playground? I wondered. How long before I could find some other women with babies who would just sit and talk on the edge of the sandbox, or around the kitchen table, as Mother once had with Sandy and Rita. I longed for sunshine and something other than my own four walls. Two of my college roommates lived in Manhattan, but they both worked during the days, and John left the house at seven every morning and didn't return until nearly eight every night.

What sort of a mother was I that I did not know how to fill our days? That I felt lonely instead of complete? Emotions from my own childhood began to plague me. Through his small life, my life replayed itself. I was terrified of leaving Alexander alone; I was terrified of being left. I couldn't imagine finding a baby-sitter so that I could go get my hair cut or have my teeth cleaned. I began to sink under the stress of not being able to leave my child with anyone except his father, even though I needed desperately to get out for just an hour or two.

I was twenty-nine years old, in contrast to my mother's twenty-five when she gave birth to me. I had no family near who were able to help with the baby, or even to advise me on matters of babyhood. I craved Nana's input, but whenever I called her in Boston she was either too sick or too tired to talk very long about Alexander. Her health had been slipping for several years by then, and, if anything, she needed mothering herself. The woman who had once mothered me so expertly was now eighty and with her own difficulties.

Diane Middlebrook came to visit, spending an afternoon with Alexander and me. I had looked forward to her arrival for weeks. We talked about her work on the biography, and she held my baby and pronounced him handsome. When she left that day, however, I crashed, oddly depressed and disappointed. Unconciously I had hoped that for one afternoon Diane — the bearer of my mother's story — could somehow *be* my mother. I hadn't missed Mother this much in a long, long time.

She hadn't been a good mother, I thought, not the kind of mother I would be — and yet I wanted to share my mothering with her. I wanted to see her cuddle my son, laugh with him, tell him a story. I wanted to tell her of my loneliness and my fears and hear her reassure me. I wanted to laugh with her. As the years passed, my longing deepened.

My fantasy had been that if only I could *have* a child, I would not go back to work. I would be *only* a mother until Alexander was grown, or at least I would work only part-time. A better mother than my own, something like Nana, but not just like Nana. I had daydreamed about a large family, of perhaps five or six children. What a shock then to find myself ready to flee our small apartment at four in the afternoon, when Alexander began what had become his routine three-hour crying jag.

Our pediatrician diagnosed colic. Hold him this way, I was told, fly him like an airplane over your arm. Make sure he burps ten times. Slide a thermometer up his rectum to help him bear down: sometimes a bowel movement helps. (The doctor neglected to suggest standing back from the changing table while executing this maneuver, and so while trying his suggestion one day I was covered by an explosion of loose and yeasty stool.) The four-to-seven arsenic hour persisted. There was no one to take over, no one to keep me company, and nothing I did helped. *Where the hell are you when I need you?*

When I picked Alexander up and let him know he was not alone (for me, a particularly poignant image), he did not respond by relaxing. He kept right on crying. And I got more and more tense, my arms becoming a stiff and uncomfortable cradle. Now I understood *why* a mother might want to hit her baby. I saw in my mind my own mother, her hands around my throat as I lay as an infant in my crib. The image haunted me, frightened me, as I paced the floor with my baby. In desperation to stop his noise I fed him and fed him again. I gritted my teeth against the pain in my sore nipples, against my own frustration. At last I sat on the sofa and cried with him, defeated. This wasn't at all the way the books had promised it would be.

During these weeks, I sat every night in the bathtub and cried, waiting for him to wake for his eleven o'clock feeding, which was followed by the two A.M. and the four A.M. (He didn't sleep through the night until he was six months old.) John kept pleading with me to get some help, but I was stubborn. "I can do it," I insisted, craving help but enraged by the idea that someone should suggest I needed it: I was sure that only working mothers or bad mothers needed help.

I had prided myself on being self-sufficient and totally different from my own mother. Alexander's needs, however, evoked in me a response not unlike that which I had felt at nine, when Mother had put her head down on my flat little chest and said, "Now you be the mommy." When Alexander cried against my milk-laden breasts, once again I was transported back into the role of the mommy. This time there were no words that could reverse our positions.

Surprisingly, it was my father who pulled me through those impossible first months by mothering me. He began calling around 5:30 when he got home from work. By then Alexander would have been fussing nonstop for an hour and a half, so I had worked up quite a lather of fury and frustration.

"Has he been fed?" Daddy would inquire.

"Three times."

"Did you put him in his bassinet?"

"Three times."

"Where is he now?"

"Can't you tell?"

"Why isn't he in his bassinet?"

"He's screaming."

"Did you change him before you put him down?"

"Twice."

"Has he got a pin sticking him?"

"Disposable diapers have tapes, Daddy." Even in the midst of a symphony of Alexander-thunder, this difference between the generations made me smile.

"Then," he instructed, "put him in his crib, get a *big* glass of wine, go into the bathroom, and turn on the shower." This advice ran counter to every bit of childhood-development reading I had done. This was the old-fashioned approach I had sworn I would never take.

Still, I was desperate, and so, given permission to be so irresponsible as to ignore my baby's cries, I did just what Daddy prescribed. It worked. Alexander still cried — but only for a little while, and because I couldn't hear it, I wasn't compelled to fix it. Gradually I began to believe that Alexander did indeed "need to cry" — just as adults sometimes do — to relieve himself of frustration. The desire to comfort, to smooth out the difficulties of my child's life, ran strong within me: identifying with his small and helpless state, I desperately wanted to fix every hurt, even those that could not be fixed. Once left to his own devices, however, Alexander began, within a few weeks' time, to go to sleep easily on his own, or just by being rocked, without the hysterics.

When he was a month old, I began to revise the manuscript for *Mirror Images*, holding him in my lap or over my shoulder as I sat at my computer. Suddenly it seemed terribly important that some part of every day not revolve around his schedule, that a few hours be marked by *me*. Working with him on my lap sufficed for a month or two more, but gradually I began to realize that I needed to find someone to watch him so that I could work without interruption. I was ashamed to admit that I wanted — no, needed — to go back to work. In my mind's eye, I saw my mother hunched over the typewriter while a two-year-old Linda hid in the garage or sat in front of a meaningless soap opera; I rejected one-half of the image — but not the whole.

With John's help, I found an older woman to baby-sit. At first Hazel came to our apartment an hour or two a day and took care of Alexander in his bedroom while I hovered suspiciously in the living room, trying to write. Soon, however, even I acknowledged how ludicrous such an arrangement was, and within a few weeks I arranged instead for Hazel to take Alexander to her apartment for four hours four days a week. There she wrapped him up in a grand-mother's love, adored him unreservedly, and wrote me progress notes of his daily activities.

During those hours I wrote like a fiend, and then did a few se-lect errands, filled with guilt at my secret pleasure: what luxury not to have to take a cranky baby through the narrow aisles of the local grocery store, with the stroller dragging behind me and the cart shoved ahead of me; what freedom not to have to think about him for four whole hours. On the playground that spring I finally met a few other women with children the same age. We had nothing in common except our babies, but that was enough. I really didn't care what these women had done before they had their children, I didn't care if our backgrounds were as different as Beverly Hills and Bangladesh — they were *mothers*. I joined a play group in an osten-sible search for friendship and socialization for Alexander, though what I really sought was companionship in motherhood for myself.

In spite of my anxieties, I adored Alexander without reservation. Having found Hazel improved my mood immeasurably; reestab-lishing my connection with my work made me feel steady and competent for part of the day, and those emotions made me more patient with Alexander when I picked him up at one o'clock. Once again I was feeling a little smug: despite my initial depression, I hadn't beaten Alexander or tried to choke him, and I hadn't been hospitalized either. I had a dream in which I told my therapist that having the baby was like taking a test. "I passed!" I said exultantly. "I passed!"

Just before Alexander's first birthday John and I decided to try and get pregnant again. Who knew how long it would take us to create the family we envisioned? Alexander himself was by then at a lovely stage — a just-turned toddler busy investigating, but not yet a two-year-old ready to say no and challenge me for control.

This time I became pregnant quite easily and stayed that way without spending a day in bed. Nicholas Gray was born on

October 4, 1984, twenty months after Alexander, and ten years to the day of Mother's suicide.

༞

Needing more living space than we could afford in the city, we moved shortly before Nicky's birth to a suburb outside Manhattan. Hazel obviously could not move with us, so, at last, I acknowledged my need for some sensible, live-in help if I were to keep working and mothering simultaneously. We hired Wendy, an au pair from Salt Lake City, to live with us and watch the children in the mornings so that I could write.

Just after Nicholas was born, the essence of my third novel, *Points of Light*, began to waft through my mind. I constructed the plotline around one of my most passionate fears: the devastation a mother would experience at the death of her young child. I made this fantasy into my own story by living every day through Allie, my main character, sitting before my word processor and weeping as I gave voice to a terrible pain, the event a mother dreads above all others — permanent separation from her child. The novel became a magic amulet, a talisman to ward off the possibility that my fiction could become my reality, just as *Mirror Images* had ensured that Alexander be born rather than miscarried.

With the arrival of my sons, a transformation had begun inside of me: a long, slow shift, as if I were a riverbed whose shape and substance were being irrevocably altered by the turbulent water of my children's childhood, which stirred up the gravel and silt of my own. It was no accident that my fourth book departed abruptly from the three that preceded it. Instead of being written from the daughter's point of view, as had *Between Two Worlds*, *Rituals*, and *Mirror Images*, *Points of Light* looked outward through the eyes of the mother of three small children. I was writing at a furious pace and couldn't seem to slow down.

Unfortunately, when I sent my editor at Doubleday an excerpt, she did not like *Points of Light*. Suddenly I found myself on the open sea of seeking a new publisher. Mother looked on with concern from her airplane in the sky, saying, "Bear up, honey. I know it's hard." Suddenly I realized how lucky I had been with the other books, how much I had taken for granted, and, once again, how much I still needed her, still relied on that warmth I believed surrounded me in troubled times like these.

I switched agents, I switched publishing houses, I started over. It took nearly a year, but eventually I found a new home for my work. Fredrica Friedman, my new editor at Little, Brown, spent long hours reading and rereading the manuscript and then offering line by line criticism. At last I had found the sort of working relationship I had shared with my mother. The book grew stronger, cleaner, better. I dedicated the book to Mother and turned in the final draft sometime the next spring. About a month after I submitted the final manuscript my agent phoned to say that the book had been seen by several paperback publishers and that a very high "floor" for the auction had already been offered.

Points of Light went on to be reprinted in eleven foreign languages. Twentieth Century–Fox acquired the rights for a full-length feature film, and Avon printed half a million copies of the paperback. Perhaps I had finally achieved, albeit in a small way, a measure of the success Mother once had. For the last decade, ever since turning aside from Mother's work in pursuit of acquiring a readership of my own, I had burned not to be known as "Anne Sexton's daughter." I wanted people to know that I, too, was a writer with an identity all my own. As if to confirm this, an editor at the *New York Times Book Review* called me and asked whether I would be interested in writing my first book review for them. I felt as if I had overcome this hurdle, at last.

For Thanksgiving that year, Joy and her husband, Steve, came down to New York. John was away for business the weekend that followed the holiday, and I was glad for their company. We were sitting in the family room of our new home, talking and drinking after the kids had been put to bed, when I heard Nicky, then four, climb out of his bunkbed and start down the stairs, calling my name.

When I got to him — feeling annoyed that he was up and intruding on the first peace and quiet I'd had all day — he was crying.

"Zan won't share!" he informed me when I asked what was wrong.

"Share what?"

"Zan won't share the purple soda!"

Purple soda? Taking Nicky's hand, I climbed up the rest of the stairs to investigate.

On the top bunk, Alexander sat like a pasha, licking his lips.

"You're supposed to be asleep," I growled. "What are you doing?"

He answered me with a five-year-old's giggle and held out an empty bottle of Dimetapp. "I love the candy medicine," he said. Then he handed me the child-proof cap.

The bottle had been full the day before when I had given him some for his stuffy nose. *How did he get the cap off?* I wondered. A tremor of anxiety rippled through my mind. I took the bottle and read the label in the light. *In case of accidental overdose, call poison center immediately.*

Joy put her head around the corner. "What's going on?"

"He drank this."

We went out into the hall. She looked over the label. Joy is a nurse, and that night I hoped that she would tell me not to worry about it, to go back downstairs and finish my drink.

She didn't.

The poison hotline advised me that the dose Zan had swallowed was "potentially lethal." My hands started to shake. I knew I should never have written *Points of Light:* having tempted the gods, now I would be punished.

Joy and I dashed back upstairs, asked Steve to take Nicky downstairs, and then got out the Ipecac that I always kept on the top shelf of the locked linen closet — where the Dimetapp ought to have been, rather than in the medicine cabinet, because little monkeys like Alexander have no trouble standing on top of the bathroom sink when they are feeling curious. Joy stopped me as I turned to go back into Alexander's bedroom. "Wait," she said, "I'm a nurse, let me do it."

"I'm his *mother*," I answered fiercely. I might have been scared beyond logic, but no one was going to take my job away from me.

I was glad to have Joy there, however, as Alexander began to stagger around his room, drunk from all the alcohol in the cold medicine, as he refused to take the Ipecac, as he began a long vomiting marathon. God, I was so scared — and she was so calm. Once again, we were a team in a dangerous situation. When Alexander wanted to go back to sleep and I had to keep him awake for another hour just to make sure his system was clear, Joy helped me tickle him, tell him stories, shake him awake. I was glad to have Joy beside me when Alexander lifted his small face to mine and said, in the clear tone of innocence possessed only by a child, "I hate you, Mommy. I hate you for making me throw up."

"Do you remember," Joy asked me, as we mopped up the bathroom floor sometime past midnight, "that little boy at our house on Clearwater Road? The one who locked himself in the bathroom and ate everything in the medicine cabinet?"

"Mother had someone over for lunch? Was that it?" I asked, my memory slow in returning.

"They were eating downstairs in the kitchen and the kid locked himself in the upstairs bathroom," Joy went on. "I went and told Mother he was there and she rushed up — remember how she could take the stairs two at a time?"

I laughed. "She hammered on the door, I remember that. And his mother was sobbing."

"I think his name was Dougie. Mother shoved us all in her car. It was that old green Ford then, wasn't it?'

I nodded. "She went through all the red lights, and I kept worrying we were going to get killed."

"We got him to Emergency in time, though," Joy said, as we tucked Alexander's comforter in around him. "Mother was pretty good in a crisis."

"And who'd have thought that. She was so bad at managing everything else."

We went downstairs to find Steve and Nicholas. "Do you remember the time the frying pan caught on fire?" Joy said. "Or how about that blizzard when Daddy couldn't get home and there was no food in the house and Mother invented her weird casserole?"

"Anne's Blizzard," I answered, thinking that Joy, too, was a storyteller. "That's what she called it — potatoes, hamburger, frozen string beans, and canned tomatoes. Not too bad." We turned the corner into the family room; Nicholas and Steve were asleep on the couch.

༃

Alexander reminded me of Joy as a little girl: he was always getting into trouble, always up to something. Watching him grow gave me a snapshot view of our early time together as sisters — Linda the good but whiny and Joy the naughty but vibrant. Joy had been the one to stuff her mouth full of purple beets and then spit them out in the driveway, and Alexander was the one who stuffed his pet dinosaur down the toilet — "because it bited me ferocious" — and backed up the plumbing to the tune of one hundred and fifty dollars. Joy was the one who dared walk the railroad trestle over the river as a shortcut to downtown Newton Lower Falls, and Alexander was the one who climbed onto the roof of the house, or to the crown of a thirty-foot tree.

When I had conceived Nicholas less than a year after Zan's birth, I had not anticipated how hard it would be to have two small children at once; my sons' birth dates were even closer together than Joy's and mine. And, of course, I was still planning to have perhaps one or two *more* children, breaking with the tradition my parents had set and that Joy herself — in a younger marriage than mine — had yet to test. If I had, as in my dream, "passed the test" of motherhood, perhaps I could become a different sort of woman than my mother entirely. But as Alexander moved deep into the tunnel of two and three years old, I began to find him harder and harder to cope with.

He had his own room, in which I had set up two tall bookcases filled with all the children's literature I could find, from pop-up books to hard-backed classics. John and I both fantasized that Alexander would be an early and avid reader, just as we had been.

One day shortly after his third birthday, he picked up his child-safe scissors and cut the pages out of every book he could reach. I cried, on my knees, as I cleaned up the chaos he had created. Already alarm bells began to sing in my mind, but I refused to acknowledge them.

On his first day of nursery school I tried to summon a semblance of calm and override the anxiety I felt. I didn't get angry when Alexander stopped on the walk in front of the building and refused to go any farther, sucking furiously on his pacifier, as other mothers and their willing children passed us. Finally, I picked him up and carried him in, whereupon the teacher reprimanded me: "Look at your body language — is it any wonder he's terrified of his first day?"

Her words provoked me to look beyond the immediate for some larger meaning. Why had I picked him up, rather than insisting he walk on his own power? Why had I not implied with my action that I had confidence in his ability to make this difficult step? After a while, I had to admit the truth: Alexander's first day of school reminded me of my own fear from years before — that anxiety-ridden moment when, finally, I had to face a room full of children I didn't know and an unpredictable adult in charge. And the days before, when I hid in the garage rather than experience again the separation from my mother. I didn't want Alexander to feel alone the way I had.

My reassurances in the car on the way over that day had no doubt made Alexander absolutely certain that we must be headed toward some terrifying destination; he spent the entire two hours of that first session sitting on my lap rather than participating with the other children in the classroom. Already the teacher had us pegged as a troubled pair.

This confusion about the boundaries between my past experiences as a child and Alexander's current experiences as he grew continued to plague us both as my unresolved emotions came flooding back to me through the conduit of his childhood. Without intending to, I had appropriated his life to reexperience mine in both its terrible and terrific aspects, in a futile attempt to reenact and heal the past. The act of others leaving, even temporarily, re-created in me that old sensation of abandonment. Watching my son at these same thresholds filled me with an anxiety so intense it threatened to sweep me away.

As his curiosity and independence and misbehavior increased, I found myself stretched to the point where I snapped at him or Nicky or both, hating myself as soon as my mouth opened. "Stop it!" I would scream when he punched Nicky in the backseat of the car. "Do you want me to pull over and put you out?" His face paled as I threatened him with the same separation — to be left alone and frightened, discarded by the side of the road — I myself had endured. I was sick with guilt. I never said it again, but what did that matter? I had said it once.

An undercurrent of rage began to grow in me, one I didn't want to look at at all. Having been beaten by my mother and father and by Uncle Ed when I was a child, I had always resolved I would never touch my own children with anger in my hands, yet several times I found myself close to spanking Alexander. One day, when he was screaming in the bathtub because he didn't want his hair washed, his shrieks reverberating off the tiles and bursting inside my head, I lost control. I smacked his bottom until we were both exhausted, tears running down, faces red from the moist heat. And then we sat there and hugged one other as if we were the last survivors in a shipwreck. I remembered the way Uncle Ed would hug me after he had beaten me with his strap, how sweet the pleasure of being forgiven can be. Love follows the purge that violence provides. Would I now teach this brand of perversion to my children?

The guilt swept in as my mind filled with images: Linda as a little girl, bent over Mommy's lap; Anne, her face enraged, a sneaker or a brush in her hand as the weapon by which she made her blows smart. My father, his hand descending on the hot target of my naked fanny. As that summer wore on and I struggled not to express the rage I felt toward my son in physical ways again, sometimes I did not succeed. I spanked him though I knew better, though I knew it was wrong. Desperate to make some distinction between Mother and me, I never used anything more than my palm so that I could tell how much it hurt. Inside me, however, I knew: regardless of my rationalizations, I was spanking him out of anger, as once I had been spanked. And it didn't work anyway — he just got naughtier and naughtier, as if to say, "You can't make me do what you want just because you're bigger."

Nicholas, too, was becoming more independent as the days went on. I was getting more and more shrill, all without meaning to. At the back of my mind I must have realized the parallels between my emotions and those of my mother: when I was three years old and Joy nine months, Mother had truly disintegrated. This was the time frame during which my sister and I were sent to different homes. Was I unconsciously replicating that old pattern of events? I buried that idea as quickly as I could.

One day in that summer of 1987 finally destroyed my illusions of how distant I was from my mother's "weaknesses." The trouble began in earnest one Monday morning when my new child-care helper did not come to work and did not call. I had a panic attack: I couldn't breathe, my heart felt as if it had grown wings and was beating an escape out of my chest. I was desperate. John delayed going to work. I called a friend who was a psychiatrist, who in turn recommended a doctor he thought could help me.

Under the care of this man, I stopped spanking my children and wrenched myself back under control. I accepted my first "psychiatric" medication, the anti-anxiety drug Xanax. This I used reluctantly for a few months until I learned that I could live through anxiety attacks, even when they happened daily. I taught myself how to keep my temper in front of the children, no matter how difficult. Some days I failed but increasingly I succeeded. Little by little I was putting distance between the kind of mother my mother had been and the kind of mother I wanted to be.

I found a new baby-sitter for the children and began to calm down. Alexander calmed down. Nicky smiled nonstop. Gradually my anxiety left me. I could breathe again. Control was returning. I began to understand that although my alternatives might be limited by who I was, or by what my childhood had been, I still did have the ability to make some choices — intelligent choices that

took into account my own weaknesses and needs rather than cater-
ing to them. For the first time, I was determined to be a better
mother than *I* had been.

When it came time to enroll Nicholas in nursery school, I pur-
posely chose one where our new nanny, Jana, could take him on his
first day. I stayed at home and paced the floors, determined that he,
at least, would not be subjected to my anxieties on a day when he
had his own with which to deal. To my surprise and joy, Jana returned to report that Nicky had simply walked into the room and
begun to play with the other children. He'd never given her a second glance.

Jana would stay for two years, and then send us her friend
Cindy, who stayed for another eighteen months. This time was
blessedly free from worry. I knew the luxury of wonderful help and
stopped being ashamed for needing it. Once the kids were enrolled
in the public schools from nine until two I discovered I could manage writing and mothering without help. The crisis period seemed
to have passed.

As the children grew I found myself called upon to do the sort
of volunteer activities my mother had always successfully avoided
and that I initially scorned, following the example she had set.
Gradually, however, I allowed myself to be drawn in, juggling this
work with my own because I could see how important it was to become involved with my children's school. I helped in the classroom,
I drove field trips, I joined the PTA Mother had so disdained. I sat
on our school's Site Council to make budget decisions, chaired a
committee that awarded grants to teachers for special classroom
projects, and became a member of the Board of Directors for the
foundation that supported our public school system in the lean
nineties. I learned how class placement can be political and I became my children's advocate. I felt more and more secure in the
kinds of roles my mother — with her agoraphobia — had found
impossible. I might be anxious, but I was managing. I was not
Mother.

My mother loved to play Monopoly, and for her marker she always chose the iron, a metaphor heavy with irony, for she never

lifted an iron in all the years I could remember. Now I am the mother who chooses this symbol of domesticity to play long afternoon wars over Boardwalk and the railroads with my children, and I, too, delegate most of the ironing to my cleaning woman. Now I am the mother who helps my children memorize their poems for performance in class: I stand at least a room away, just as she did when teaching me to project my voice. She taught me all the secrets of her spaghetti sauce, long-simmered all day in a deep pot, rich with whole Italian tomatoes. Spaghetti was one of the few meals she enjoyed making, instructing me to use the can of plain tomato sauce her recipe indicated "with creativity." I could never understand how canned tomato sauce could be used creatively, and I have never used it. Maybe she never did either. Over time I have added ground carrots for sweetness, sausage for spice, and more garlic and oregano than Mother ever would have dreamed of throwing into the pot.

Little by little I have grown into being a mother. No more sensitive or empathetic than Anne, but more controlled, more able to draw boundaries, more able to be the adult my children need. When I was eleven Mother did not allow me to remain at camp because she needed me too much. This year my children expressed the desire to go to the East Coast for camp, to leave their home here for a summer in Maine. When I told friends and family that Nicholas and Alexander would be spending July, and possibly August — if they so chose — at sleep-away camp in another state far away, many expressed their horror. "Are you ready for the separation?" they asked. To ask about *my* readiness is to ask the wrong question, I think. I need only to assess whether or not *the children* are ready. In retrospect, I'm sure Mother would have agreed, despite her inability to manage it that way herself.

I imagine how she would sit around the kitchen table with my children now, throwing her head back with laughter at one of Alexander's jokes, applauding Nicky's innumerable and dramatic antics; she would have enjoyed watching them grow, strong and inquisitive as they are, both of them ardent story writers, both of them proud enough to take Grandma Anne's books with them to school — along with mine and John's — for display when it is their turn to be "person of the week." Earlier this year, I walked through our local bookstore with Alexander — now ten years old. The paperback edition of Diane Middlebrook's biography was prominently displayed, its cover the signature photo of Mother in her black-and-white dress, legs twined, facing outward. Alexander stopped in front of it. "Look," he said, "there's Grandma Anne."

I put my arm around him. "Isn't it strange to see your grandmother here like this?"

"It's stranger never to have met her."

We stood in silence for a moment more, then turned and walked toward the door.

"I miss her," I said then.

"I'm sorry, Mom," he answered, and then, overcoming his burgeoning distaste of physical contact with his mother in public, he took my hand and squeezed it. A gift. "I wish I could have known her."

I squeezed back. "Me, too."

My children have helped me to grow up, and I feel gratitude for this. The battle I fought with myself — to provide for them a reasonable level of predictability, a set of rules they could live by, the emotional security that comes from knowing there will be no more sudden surges off the cliff into an abyss of anger — is the most important achievement I have ever made.

How many emotions come to me now, rapid-fire, in the course of overseeing their days: sometimes weariness or impatience, sometimes firmness, sometimes anger, but more often tenderness and empathy. They call me mother and my voice answers, sounding the joy I feel in my ability to do just this — what for many lucky women may come naturally or simply, but which for me was so difficult to learn.

Mother, I have improved upon your recipes for spaghetti sauce and for mothering. I have taken your ability to create and to love and made them my own. Bless me as I offer these parts of you to your grandchildren. Though they will never meet you, in this way they do indeed know you.

Exposures

A woman
who loves a woman
is forever young.
The mentor
and the student
feed off each other.
Many a girl
had an old aunt
who locked her in the study
to keep the boys away.
They would play rummy
or lie on the couch
and touch and touch.
Old breast against young breast.

— Anne Sexton
"Rapunzel"

I EXPOSED MYSELF to Diane Middlebrook's tape recorder in private, sitting in her study or mine, drinking endless cups of strong black coffee. Like the slow unfolding of a rose, petal by petal, each motion deliberate and in its own time, the process could not be rushed or forced. Some revelations took years for me to release.

My desire to emerge from Mother's shadow had grown even more intense during these years. Diane had boxed up and carted off the story of Mother's life, but I still had to face the fact that I had chosen to work in a field in which Mother had achieved fame, notoriety, and respect. Although immediately after her death I had given a few readings of her poetry, now I always refused and turned down offers to speak about her to the press as well. Every time I had one of my own books published, I told the publicity department I would not exploit Mother's name and that they must make sure I was going to be interviewed about my own work and not about my family tree. I was getting sick of stumbling over Mother every morning when I turned my word processor on.

I had begun to feel like a ghost. I never volunteered the fact that I was Anne Sexton's daughter, even if I was among other writers; if others asked me about our relationship, I answered abruptly and changed the subject. I wanted to erase all my connections to her. However, being a writer made it very difficult to put distance between us.

Though I continued to work steadily on trying to develop my own career as a novelist, the themes and situations about which I chose to write kept returning, however unconsciously, to that primary relationship with Mother. In *Mirror Images*, I explored my feelings about having been too closely entwined with a strong, dependent mother. I cast this theme in a fictional disguise, an erotic relationship between the mother, Vivian, and her daughter, Mira. In the process of writing, however, an odd phenomenon occurred and continued to recur whenever I was creating the scenes of incest in the book: working on my first word processor, I began to type, quite unconsciously, in the first-person voice of the daughter and in the present tense as well — even though the rest of book was crafted in the third person, using the past tense. Although this shift in the novel's point of view created a break in style, it felt oddly compelling to me and I left it intact. Why did it sound so much stronger? Why did I feel so mesmerized by, so submerged in, my young character's pain? Why did my body feel as numb as hers? At that time, I was not prepared to ask these questions nor to find answers.

Years after writing those scenes, however, in the midst of that period of depression and anxiety that began when Nicholas and Alexander were babies, I went one Wednesday to my therapy session and something unexpected happened.

I was lying on the couch, my eyes lingering on the window and the tall plants at the far end of the room as I mused aloud. As always, my analyst sat behind me, out of sight, silent except for the creak of his rocking chair. I had begun talking about one thing, speaking — as the analytic contract requires — of whatever came into my mind, without editing or revising the thought, when suddenly I felt restless. I shifted uneasily on the couch under an attack of nausea. I thought about asking to leave but didn't. Couldn't. Something was coming up at me from behind, like an idea trying to get written, but worse. Bad. I closed my eyes to get away from it.

"Go on," he said, after I had paused mid-sentence and not picked up for a while.

I was spinning dizzily on a sea of anxiety. "I can't," I said, beginning to cry. "There are these pictures I see, in the blackness in my mind."

"What kind of pictures?"

"Mother's body. My body."

"You mean the times when you saw her masturbating on the bed, or in the tub?"

"Yes. No. More than that. Oh, it's getting worse. I feel so sick."

"Let it go."

As a print in a bath of darkroom developer acquires sharp edges, definition, substance, I saw before me not just a snapshot now but a scene entire. I moaned.

"Where are you?" he asked.

"Asleep. Somewhere. Not my bed — the blanket isn't heavy enough for it to be my bed — it's the electric blanket on my parents' bed. I'm keeping my eyes closed. Don't want to open my eyes, don't want to wake up. I'm pretending."

"Pretending what?"

"To be asleep. I always pretend, if I pretend then after a while the bad feeling goes away. But now I'm opening my eyes. It's so dark."

"Who are you with?"

"Daddy's traveling. I can see the orange light of the clock across from their bed."

"How old are you?"

"Seventh grade. I had a fight with my best friend and her mother says I'm a bad influence. Oh, I have to keep my eyes closed! Keep thinking. The bad thing — I can smell it, it's getting closer. I can't breathe! There's no air here! The weight is horrible, it's like dying under a truck. I'm suffocating!"

Sobs choked me. At the same time I was back in my parents' bedroom I was also there, right there, on the psychiatrist's couch. I could feel my doctor's presence. He said nothing, waiting.

"The bad thing — on top of me," I blurted out. "I can't breathe! Oh God, she's so disgusting!"

"Why is she disgusting?"

"Her tongue — it's in my mouth. Wet and slimy. She's putting the poison down deep inside! Why doesn't someone come to help?"

"There's no one else there," the soft voice behind me said.

"Why don't I get up? Why don't I push her off?" The sobs boiled out of me, mucus streamed from my nose.

"She's very heavy."

"I want to scream — get off, get off, get off! I hate you! I'm going to throw up. Let me up! She's following me to the toilet. I'm throwing up the poison but it burns. I'm crying and she holds my head. She's pressing a cool washcloth on my forehead. Now she's being my mother again."

I gagged, swallowing down a pool of saliva and tears. My chest ached as if I had vomited up an enormous stone — the stone was the words I never said all those years before. My mind had held time a prisoner; once memory was released from behind the bars I had so carefully kept in place all those years, I had been assaulted by the past. Memory turned on me, caught me by the throat, shook me with a leer: *So you wanted to know? Well, now you do.*

"Was she masturbating on me again?" I asked him, desperate, wanting to throw myself on his lap and be hugged, but I just lay there, hugging myself and shaking with a terrible chill. "Did it happen more than once?"

"Does it matter?"

"What do you mean?"

"What she did was enough." He kept rocking. "What you know is enough. You don't have to be raped by your father to call it incest. When there's radioactive fallout over Europe you don't need to be told there was a nuclear explosion at Chernobyl."

My time was up. I wanted to go home and be held by John. "Will he think I'm disgusting?" I asked my analyst with anguish.

"Why would you want to let him know that you fooled around with your mother?" he replied, looking appalled that I would even make such a suggestion.

He escorted me to the door. He did not pat my shoulder or my hand. He did not tell me I had done a brave and painful thing in exposing myself to my memories. He did not tell me that I might want to calm down in his waiting room before trying to drive my car. I felt overwhelmingly alone. And dirty.

I sat in my car in the driveway. I couldn't stop crying. I hyperventilated until the gray sky above my head spun. Finally I crept home, hands shaking on the wheel. I went to bed and hibernated, allowing my au pair to care for the children for the rest of the day.

My shame was deep, my voice silent again. I did not tell John. Not then. Several days went by before I got angry. *I* had been fooling around with my mother? By what stretch of the imagination could this interpretation be valid — *she* had been fooling around with *me*. Out of the anger came a small but growing certainty: parents bear the responsibility in setting limits — children don't.

Over time I have accepted the useful points my analyst made: this single memory, coupled with the others of Mother masturbating on me early in the mornings, or in front of me when I was small, was ample. The knowledge I had retrieved stood as yet one more confirmation of the terrible complications I knew our relationship had suffered. As for definitive answers and precise facts — memory offers no such luxuries. Memory insists I gamble and take what I can get without bankrupting myself. What I have remembered is more than enough already. As for my analyst's cold attitude during my pain that day: even though I am resentful about his lack of compassion, I discover I am simultaneously grateful to him — for his long silences allowed me to move into discovering the truth for myself.

How easy it must have been for Mother to take advantage of me, infinitely trusting as I was, desperate to please her, wanting her love and adoration above all. I asked myself over and over why she couldn't have controlled herself when failing to do so brought such trauma? I was nowhere near ready to forgive her. But the entire incident brought new light to my own unfolding relationship with my children; it explained why I felt so haunted by the importance of establishing these same boundaries my mother had been so incapable of observing.

To this day, I sometimes feel the irresistible pull of my sons' unconsciously provocative behavior. A rain of tiny kisses from my child's soft sweet-scented mouth can tempt me, tender unlike any other caress. My body, like any body, an odd collage of instinctual drive and continually engageable nerve endings, can still react on a level purely biologic, even in the most inappropriate of situations.

Unlike my mother, however, I draw lines none of us can cross: as a family we cuddle plenty, but with pajamas on, and only at the children's invitation. I remain willing to discuss the sexual questions my children ask me, but I volunteer nothing, careful not to pressure them to grow up too fast. I never slam the door in their faces if they walk in on me as I am dressing, but I don't parade around naked either. Today Alexander and Nicholas initiate discussions about homosexuality, contraception, and AIDS, which they learn about in school classes and through the media. They see me as someone they can turn to with questions but they also know I set limits. I love my children — and so I fight hard to guard against my own unconscious desire to re-create my past.

When I first came to admit my memories of my mother in inappropriate sexual situations, and then when I heard some of these memories corroborated in her own words in the taped therapy sessions,* I judged and hated her for what I considered her weakness and her selfishness. Still, I kept asking myself, why did I not push

*For example, in a therapy session with Dr. Orne in 1961, when I was nine and Joy seven, Mother struggled to examine her relationship between us and the sexual feelings we aroused in her. "You said [talk about] sex. — Could talk about my children. — I don't want to say what comes to mind. . . . The children's relation to my body: six months ago taking a bath, touching [my] breasts, later in bedroom with Linda says did milk really come out? Can I find out? I said yes. I didn't know at what point to back

her away that night when I was in the seventh grade? Why did I not scream, "Get off! Get off! Get off!" as I had done in my therapist's office? Why did I swallow the words and vomit instead?

I could not claim rape, as if she had been a strong man who gave me no choice, and this question in particular haunted me: did I have an alternative? The answer, arrived at reluctantly, but also with relief because it felt honest, was yes. I did have a choice. I chose not to push her away because my priority when I was twelve and thirteen was to minister to her desires and needs (whether she was crazy or well) rather than to my own. I would always, it seemed, be the gatekeeper.

Still, I wasn't a martyr: I had my own needs answered as well — emotional needs. I had endured the loss of my mother repeatedly as a child; risking it again as an adolescent had seemed too painful. By becoming her best friend, her confidante, even her companion in bed, I ensured my position at her side. I would have allowed her anything she wanted to remain thus situated. And so, like my character Mira, I made myself numb, made my body a stone in exchange for my mother's love. When I reread Mira's words and hear my own voice, I still want to cry, to mourn the childhood I lost.

To keep these events a secret from the man with whom I shared my life — as my analyst had suggested — only increased the shame that had crippled me for the last twenty years. Healing the damage began when I felt comfortable enough to let down my guard and share this part of my history with my husband; only when I was

---

out. . . . They make me feel more womanly. Joy kissing the other breast, I wonder if I'm taking it a little too far. . . . Linda got sand in her bottom at the beach. I gave her the washcloth and told her she could wash it off herself. She pointed to her clitoris and said her friend Nancy said this was just like a boy, that it will grow. I said that's your clitoris and it won't grow, but when you have intercourse, mating, it will feel good there. She said you don't have one of those all you have is hair. So I showed her. So I told her she should masturbate then she'll know that it feels good there. But maybe this is too intimate. This is usually what you do with your friends, not your mother." Orne: "Why do you want her to masturbate?" Anne: "I'm just making it a little more right if she does."

able to acknowledge what had happened to me could I begin to dig a grave for those events.

I spent years more in therapy, shouting my resentment, stoking my anger over the betrayal I still felt. I wanted to reclaim the childhood of which she had robbed me. I hated her for having refused to mother me, for using me sexually and emotionally.

After a time though, my fury began to exhaust itself with its own combustion and to burn less brightly. I began to remember the other times I had spent with Mother, those that had nurtured and inspired, not just those that had damaged. Little by little I began to miss her again as well as hate her. As the years have passed I have discovered that love and empathy play side by side with anger, fear, and resentment.

Still the stain of trauma remains, and probably always will, especially when sex is *expected* of me. Then sometimes, at the first embrace, a kiss, or my husband's hand on my breast, I am flooded with pictures I try to beat back. I lose my place in time, and once again my throat closes down and I choke back my scream: *Get off!* No matter how hard I try to change this scenario — through years of psychotherapy or with sheer determination — I sometimes come back to that dark night when my mother's sticky body lay tightly on mine, the stink of her booze breath, the legacy of fear and self-hatred with which she left me. Of all the mistakes Mother made, this one was the hardest to forgive.

ﾞﾞ

Several years after my therapy roused this particular memory, I read another draft of Diane Middlebrook's biography, then nearing completion. In possession of my own history at last, I began to see some startling parallels that remained invisible to Diane. As with everything else in Mother's life, her work of the imagination tapped down deep into her daily existence, both present and past.

In the mid 1960s, the period during which she pushed me for an increasingly inappropriate sexual and emotional intimacy, Mother was absorbed in writing *Mercy Street,* her loosely autobiographical play, produced off-Broadway, about a daughter's incestuous entanglements with both her father and her loving aunt. The play exposed many of her most deeply intriguing — and troubling — fantasies and ideas.

The source of the plot for Mercy Street stemmed from Mother's questions regarding certain memories she had of her father, Ralph, and her Nana, Anna Ladd Dingley. Mother's recollection of her father sitting on the edge of her bed, drinking and fondling her, and then of being discovered there with her father by her Nana, was also mixed up with the sexual feelings engendered by special "cuddles" with Nana on the couch in the older woman's bedroom, cuddles whose essence would also be caught in suspension in the poem "Rapunzel," from *Transformations*.

During the eight-year course of her analysis, it remained unclear to both Mother and Dr. Orne whether these elusive memories were real or just stories spun from subtle events and sexual feelings that never bloomed into outright acts of incest. However, Mother had an interest in understanding the emotions these scenes had created in her so that she could use them as fuel for her writing. Whether the incest actually occurred did not matter to her as much as it might have to other people. The draft of the biography I was reading — drawing from the wealth of material from the taped therapy sessions, and tying it to the scenes of incest in Mother's play — outlined all these questions in frank detail.

At the time Mother was writing *Mercy Street* and was tapping her own unconscious for emotions long buried, I was in the midst of puberty much as was Daisy, her heroine — close to the age Mother had been when her relationship with both her Nana and her father became so complicated. In reading Diane's manuscript during the summer of 1989 with my own memories of incest near the front of my mind, I suddenly saw how all these complications had merged in Mother's mind twenty years before to form a knotted and inseparable tangle of emotion and action.

In the letter Mother gave to Maxine for safekeeping in 1969, she alluded to the confusion she felt between Nana and me. "I wonder about your sexual self and if it will be happy . . . My relationship with you is like mine with my nana." As I perused that nearly final draft of Diane's, I once again entered that period of our time together when Mother was consumed by the incest depicted in *Mercy Street*, the incest that still burned so hotly in her own unconscious. New questions and conclusions boiled through my mind. When Mother came to my bed and masturbated on me, was she perhaps re-creating what might have happened to her as a child and what was also happening to her character Daisy, on stage in *Mercy Street*?

And then, when I at last escaped from her sexual needs, had she not insisted upon replacing one intimacy with another by making me the confidante for her descriptions of adultery? Once her Nana had supposedly stood at the threshold of Anne's bedroom to witness what my mother and her father were doing on the bed. Surely Mother's confessions to me of her adultery were a metaphorical re-creation of that scene as well: at fifteen I was assigned Nana's role, a disapproving figure in the doorway.

That summer of 1989, I lived inside Diane's version of my life with Mother — poems, text, play — and all of it seemed to reverberate with the themes of intense love among family members — sometimes sexual, always complicated. "Little Girl, My Stringbean," "Rapunzel," and "Sleeping Beauty" wrestled with these same issues, and many were written during the same period:

> *There was a theft.*
> *That much I am told.*
> *I was abandoned.*
> *That much I know.*
> *I was forced backward.*
> *I was forced forward.*
> *I was passed hand to hand*
> *like a bowl of fruit.*
> *Each night I am nailed into place*
> *and I forget who I am.*
> *Daddy?*
> *That's another kind of prison.*
> *It's not the prince at all,*
> *but my father*

drunkenly bent over my bed,
circling the abyss like a shark,
my father thick upon me
like some sleeping jellyfish.
What voyage this, little girl?
This coming out of prison?
God help —
this life after death.

— "Briar Rose (Sleeping Beauty)"

I kept thinking about telling the entire story to Diane. Mother's poem about Briar Rose felt as if its voice had come straight from my own heart. Was it possible that the biography might benefit by drawing these disturbing parallels between Mother's childhood and mine, as well as between Mother's daily reality and the imagined life she created within her work? Was it possible that out of my own shameful event, which I had so longed to bury, Diane could harvest some worthwhile truth?

Perhaps reading the drafts of the biography that summer helped me — for the first time — to understand and empathize with the sexual complications Mother's own life had contained. While reading the introduction Dr. Orne, Mother's first psychiatrist, had written for the biography, a new insight jolted me regarding her love affair with Dr. Duhl: however hurt and angry the rest of us might feel, Mother was the one who had taken the worst of the impact when Duhl curtailed the affair and the analysis.

Having ended my own analysis of four years' duration only the year before I read Orne's introduction, I was keenly aware of how vulnerable a psychiatric patient can be and of how much trust must exist for therapy to be successful. As is common, many of Mother's fantasies were of a sexual nature, directed toward the doctor, as she worked out feelings transferred from other situations in her life. Just as a child discovers her early sexual self through expressing her erotic feelings toward her parent, both parent and analyst must allow the expression of these complicated emotions within the safe harbor of reassurance that such fantasies will never be acted upon.

I found myself identifying with what Mother had gone through; I found myself feeling curiously empathetic.

Still, how could I bring myself to speak openly about any of these ugly events to Diane? How could I allow their inclusion in a book many thousands might read? Filled with dread, I explained to Diane that there was one final topic I wished to discuss off the record. And thus it was, sitting at my kitchen table on a sunny day, that I exposed this part of the story — awash with humiliation, but with determination as well. I cried, I trembled, I hoped Diane would understand. She held my hand, and tears stood in her eyes too.

We sat silently for a while. I could see she was shocked by this aspect of the story of the relationship between Mother and me, but not surprised. We both understood, intellectually at least, how those who are wounded seek unconsciously to re-create the original trauma. Sometimes we are lucky enough, or persistent enough, to achieve the insight that enables us not to act out these earlier scenes of our lives. Mother had been unable to do that.

Once I had thought that my mother didn't love me enough to keep herself from hurting me. Once I had judged her to be selfish and weak, but by the time Diane and I sat at my kitchen table I had come to a new understanding: Mother just hadn't perceived this aspect of herself and her history well enough to guard against the inevitable compulsion to repeat, re-create, and recast the past. Even if she had, her sickness would have prevented her from controlling herself well enough to have avoided it. However I might rail at the unfairness of it all, that was the truth of that time. The day I began to accept this was the day I began to forgive.

Diane and I agreed that I would read the material I had given her in the context of the final draft, and then decide if I could bear to see it published. Sometime later, as she approached the final stages of manuscript editing, she was having difficulty reconciling her desire to tell Mother's entire story with her desire not to cause pain — either to me or to other family members, particularly my father. It was the summer of 1990, and I was in the midst of finishing the last draft of my fourth novel — ironically entitled *Private*

Acts. Sparked by Diane's concerns and my own feelings of vulnerability, I recalled my mother's answer to her friend and early critic John Holmes, regarding the personal revelations her poetry required: "At first it was private, then it was more than myself."

I urged Diane to press on. "Why include that Anne crept into bed with Linda and masturbated on her," I inquired rhetorically in a letter written that July,

> except that it had everything to do with writing *Mercy Street* and "Little Girl, My Stringbean" and remembering her own experiences with [her] Nana and even perhaps (I would think) a good deal to do with the affair with Anne Wilder? Why include that she beat her children — except that it follows the thread of her own childhood, that thread of travesties which (without insight) we are doomed to compulsively and vengefully repeat? If we must hear the truth, let us hear it all. Let us be able to say at the end: this is the price and reward of madness; this is the price and reward of genius. This book must now move onto a new level and stretch for the ideal she aspired to and quite often achieved: to tell the truth no matter how painful. You have already written a great deal that is painful. This has been very difficult for me to read, more so than at any other time. No family member will ever like this book. You must not care about that any longer: it is an impossible task. We are all hurt by it. We were all hurt by having lived through her life beside her, behind her, in her shadow, holding her hand: that is reality. Of the joy we have also spoken. The only way to transcend the hurt is to tell it all, and to tell it honestly.

Diane gave me one last chance to back out before she sent the book to her editor. I wavered. I talked to John, for courage was required of him as well. He encouraged me to let it stand. I told Diane to leave it in when she submitted her manuscript.

On that afternoon in my kitchen with Diane, I did not foresee that my decision to be open about Mother's sexual relationship with me, as well as my other decision regarding the release of the psychiatric tapes — so calmly and logically arrived at in 1985 —

would later be transformed into a hornet's nest of controversy. I was not yet wise enough to anticipate that exposing myself and my deepest feelings to a biographer in the privacy of my kitchen in no way resembled speaking to "the common reader" from the front page of the *New York Times*. Nor was I savvy enough to predict that, despite the pain the controversy would bring to me personally, it would also create, quite unexpectedly, a *Times* bestseller. Once again, Mother would be front-page news.

The phone drilled into the dark middle of night, smashed open the cavern of sleep. In the instant in which I opened my eyes I was once again sixteen, and an old story reverberated through the darkness: Joanie dying, dead and gone in the instant between a ring and an answer.

But no. This was July 1991. I was thirty-eight, and this intrusive sound did not signal a phone call at all but belonged instead to the fax machine, which was attached to an old-fashioned phone with a bell rather than an electronic titter — a phone like the one that rang in May of 1967. It sounded into the dark only one time. From my bedroom, I heard the machine chatter, sending the sheets of slick paper down onto the floor of my office, a room away.

I looked over at the clock that glowed in green display: 5:30 A.M. I turned on my side and tried to go back to sleep, breathing deeply to slow my heartbeat. John shifted position three times, pulled the pillow over his head, then rolled onto his back and sighed. He padded off, naked feet drumming the hardwood down the hall to my office. A few minutes later he was back and settling himself in again.

"So what was it?"

"Nothing."

Instantaneous adrenaline. Awake — as in a fire drill. When John says something is nothing, you can be damned sure it's impor-tant — and unpleasant.

"What's nothing?"

"Just a fax from the East Coast."

"About what?" I was starting to get drowsy again.

He hesitated. "It's an article from the *New York Times*. About Diane's book."

Diane's book. I rolled onto my back and stared at the ceiling in the dark. I had spoken to Alessandra Stanley of the *New York Times* a week before, in an interview about the biography, but I had shelved that phone conversation at the back of my mind. The book wasn't due for publication until September.

"How can a piece for the Sunday *Book Review* be out when it's only Monday?" I felt confused. "And it's two months early."

"It's a *news* article. On the front page. About Dr. Orne and the tapes."

I got up and went in to read the fax.

Then I walked to the end of our driveway in my pajamas, picked up my *New York Times* and read the article again — just the way a million other people were reading it up and down the eastern seaboard over their coffee.

Even though I had been helping Diane for ten years and knew perfectly well that the book would raise controversy, I was in no way even remotely prepared for the sensation of standing up naked in public and letting people stare at me. The phone calls began: from newspaper people and magazine writers, from television publicists and my friends.

Had I been stupid? Had I been smart? Had I been motivated by anger, greed, by self-aggrandizement? Had I been acting in Mother's best interest? In my own? All these questions to which previously I had had sturdy answers began to spin through my mind that morning as I sat at the kitchen table and stared at my mother's picture on the front page of the *New York Times.* I thought to myself how easy it would have been simply to have kept quiet, to have burned what I did not like, how easy it would have been to shut the door to our lives instead of *inviting* everyone in.

A few days after the first article in the *New York Times* appeared, my phone rang one more time. I was in the kitchen, preparing our supper late in the afternoon. I answered to hear my cousin Lisa's voice over the line.

Lisa Taylor Thompson had appointed herself spokesperson for her branch of my mother's family, as the eldest daughter of Mother's sister Blanche. She had had a career in television production before retiring into marriage. Several years my senior, Lisa has always spoken with authority.

I had not seen her since about 1980, when Joy and I had been invited to Blanche's house for dinner. That was the first time in many years we had gotten together with this part of the family, although we all lived in the Boston environs. That dinner had been stiff and awkward for me, not one I wanted to repeat; seeing Uncle Ed again had brought on an anxiety attack.

This afternoon some eleven years later, Lisa was angry: she and her mother were very upset about the impending publication of the biography. Initially Blanche had been most cooperative with Diane, happy to have the opportunity to air her belief that my mother had had a very fortunate childhood — despite the manner in which Anne would later depict that childhood in her poetry. This alternative viewpoint was pivotal to Diane in creating a complete and balanced picture of Mother's early years. Yet, even though Blanche's opinion of the family had been represented in the manuscript as one of several different perspectives, when my aunt was given a draft of the chapters regarding her sister's early family life, she asked that her own name and direct quotations be withdrawn from the book.

Evidently, Blanche was upset that her perspective on my mother's childhood was not the *only* one Diane had used. She was outraged at the portrait Diane had drawn of her parents, Ralph and Mary Gray Harvey, as capricious adults who gave and withheld love on whim. Though Diane had included Blanche's stories of wonderful Christmases and summers on their Maine island, tales of Anne's antics with friends, of the wealthy and privileged life they had all led, she had also included Anne's judgments — excerpted from poetry, letters, and psychiatric records — that her parents were emotionally abusive alcoholics. The speculations that Anne might have been molested by their father came in a later draft, a draft that Blanche had not seen before the front-page article ran in the *Times*. Why had she not seen that draft? Lisa demanded. Why hadn't I stopped this travesty of a book? One more time I explained that I was not a censor and that I had no approval rights over the manuscript.

Lisa reminded me that Mary Gray and Ralph were my grandparents too. This brought me up short, for I realized that I didn't think of them as my grandparents at all: to me they seemed more like characters in a book. They had died when I was only five, but Lisa had known them far longer.

Later Lisa and her sister would write to the *New York Times* to protest the negative portrait the biography had drawn of the Harvey family. In her letter she claimed that my grandparents' family was normal, even though my mother's sister Jane had also committed suicide; even though Ralph Harvey and his sister Frances were both treated and intermittently institutionalized for alcoholism; even though Frances would also kill herself; even though Mary Gray's aunt, Anne's Nana, was institutionalized for a mental breakdown at the end of her life.

Alessandra Stanley's article on the front page of the *Times* was only the beginning of a two-month period during which I lost my privacy, but what a beginning it was. Ultimately, in scores of articles, the press did not damn me for having censored my mother's life — as they did Sylvia Plath's family for destroying her private diaries after her suicide. Instead, they vilified me for having exposed her, for allowing her to be seen where she had placed herself throughout her life: naked and quivering on the examining table of her art.

Newsweek cast me as the disgruntled daughter who had "settled the score" by despoiling her famous mother's image. Some of Mother's friends did as well, and their accusations cut deeply. I retreated inward. I couldn't deny that I did still have feelings of anger toward my mother. However, was that anger so in need of vengeance that it constituted *the reason* I had chosen to give Diane Middlebrook access to the tapes and to expose the other painful material about our relationship?

By reexamining this question over and over again in my therapy sessions, I was finally able to reassure myself: though I was still angry, that anger was not why I had released the tapes. I had made my decision based on the knowledge that the tapes would illuminate the roots of the poetry; that Mother considered them important enough to have placed those in her possession — and her transcriptions of them *all* — in her archive. During her lifetime my mother had never held back her private life.

What did I have to gain by releasing the tapes? A loss of my own privacy, the anger of the family and many of Mother's fans. Releasing the tapes neither improved my life nor eased the anger I felt.

The subject of the tapes had become a cause célèbre in the press, but no one was more affected in a negative sense than Dr. Martin Orne. The American Psychiatric Association required him to answer charges of violating medical ethics through his involvement with the biography. This review by a board of his peers struck both me and Maxine Kumin, who, along with thirteen others, came forward in support of his case, as a very sanctimonious witch hunt. If he hadn't allowed Diane Middlebrook to listen to the tapes, if he had tried to deny me access to Mother's records, I would have obtained a court order for their release, as I had done with McLean Hospital. In contrast, how ironic — and how tragic — that the APA appears never to have bothered even to investigate — much less censure — Frederick Duhl for his sexual relationship with my mother while she was under his psychiatric care.

I loved my mother when she was alive; I love her still — despite anger, despite her mental illness and the things it allowed her to do. I never wanted her to seem like "a monster" to anyone. She was loving and kind, but she was also sick and destructive. She tried to be "a good mother," but in truth, she was not.

Mother was simply human, subject to all sorts of frailties and problems. Other people want to remember her only in certain lights, a legend of sorts. They may not want to hear that anything Anne Sexton did was less than perfect, or less than helpless, or more than a mere inevitable result of the society in which she made her way. In enriching the reality of the woman she had been, perhaps the biography had destroyed the very limiting image of the woman who was victim: to her mental illness, to her abusive husband, to a society that had oppressed her as a female by asking her to be solely a housewife and mother. Until the publication of the biography, none of the tragedy in her life had been her fault. Yet in her relationships she was often capable of, and insistent upon, taking responsibility for her share of troubles: insistent upon shouldering blame and apologizing; insistent upon reconciliation. However she might have felt during her most self-pitying periods, when she was at her strongest and her most creative she would never, ever, have wanted to be viewed as a victim.

Just as I do not see her as either victim or monster, I do not see myself as a victim of abuse or a monster of revenge either. The rich yet troubled relationship my mother and I shared is too complicated for labels as simplistic as these.

Rather than remembering the angry reactions to the biography, I try to keep Mother's last letter to me — the one in which she asked me to be her literary executor because she trusted my judgment — foremost in my heart. Despite the difficulties, I treasure her faith in me and the resilience she nurtured in me — for this, at last, is what brought me from anger to forgiveness.

On the Back of Love

I have gone out, a possessed witch,
haunting the black air, braver at night;
dreaming evil, I have done my hitch
over the plain houses, light by light:
lonely thing, twelve-fingered, out of mind.
A woman like that is not a woman, quite.
I have been her kind. . . .

I have ridden in your cart, driver,
waved my nude arms at villages going by,
learning the last bright routes, survivor
where your flames still bite my thigh
and my ribs crack where your wheels wind.
A woman like that is not ashamed to die.
I have been her kind.

— Anne Sexton
"Her Kind"

BY THE TIME *Anne Sexton: A Biography* was published in the autumn of 1991, the publicity had almost exhausted itself. Diane Middlebrook went off to tour many cities, the book moved onto the bestseller list and then off it. I was left with a strange feeling of dislocation and depression. Gradually I began to realize that I was envious of Diane's success — and Mother's as well.

Although I didn't admit it to myself, in the last year before the publication of the biography, I was struggling not to get discouraged about the progress of my own work. My latest novel, *Private Acts*, was not finding an audience, and sales were flat. My mood dipped lower and lower.

As the winter wore on, the disappointment over the novel led me to worry about whether Little, Brown would be interested in

my next book. Mother's voice, prophetic, whispered once again in
my ear: her warnings of the ego blows, of the lean years, of the
emotional hardship that accompanied the inevitable rejections —
"Don't be a writer, Linda." I tried not to listen, but in truth I felt
discouraged. I wished she were there to talk with and discovered
that I had begun to miss her again. *Where are you when I need you,
Mother?* Having revealed my anger to Diane about my sexual experiences with my mother, the anger itself had grown dimmer. I grew
depressed over losing her again, as if her death were an old wound
that ached on rainy days.

Disappointing sales figures affect everything to come, as if the
writer is a dog chasing his tail in a downhill tumble: if the figures
go down for one book, the publisher doesn't want to advance much
for the next; if they don't advance as much for the next, the book
gets less in the way of advertising, because advertising and promo-
tion budgets are often based on the financial stake the publisher already has invested in the book. It takes a certain amount of luck, as
well as the right manuscript, to break this vicious cycle.

I knew that this time Little, Brown was going to be very careful
about signing up what I chose to write next, and so I made a radi-
cal decision. I would try to write a different kind of book, one with
less risk of getting buried — a psychological thriller. Maybe it
would be fun to get away from the more intense and emotional
writing I usually did. I centered *Bedside Manners* around the story of
a female serial killer who retaliates for the sexual abuse she endured
as a child. Rapidly I discovered that working within the format of
a thriller was fun. The form had well-defined boundaries, and I
didn't have to sit and weep over my characters' lives as I did so often with my more emotional books. Maybe I had just gotten tired
of sitting around and crying.

A thriller took more plotting than I was accustomed to, reminding me of a jigsaw puzzle in reverse: beginning the work from the
middle and then moving outward to the edge pieces. Despite the
elaborate outlining required, the pages bloomed up quickly on my
computer; suddenly I felt happy and optimistic again, as if I were
standing on a beach after a storm had blown out to sea, sand and

surf swept clean by the wind. My writing felt solid and clean, and I looked forward to sitting down at the computer every morning. When it was about forty pages long, I sent it off to my literary agents.

They hated it.

Never before had my agents disliked my work. With a tinge of desperation, unwilling to accept the calamity of their negative response, I told them I would revise it, enrich it with more pages and more fully developed characters. Perhaps it was still too much a creation in my mind, not yet fully alive on the page. After that they could send it to my editor, who would have to be the final judge.

The approaching publication of the biography intensified my unconscious need to have a project of my own well under way — immediately. I felt that without the shield of my own writing, I would be caught naked when the spotlight came up on Mother. Two hundred pages later, alternating between fear and confidence, I sent my manuscript back to the agency. The good news: the book was considerably stronger. The bad news: my editor didn't like it at all.

Both my agents and my publisher thought *Bedside Manners* would damage my career. By this time the biography was on the bestseller list; for the first time since I had begun writing sixteen years before, my accounts were in the red. Mother's star was once again in the ascendancy; mine was in the gutter. Depression overcame me again, but I would admit it to no one, certainly not myself. Determined to appear undaunted, I told myself I would get back to work as soon as possible, as if nothing terrible had happened.

But how to go back? What to do? I began to sit and stare into space instead of working.

I had been well advised by this publishing team in the past. To ignore their reactions would have been crazy. But was it possible they could be wrong? Secretly I was very angry, suspicious that they were negative simply because they could not envision me writing anything other than the same kind of novel I had always written.

I took a break for a month and then decided to reread the manuscript: if I still believed in it, then I would push ahead. For that month I drifted, fighting depression, longing for something totally apart from my writing life. I decided to check out Dalmatian breeders. Our Dal girl came to us, like Penny, when she was about a year old. At the home of the breeder who cheerfully took my pet puppy deposit, show-girl Rhiannon laid her head upon my lap and studied me with eyes that knew my heart. Mother had called Penny's eyes soulful, and Rhiannon's were no less so. They comforted me. It seemed a sign.

When I went through the new novel again, I decided perhaps I had trivialized the issue of sexual abuse — a subject about which I obviously felt quite passionate — by setting it in a genre format such as a thriller. I rubbed my hands together at the thought of a new project, and my mood swung upward once again; I decided I would lift the scenes of sexual abuse and locate them in a book more traditionally my style — psychology, high emotion, a plot built around family relationships rather than murder. I plunged right back in. It never occurred to me to take more time off because my life was now dominated by the silent fear that I would never again write something publishable. Depression was waiting in every day of silence. I filled extra hours with volunteer work for the schools, working and showing my new dog, planting elaborate gardens. I kept myself as occupied as possible. The old dichotomy stood in my mind: Mother working; Mother sick. Working had always pushed back depression for me. I craved it now as never before.

Late in 1991, while winter was setting in, I chose a new title, *Night Vision*. I used, in transformed version, some of the characters from *Bedside Manners*, and some of the scenes of sexual abuse. The writing came very slowly to me now, but by early 1992 I had twenty-five pages and a well-developed outline. I sent them off to both editor and agent simultaneously, an act that indicated my desperate need for quick approval. I pretended to be certain of the manuscript and cheerful to have weathered the earlier storm of rejection. I told myself how happy I was to be writing once again and congratulated myself on not allowing depression or discouragement to overcome me, as they might have Mother.

When both editor and agent called to say they didn't like *Night*

Vision any more than they had liked *Bedside Manners,* my world simply stopped. I went into shock.

My agent, forever kind, demonstrated her concern by being gentle. "You *are* a writer, Linda," she said. "You're just going through a terribly hard time. Why don't you take some time off?" Feeling angry and betrayed, I informed her I *certainly* wasn't going through a hard time and that I was *certain* the material was solid.

"I just don't see your usual passion in it," she replied.

I was now at the bottom of a deep dark well. Far above me shone the world of my children, my husband, my dog. How would I ever climb out? Did I even want to?

Knowing that the book had been rejected by an editor whose opinion and skill I held in high regard made writing nearly impossible. Anxiety assaulted me every morning when I faced the blank screen of my computer. Some days I would reread the previous morning's work and be pleased, but three days later it seemed insipid or obvious — or even worse, boring. Riding these wild swings, I revised and revised as if I were a dog worrying an old wound, and it became increasingly difficult to move forward into new material. Although I was accustomed to working steadily, a few new pages a day, remaining mired in old chapters now felt safer than summoning the strength required to make the unconscious leap to create new ones. Finishing a single chapter sometimes took more than a month.

In July the problem came to crisis: a major block, unlike any I had ever known. I couldn't think of a thing to write. I was dry. My throat felt parched, as if in literal imitation of my voice having evaporated. Now I sat alone, deserted by my editor, my mother, my muse. At the bottom of the well, I slumped into nothingness. I was no one. I had nothing inside to offer. And now a voice came to me, a voice that hissed in my ear, dangerous as a hornet: *"You'll never write again."*

A migraine headache descended together with the depression — but far worse than the migraines I had had on and off for many years. Mother, too, had suffered from migraines, though not as intensely. Earlier that year I had tried Prozac, an antidepressant, to relieve the stress I believed was causing my steadily worsening headaches. I could not admit to myself, however, that secretly I hoped the antidepressant would do what it had been designed for: help my depression and anxiety. I did not want to admit that I was depressed because I did not want to seem like Mother. And, it seemed, there was always a mood swing that brought me back to the top, that made me know I was *not* like her.

This headache, however, lasted for three weeks. Hours every day floated by, fuzzy hours woozy with painkillers — and still I had the pain. And the nausea. And the dizziness. The pain and vomiting escalated; I made an emergency trip to the doctor for an injection of Demerol and Phenergan.

As adolescents, both my sister and I had had fantasies about substituting sugar in the capsules of Mother's nightly rainbow assortment. We hated her addictions, which seemed symbolic of her mental illness — her lack of control, a metaphor for *our* lack of control. We wanted to believe that she could get off the drugs if only she would make her mind up to it. We wanted to believe that she, and therefore we, had a choice.

The internist finally told me that my migraines had become chronic because I had taken so much medication that I had become addicted to the painkillers.

> *Sleepmonger,*
> *Deathmonger,*
> *with capsules in my palms each night,*
> *eight at a time from sweet pharmaceutical bottles*
> *I make arrangements for a pint-sized journey.*
> *I'm the queen of this condition.*
> *I'm an expert on making the trip*
> *and now they say I'm an addict.*
> *Now they ask why.*
>
> — "The Addict"

Mother, have I borrowed too much from your book?
I told myself I had to fight it. I couldn't give up. I'd been on

codeine and Fiorinal for three weeks, and now I stopped taking it all at once, lying in a dark room, waiting for the continual and terrible pain to leave me. It took nearly two weeks, but eventually the headache did disappear. At this point my internist took me off Prozac and substituted Nortriptiline, a stronger antidepressant reputed also to be effective at preventing migraine and depression, but which had the side effects of drowsiness and muddy thinking.

As a teenager I had watched Mother endure the "wooliness" associated with Thorazine, and I had never really empathized with how she felt. If she couldn't write, I reasoned, at least she wasn't trying to kill herself. But now I understood: the doctor was treating me with a medication designed to alleviate my depression — but, because the medication was making me too groggy to write, the depression was deepening instead of lifting. An important purpose in my life had been compromised: writing was the balancing bar both Mother and I carried across the tightrope of our daily lives, a weight that kept us upright. Without that, I now saw, neither one of us could get up in the morning and face the minutes and hours that were to come.

I went off this drug, too, and tried to get along without any medication at all. But I lived in fear of another migraine attack, of the intense pain that only drugs could mute. My depression deepened, although I would admit it to no one, not even to John. Surely, I told myself as the summer wore on, this must be the bottom of the pit.

By the time August came around, not a new word for the novel had been entered on my computer since May. I went back into psychotherapy and spoke often of Mother. In fact, suddenly I couldn't seem to stop talking about her. My psychiatrist called my attention to this, and we pondered together how we were going to get Mother out of the middle of my life.

"How often do you think about your mother?" he asked. "Once a week? Once a month?"

"How about every day," I replied.

Then, quite suddenly, a new idea for *Night Vision* came to me. I scribbled it down: add more of the relationship I had had with my mother to the life of the novel's main character. It would still be fiction, but it would be a story about which I could feel passionate.

Inspiration provided energy. Quickly I was able to add a good twenty-five pages to the book. My mood cycled upward, and I felt more confident, certain what I had written was excellent. Perhaps this long battle with myself was finally ready to be resolved. But as September faded toward October, I crashed again — harder than ever before. Once again the idea of work became absurd, the characters ridiculous, the novel itself dull and boring. I couldn't move ahead into new material, and once more I doubted that I would ever finish the book.

Mother had often endured writer's block, ups and downs, in whatever she was working on at the time. I had seen her sink into depression when she could not work. I had seen her become suicidal. Never before had I understood it so well.

Previously depression had meant a gloom to me — a gloom, nearly visual, that descended before my eyes and made it difficult to think or see clearly. I became a gray person. But this felt different: this time my depression had developed into a physical pain. I found myself stooping as it gnawed at my stomach. Like a tumor, it went with me wherever I went, for whatever I was doing. It spread its tentacles wide, and took deep root. "*Your writing is worthless,*" hissed the voice I didn't want to admit I could hear. "*You are worthless.*" Inspiration sputtered out, and the whole world went dark. Once again I was a child, groping and hurt, hiding in the garage with the spiders, desperate to go home and sit in my mother's lap. I believed I would be punished the rest of my life. Desperate to get away from the pain, I could escape only in sleep.

The date of her suicide approached. Beginning eight years before, the anniversary of her death had been supplanted in my mind by the birth of Nicholas — born ten years later to the day. Initially I had been pleased by the macabre circumstances: on the day I had lost my mother I had gained a son. But this year the fourth of October seemed dark indeed. As I went through the motions of celebrating my son's happiness, inside I felt only my own anguish.

I tried to hide these feelings from my family, but they were too sensitive to be fooled. John explained to the boys: "Mommy is having a hard time. She needs you to be good to her." I hated the burden this put on them, so reminiscent of the way Joy and I had tiptoed around Mother when she was having a major depression. Nicholas had become more eager to please, more malleable, just as I had as a child; Alexander struggled not to act out, just as Joy had. All in all, the anxiety level in the household had risen to an unacceptable level.

How often had I castigated Mother silently: too depressed to make the beds? Too depressed to drive us to our after-school activities? Too depressed to put the potatoes into the oven for dinner? I had always believed that she only needed to be strong enough to stand up and overcome it. And then, suddenly, here I was, unable to stop crying, doing my marketing with sunglasses on so that no one could see the tears that would not cease; picking up the car pool and staring lifelessly through the windshield as I made certain to drive safely.

Was I turning into her? I wondered with a flat sort of horror. Had I become "her kind"? I kept telling myself that the crucial difference between Mother and me was not in how we felt, but in how we acted. I *would* do the marketing. I would *not* make my children afraid by putting my head in the mashed potatoes or staring off into space for hours. I would not *be* her.

I had always prided myself on being a fine cook, yet here I was, resorting to hot dogs and canned soup, though no one objected save me. Smiling at John when he came through the door from work became an insurmountable duty. For a few weeks, a new morning routine developed as he reassured me that if I needed him all I had to do was call the office and he would come home from work immediately. He sensed how near the edge I stood, while I continued to deny my depression and insist that I was fine. He didn't get exasperated with my depression the way my father had with my mother's, though perhaps the situations were not truly comparable. Still, he was supportive and kept encouraging me to open up about my feelings. Only later would he tell me of his own fear, anxiety, and anger.

I sat in front of my computer during the mornings and stared at a blank screen. I still managed to accomplish the chores and mothering that I absolutely had to. Inside me the pain escalated every day. I despaired that it would ever end. For the first time since adolescence, thoughts of suicide began to occupy my mind. Shame overwhelmed me. *"Not only are you worthless,"* the voice hissed. *"You're weak. Just like her."* I pushed the self-destructive ideas away, but more and more slowly each time.

One morning in October, after John had dropped the kids off at school on his way to work, I made my household rounds, making the beds and straightening up before going to my writing room. Slowly I walked back to our bedroom to get dressed. I had made our bed first, as a way of preventing myself from getting back into it. I sat on the edge of it, and pulled on a sock. Once on, I realized it was one of Nicky's, which had been put away in my drawer accidentally. I looked at that piece of cotton, stretched small and tight over my foot, and grabbed it angrily. I tried to pull it off but it was stuck. Time slowed. I started to cry. Even as I sobbed I told myself I was being ridiculous, acting like an overgrown toddler. Even worse, absurd. A picture came to mind: my mother, unable to put the potatoes into the oven in time for dinner. My mother, sitting at the kitchen table, nervously twirling her hair into masses of snarls.

The pain inside me took off like a horse running free on a winter's afternoon, blotting out all rational thought. *"You're going to die,"* the voice said triumphantly. *"You're going to die."*

I looked up at the closet where I stashed all our medications: Percodan left over from a root canal, Vicodin from a sinus infection, plenty of codeine and barbiturate for migraine, a few Valium for plane flights. Yes, there was plenty here to do the job, and I no longer cared whether it was right or wrong, whether it was weak or courageous. I thought of Mother's signature poem, the poem with which she began every reading, the poem that ended with the words: "A woman like that is not ashamed to die. I have been her kind."

I sat there, looking up into my shelves of pharmaceutical riches. As I reached out, I saw my children's faces, struggling to cope each day and night, alone. I remembered my own grief as a child: alone at Blanche's trying to go to sleep; alone at Mary Gray's, playing forlornly with a beach ball that the wind blew over the cliffs and into the ocean; waiting at the locked door onto the ward at Mass General Hospital to see Mother.

With violent effort I pulled off the sock. I slapped my face, as if I could wake myself from this terrible nightmare. I dialed John's office, sobbing so hard the secretary put me through without asking. He came home from work and carted me off to the doctor's office.

I kept crying, the hurt inside overwhelming. Breathing difficult, I struggled for air. *"Die,"* the voice said, *"you are alone,"* but the sound of it was fainter now that other people were around. The nurse gave me a sedative. John took me home and sat with me while I hiccoughed myself to sleep. The pain lessened for a moment. I *wasn't* worthless. My family loved me, counted on me. I *wasn't* alone. And somewhere, somehow, Mother, too, was holding my hand.

The next day John took me to a specialist in psychopharmacology, who put me on an antidepressant again — Zoloft this time, which had fewer side effects — to help control the depression as well as treat the omnipresent migraines. "I'm in a trap," I told this doctor with panic and despair. "I want out, but I can't leave my children like my mother left me."

As the weeks slowly moved toward the holidays, and the drug gradually took effect, my mood began to improve a little. I had made it through the crisis by riding on the back of love: love for my sons had kept me from acting out the impulse to kill myself, just as, for a time, love for her daughters had motivated my mother to fight her powerful demons.

Gradually, my acute pain and strong suicidal desire began to wane. Nearly two months would pass, however, before I felt safe again — two months before I did not wake up and dread the day before me.

The Starting Point
~

*Depression is boring, I think,
and I would do better to make
some soup and light up the cave.*

— Anne Sexton
"The Fury of Rain Storms"

S UICIDE is an immediate and permanent solution to pain. The pain can be either physical or emotional: emotional pain of an intensity sufficient to drive the sufferer to consider suicide often manifests itself in physical symptoms so powerful that to quibble about origin is beside the point. Pain is pain regardless of its source. None of these conditions can necessarily be conquered by willpower; neither are they induced by laziness, lack of moral ethic, or selfishness.

In my mind I had accused my mother of these failings many times. Now, my own experience had taught me a different and quite simple lesson: suicide is a synonym for escape. My mother had known, by the time she was forty-five, that she would never get well, that she would suffer recurring bouts of intense and debilitating depression. I had never quite understood this before. I had been unable — and unwilling — to empathize with her and to acknowledge the similarities between us. Now I understood her depressions and wished I did not. She had sought death because she believed she had no alternative. A life of pain is not a life worth living. She was not a coward, but instead a realist.

On October 4, 1974, my mother wrote no note, made no phone calls. She did not reach out for help or rescue, and she chose a method far more certain than her old routine with sleeping pills. With the fine autumn sun streaming down onto the roof, Mother rolled the garage door shut, climbed into her car, and turned the key in the ignition — not as a cry for help but as a solution. She took her life to end her pain.

My mother died of depression. Untreatable, unceasing depression. Why, when we refer to depression, do we think of it in the main as a state characterized by numbness and low spirits rather than intense suffering? Why, in fact, is the word *pain* rarely used when describing depression? The dictionary uses synonyms such as *melancholy, despondency,* and *sadness.*

In the end, my mother knew that all the therapy in the world would not save her. At that time the psychiatric community did not have available the class of antidepressants now widely prescribed, like Prozac and Zoloft, with maximum efficacy and minimal side effects. Mother did not want to remain reliant on sedating drugs or alcohol. Her life did not have quality sufficient to create the desire to continue. She wanted to die, and her desire came not from anger but from despair. At one time writing had lifted her beyond herself: using words, she escaped her own pain by offering it to others. She was able to expand herself — to imagine Anne into other lives, other bodies, other sexes, other situations — by drawing similarities between herself and her readers, herself and her subjects. Poetry contained the magic of temporary healing. But, with her unerring instinct, she knew that her writing had slipped. The old tricks of expansion and identification worked less and less as the poetry lost its center of gravity and began to spin out of control. Soon even the old black art brought no comfort to its creative witch.

How often has it been speculated that the madness makes the art? If Mother were alive today she would shake her head in disagreement and remind all questioners that when you are submerged in pain and confusion you are not able to create anything at all. You work too hard simply to survive.

Now I understood what she meant in a whole new way, since my own episode with depression had lasting side effects on my work. Although by December I was once again cooking family meals and negotiating the supermarket without tears, I couldn't bring myself to open *Night Vision* again. It seemed useless.

In an appointment with my therapist, I was struck by a new

insight: since the publication of the biography I had reentered the state of mourning that had ceased a year or so after her death eighteen years before. Now the forty-year-old Linda wished she could sit at her kitchen table and talk of any manner of things with Anne. I had thought I was finished with grief; it appeared I was not.

I needed an exorcism. Although Mother had killed herself when I was twenty-one, my thirty-ninth birthday had come and gone and she still rose each morning from the tumble of my sheets. She still lay down to sleep by my ear at night.

I looked up the word *exorcise* in the dictionary: *"To expel (an evil spirit) by or as if by incantation or adjuration . . . with an oath."* My writing was my oath, as it had been Mother's. I had been weaned on the power of the word; language had fed me when Mother herself could not. In liberal interpretation of our old Puritan standards, we had discovered that the hard work of writing brought the reward of a mind clearer for the effort, a soul cleansed and released.

To write about Mother and me would enable me to take control of the demons inside and let them know who was boss. I would be my own witch doctor. After all, if I could wield it, my pen was the only instrument required to stake the beat of grief's relentless heart.

If my goal was to exorcise Mother, would I have to let her go? Would I have to give up the idea that she still lived, and perhaps even that she still talked to me from that airplane in the sky?

As I was driving home from that session with my therapist, I wondered why the idea of release threatened me so. My anxiety was certainly spiking to new levels as I flashed through stoplights red and green. In what ways did my mother continue on inside me? Why was I keeping her there, erecting a shrine in my heart?

Later that night I had a dream. Even as I scrawled it on a sheet of paper upon waking, I could see how similar its subject was to a poem Mother had written, and I was not in the least surprised to find that I had unconsciously shaped it, at the end, into a rough-hewn poem. Her poem "Hansel and Gretel" was included in *Transformations,* the volume of retold Grimms' fairy tales that she had dedicated to me. *My* dream went this way:

I am alone in the dark, in woods where my bed is a nest. I am grown smaller than a child. Sleep is muddy, tossed by anxiety. The moon comes up, lights diamonds scattered across black soil, each a stepping-stone that will take me back. This is the path to reunion. Smaller than small, I have become a weapon forged by love.

The trail calls me, an internal song primal as birthing. It is too late to cry or say no, too late to run. I crave a brother, a sister, someone to hold my hand, to lead and to follow. I am scared to do this alone.

Crushing diamonds beneath my feet, I follow the trail, reach the clearing, the hardened house of gingerbread, the crematorium of my past.

Out comes the witch: to praise, to exclaim, to embrace. A visit, a story, let it come, let it go. She cries with delight and despair at the ways we have changed. She is my dream; how long I have guarded her. Holding hands, we dance in a circle. I brush her hair, an old habit, until it is long and shiny, a lake of light in the fire. Her voice ripples, capturing me with its magic, smooth as bird flight. How I want to listen and believe. How I want to be soothed and rocked by her lullaby.

Later we feast on coconuts. Her eyes twitch over the fat of my breast, the long sinew of my thigh. I am her Chickenbiddy. I am her drumstick. She moves with stiffness to stir the fire, offers me a baked apple. Frost has settled in her bones.

Mother,
we know
what we are about.
The oven door
is a hungry black mouth. It
waits. The bird cage is too big
for any bird. It
waits.
We do the mother-daughter dance.
Smaller than small, still
I must win.
I have what you need.

I have what you want.
Love binds
desire. Is it a dream
that I slide you
into the black
water
of the oven?

Is it a dream
that I launch your long
motionless body, well-kept
with my devotion, sleek
with my love?
Is it a dream
that you go
without a ripple
just
my face
salt-slicked
at your smooth glide
out?

   In the dream-poem that I wrote that night, I assume once again the role of the gatekeeper, guarding an important and sacred treasure hidden deep in a secret wood: the memory of my mother with her magical voice, and her gifts of words and baked apples. Here I would will her back to life, but to do so would require that I give up my life to her; to do so would require an act of cannibalism on her part, to reverse this process that every mother and daughter engage in — the mother-daughter dance, birth and death, the passing on of strength and knowledge and power. She can live again through me — but at what cost? In the end only love can bind these taboo desires and keep them in check. In the end, for me, love did not hamper her expression of the forbidden — or of the marvelous. In the end her love both damaged and nurtured.

   In the dream only one way out exists for the gatekeeper: if I can find the path in the dark, crushing beneath my feet the diamonds that I inherited from her — rings and words both — I will come upon her in the woods one last time. We will share a baked apple before I try to send her down the long black river of death.

Was Mother my muse? My inspiration? If I silenced her, would I also silence myself? Much as I resented the shadow her success cast over my present working life, her example and her words stood before me like a safe envelope of light: at this pivotal and insecure moment in my life, how frightening it felt to consider letting her die at last. Complicating these insights was the knowledge that she had killed herself at forty-five, and forty-five was only a handful of years away for me. What would it feel like to lose this powerful muse? Would I lose myself as well?

This journey of mourning my mother, which I had begun as a twenty-one-year-old girl and which I now faced as a woman turning forty, had brought me full circle, back to the place where I read her letter to the "40-year-old Linda" as if for the first time. That place was my starting point.

I asked myself more questions: Why do I mourn her again? Why do I grieve so deeply? I had not thought I had avoided her death or the complicated emotions it brought originally. Why, so suddenly, had empathy — rather than anger — become my dominant emotion?

These questions became the signposts of my journey when I had this dream. They told me where I had been and how far I had yet to go; they propelled me forward — as if I were a traveler nearly at my destination who speeds up after the highway sign that says I have only twenty miles more till sleep.

A few nights later, John and I sat in a movie theater, watching the film version of Norman Maclean's autobiographical novella, *A River Runs Through It*. It occurred to me then that I had been attempting to write about my life with my mother throughout the last three years. I had begun with the creation of the intensely personal scenes of sexual and emotional abuse in the thriller *Bedside Manners*, and then, in *Night Vision*, I had imbued the narrator with my feelings about having been a daughter haunted by her mother's mental illness.

The urge to write about my life with Mother had been there throughout all these drafts and pages, and in all these words. I had already written about Mother in *Rituals* and in *Mirror Images,* but this time felt different. This time the more I had tried to hide behind the wall of my fiction, the less I was able to produce; my interest always waned when I went back to trying to create differences between the characters and myself. Perhaps what I needed to do was to write about the issue directly. No disguises this time around. No more running away. This time I would dare to speak in my own name, to use the gift of words she had made my legacy.

I could begin by simply keeping a journal. Or I could write a memoir of my relationship with this complicated woman, from the perspective of the daughter I would always be as well as from the perspective of the woman and mother I had become. I had spent so much time trying to get away from the image of myself as merely Mother's daughter — trying to establish an independent career — that to turn around now and write a book that dealt specifically with that relationship felt intensely threatening.

Yet I sensed the time had come.

From the perspective of starting the fifth decade of my life, I now understand my mother's life as a woman in ways I could not possibly have done when I was only in my twenties. I understand the joys and frustrations of parenthood; I understand the satisfactions and disappointments of being a writer; I understand the difficulties a marriage can undergo and still survive. The very nature of suicide and depression and the choices they force now hold a different meaning for me.

Perhaps I understand Mother better because I have forgiven her, and perhaps that forgiveness comes at this time of my life because I can finally empathize with what she endured and with the ways in which she both failed and triumphed. I begin to find joy in our similarities rather than feeling threatened by them: it no longer seems a crime to admit, "I have been her kind." Mother may always talk to me from that airplane high in the sky, but finally I am able to answer her. By forgiving her, I acknowledge that she is gone, and I allow myself to miss her at last.

And so I begin again: woman, wife, mother, daughter, and writer. I cast my feelings into "Language" — the shared medium in which Mother and I reveled — to find freedom. I sit at my own desk and contemplate the long green of a late afternoon. I am not running anymore.

Two summers ago I began to show my Dalmatian Rhiannon in both conformation and obedience, reexperiencing those long ago summers of working with animals and taking them into the show ring. In February of 1993, Tia arrived: seven weeks old, filling the house with her noisy demands and her vigor, her puppy breath and her puddles, her dark and watchful gaze. This past fall I bred Rhiannon and then watched as her sides filled and her belly grew heavy. I midwifed her litter, just after New Year's, holding each small mouse of a puppy in my hand to rub it down. These small creatures have been a gift that fills our home with the scramble of life as it grows and changes in front of us. Surely my next novel will feature a black-and-white spotted dog as I remember and celebrate that impulse my mother had twenty-six years ago when Penny had her puppies: the desire to live.

Mercy Street

の

*When I first got sick and became a displaced
person, I thought I was quite alone, but when I went
into the mental hospital, I found I wasn't, that there
were other people like me. It made me feel better —
more real, sane. I felt, "These are my people." Well, at
the John Holmes class that I attended for two
years, I found I belonged to the poets, that I was real
there, and I had another "These are my people."*

— interview with Anne Sexton
by Barbara Kevles

I AWOKE this morning, still dreaming of a woman in an apron, still crying into my pillow. I wondered why. The dream itself seemed unremarkable, forgettable. I opened my eyes and began to turn it over in my mind. A few minutes later, I slid quietly from the bed so as not to wake John and tiptoed down the hall to my writing room, where I switched on my computer and began to dig for the details of the dream as if I were a gardener foraging for root vegetables.

In the dream I held a sketchpad and kept trying to draw a good likeness of the tall dark-haired woman who talked without stopping as the family ate dinner. We all sat around a table in a house resembling the one in which I had grown up, in a dining room like the one where my mother's desk overflowed from the corner and where our family of four witnessed the beginnings of art and blessed it as best we could. In the living room a few feet away, an audience waited for the dark-haired woman to come and speak to them. The dream was black and white, as if we were all moving in an old television show from the 1950s.

After a time I finished my sketch, satisfied with the intricate shading and perspective, the mystery and the revelation I had achieved. I stood to polish crumbs from the table, and then turned to the silver-framed mirror above the sideboard. I applied my lipstick, getting ready for her performance, and saw myself reflected there, a woman. The audience continued to wait, while the dark-haired woman continued to talk to the family, her voice intense and emotional. Her words rose like miracles from Jesus, out of the cloister of our dining room, to sift down onto the laps of the waiting multitude. After a time, I could hear the audience begin to clap and call her name.

"Come," I said with frustration, putting my arms around her. I drew her under the arch that marked the entrance to the living room. "They are waiting for you," I told her, opening my arms wide. "These are your people!"

She stood at the entrance to the room and stepped forward into applause.

I woke.

Outside my windows now, the morning is still dark, the lace of valley oaks thick against the pinking sky. Except for a rising bird call, I am alone at my desk in the silent house. I, too, am an interpreter of dreams, a tapper of the unconscious, a maker of metaphor. I come to this page with my arms full of words — both hers and mine.

In the end I could not save my mother nor help her find Mercy Street. Looking back, I see that ultimately I understood her longing with so much of my heart that it became a part of me too, one more lust I had inherited. While I searched for my own Mercy Street, I memorized her last letter to me as if I were a soldier on a mission; I still hear her words, so full of yearning: "Maybe, just maybe — the spirit of the poems will go on past both of us, and one or two will be remembered in one hundred years."

Mother, are you listening? Twenty years have passed since you confided that dream to me. I am still the gatekeeper, and I bring you good news: The spirit of the poems does go on past both of us — and many will be remembered in one hundred years.

Mother, I read your words and turn the corner. Here, at last, is Mercy Street.

Notes and Sources
ᴈ

SOURCES

Nearly all of my mother's papers are housed in the Harry Ransom Humanities Research Center at the University of Texas in Austin, abbreviated here as HRHRC.

Works frequently cited have been abbreviated:

CP: Anne Sexton, *The Complete Poems* (Boston: Houghton Mifflin, 1981)
SP: Anne Sexton: A Self-Portrait in Letters, ed. Linda Gray Sexton and Lois Ames (Boston: Houghton Mifflin, 1977)
NES: No Evil Star: Selected Essays, Interviews and Prose, ed. Steven E. Colburn (Ann Arbor: University of Michigan Press, 1985)

Psychiatric records used in this book consist of the therapy tapes of my mother's analytic sessions with Dr. Orne; the therapy tape transcripts my mother later made of those tapes; and the notes taken by Dr. Orne during the session. These are cited, respectively, as therapy tapes, therapy notebooks, and doctor's notes.

NOTES: Chapter References

In Exile

15 "big house with four garages": "Young," *CP,* p. 51.
16 "Her family was not": Dr. Martin Orne to Diane Middlebrook, 10.4.90.
18 "[My sisters] certainly didn't care": A.S. to Dr. Orne, therapy tape, 7.22.61.
32 "I hold a five-year diary": "All My Pretty Ones," *CP,* p. 49.
34 "Oh the enemas": "Cripples and Other Stories," *CP,* p. 160.

First Metaphors

39 "What you write is better": A.S. to Dr. Orne, therapy tape, 11.30.61.

60 "We spent about an hour pretending": A.S. to Dr. Orne, therapy tape, 2.21.63.

60 "It's something like a trance": A.S. to Dr. Orne, therapy tape, 2.21.63.

More Than Myself

77 "[My mother's] father was a writer": A.S. to Dr. Orne, therapy tape, 7.11.61.

77 "I think she was actually pretty nice": A.S. to Dr. Orne, therapy tape, 7.22.61.

79 "[Kayo] was all set to commit me": A.S. to Dr. Orne, therapy tape, 8.1.63.

80 "I thought, well, I could do that": A.S. interview with Alice Ryerson, 1.62, Radcliffe College Archive.

84 "Any demand is too much": A.S. to Dr. Orne, doctor's notes, 12.15.57.

88 "Maybe why I want Kayo": A.S. to Dr. Orne, therapy tape, 2.27.64.

Companionship

89 "I love you": A.S. to Linda, 7.23.69; *SP,* p. 342.

93 "You and Joy": A.S. to Linda, 7.3.74; *SP,* p. 417.

95 "Under every word": A.S. to Dr. Orne, therapy tape, 7.25.61.

100 "You must come home in August": A.S. to Linda, 7.8.65; *SP,* p. 246.

110 "When I feel depressed": A.S. to Dr. Orne, therapy tape, 2.62.

110 "No one would believe": A.S. to Dr. Orne, therapy tape, 11.30.63.

116 "I am married": A.S. to Philip Legler, 5.4.66; *SP,* p. 293.

117 "Linda's never flown," A.S. to Anne Wilder, 4.2.66, private collection.

120 "I feel kind of awful": A.S. to Philip Legler, 4.27.66, HRHRC.

121 "If I don't die tonight": A.S. to Philip Legler, 5.22.66; *SP,* p. 290.

Live or Die

130 "I have to be great": A.S. to Dr. Orne, therapy tape, 11.30.61.

Independence

146 "I don't like you telling me": A.S. to Constance Chase, 9.20.71, HRHRC.

147 "People flock to Bob Dylan": A.S. interview with Barbara Kevles, *NES,* p. 108.

Self-Portrait

209   "Something comes between me and Linda": A.S. to Dr. Orne, doctor's notes, 12.17.57.

In Search of a Biographer

222   "took something that was mine": A.S. to Dr. Orne, therapy tape, 3.5.63.

228   "There wouldn't be anyone": A.S. to Dr. Orne, therapy tape, 3.3.64.

228   "I was just suddenly": A.S. to Dr. Orne, therapy tape, 4.6.61.

228   "I drink and drink": A.S. to Dr. Orne, therapy tape, 6.15.61.

228   "I started to spank Linda": A.S. to Dr. Orne, therapy tape, 6.17.61.

228   "Three weeks ago": A.S. to Dr. Orne, therapy tape, 7.15.61.

229   "Writing is as important": A.S. to Dr. Orne, therapy tape, 7.29.61.

229   "I hate Linda": A.S. to Dr. Orne, therapy tape, 12.17.57.

231   "I can write": A.S. to Dr. Orne, therapy tape, 4.4.61.

Exposures

276   "At first it was private": "For John, Who Begs Me Not to Enquire Further," *CP*, p. 34.

Mercy Street

302   "When I first got sick": A.S. interview with Barbara Kevles, *NES*, p. 87.